COUNTIES LONDONDERRY & DONEGAL

A

TOPOGRAPHICAL DICTIONARY

OF THE PARISHES, VILLAGES AND TOWNS
OF THESE COUNTIES IN THE 1830s

ILLUSTRATED WITH
CONTEMPORARY MAPS AND ENGRAVINGS

BY SAMUEL LEWIS

PREFACE

BY BRIAN M. WALKER

BELFAST

PUBLISHED BY FRIAR'S BUSH PRESS

2004

THIS SELECTED EDITION
PUBLISHED 2004
BY FRIAR'S BUSH PRESS
160 BALLYLESSON ROAD
BELFAST, BT8 8JU
NORTHERN IRELAND

FIRST PUBLISHED 1837
BY S. LEWIS & CO.
87 ALDERSGATE STREET, LONDON

ISBN 0-946872-63-5

TEXT COPIED BY IRISH TIMES (IRELAND.COM)

PRINTED BY DATAPLUS PRINT & DESIGN
13 HILL STREET, DUNMURRY, BT17 OAD

PREFACE

This volume brings together three important contemporary sources of information about life and society in Counties Londonderry and Donegal in the 1830's. The text is taken from the monumental two-volumed topographical dictionary of Ireland, published by Samuel Lewis in 1837. His work covered all of Ireland in alphabetical order in a grand total of 1405 double columned pages. Maps of the main towns have been photographed from the first edition Ordnance Survey maps, which were published in the mid 1830's, and are integrated into the text. A considerable number of engravings, mostly from the 1830's, has also been included. In the case of all three components of this book – the topographical text, the maps and the engravings, the period of the 1830's witnessed new heights in the availability and worth of such sources. Brought together here in this particular form, the material presents a special view of these parishes, villages and towns in the period before the great changes of Victorian Ireland. It gives a compelling record of agriculture, industry, population, buildings and antiquities over one hundred and sixty years ago.

Samuel Lewis, publisher

Our knowledge about the life of Samuel Lewis is fairly limited. We do know, however, that during the 1830's and 1840's he ran a publishing business in London, first at 87 Aldersgate Street and secondly at 13 Finsbury Place South. He died in 1865. More is known about the outcome of his publishing efforts, in particular the very successful series of topographical dictionaries for which he was responsible. His 4 volumed topographical dictionary for England appeared in 1831 (7th edition 1849) to be followed a year later by a similar two volumed work for Wales (4th edition 1849). In 1837 he produced a two volumed dictionary for Ireland (2nd edition 1842), accompanied by an atlas of the counties of Ireland. Finally, he published a three volumed topographical dictionary for Scotland in 1846.[(1)]

Production of the Irish dictionary involved a vast entreprenurial enterprise.[(2)] Starting in early 1833, agents were dispatched to all parts of Ireland to gather information for the work and also to obtain advance subscribers. The dictionary was priced at two guineas per volume while the atlas was also available for two guineas. As was explained in the preface to the first volume, compared to England and Wales, there was less available for Ireland in the form of county histories and other such work, so it was important to gain extensive personal information. His principal sources of information were local landowners and clergy. When the dictionary appeared finally in 1837, the list of subscribers (including many of his informants) ran to a total of nearly 10,000 names, including large numbers in both these counties.

The publication of the Irish dictionary led to considerable controversy, caused not by the content of the volumes but by objections from some of those listed as subscribers to being included on the list. A number of legal cases ensued over questions of liability for payment for the two books. There seems to have been relatively little debate over the accuracy of the contents. The 1842 revised edition made some corrections but also updated the figures in accordance with the 1841 census and replaced educational material with extra material on the railways. The entries reprinted here are from the first edition and so relate to the 1830's.

This dictionary by Lewis gives a unique coverage of life in Ireland, parish by parish and town by town. No-one before had produced such an extensive survey. At the same time as the appearance of these volumes by Lewis an enterprise was underway to record Irish society and economy as part of the Ordnance Survey (O.S.) with the writing of memoirs to accompany the production of the first O.S. maps for Ireland. This project collapsed finally in 1840, however, after only the northern counties had been investigated, and just one volume was published for the parish of Templemore in County Londonderry. Only in the last decade of the twentieth century have the memoirs been published.(3) These volumes by Lewis are very valuable for us today not just because he gathered important personal information at local level but also because he availed of much of the statistical and factual information which was now becoming available for Ireland, often through parliamentary papers and reports. In particular, he used the 1831 census report, new educational data and O.S. acreage figures.

At the same time, we must be aware of some of the perspectives and weaknesses of the material. A man of his time, Lewis approached his work from the standpoint of a society run by the gentry. The parishes are those of the Church of Ireland which was the established church. We must appreciate that some of his accounts of Irish pre history and archaeology would be questioned by historians and archaeologists today. His information on these matters reflects the state of knowledge about them at the time, which changed considerably in the course of the nineteenth century, thanks to the work of people such as John O'Donovan. For example his references to 'druidical altars', and some of his accounts of the origins of the early people of Ireland would not now be accepted. Those interested in the composition of placenames should check Lewis's interpretation with modern works on the subject.(4) It should also be noted that Lewis gives distances in Irish miles (10 Irish miles equal a little over 12 miles British). Spellings of names have been left as found in the original text.

Maps and map makers

Run by officers of the Royal Engineers, and starting in the 1820's, a complete mapping survey of the whole country was carried out under the auspices of the Ordnance Survey of Ireland, based at Phoenix Park in Dublin.(5) This led to the appearance in 1833 of the first six inches to the mile maps for County Londonderry, to be followed by similar maps for all the Irish counties over the next nine years. The first maps for County Donegal were published in 1836. This surveying project was a vast undertaking which involved considerable expenditure and manpower. The result was a very extensive cartographic record for Ireland, which had no equivalent in the world at the time.

In this volume plans of the main towns in the two counties have been copied from the original 6 inch O.S. maps. For sake of greater clarity the town maps have been magnified by 40 per cent. Map publication dates have been recorded, but it should be noted that the actual surveying could have been done in the previous one or two years. We have also included a map of each of the two counties from Lewis's atlas. An advantage of this map is that it gives the location of the parishes, and, while it does not show the parish boundaries, it can be helpful to give people some idea of which parish their area is located in. The maps in the atlas were based on drawings reduced from the Ordnance Survey and other surveys.

Artists and engravers

The period from the early 1820's to the early 1840's witnessed an upsurge in the appearance of topographical views of Ireland, partly due to technological advances, such as the advent of line engraving on steel in the early 1820's. The bulk of the illustrations in this book come from the 1830's, although some are as late as 1847. The publication of the weekly *Dublin Penny Journal*, 1832–5, with its many wood engravings, was an important new departure in the level of illustrated material available at a low cost. The journal carried topographical articles and illustrations on many parts of Ireland. Besides the *Dublin Penny Journal*, there now appeared a large number of illustrated books, covering special areas or all of the country. Well known artists, such as George Petrie (who worked for the Ordnance Survey in the 1830's), were employed to provide drawings to be engraved for these works.

Of special interest in this activity is the work of a number of northern artists. Views by the Belfast born Andrew Nicholl (1804–86) appeared frequently, both in the *Dublin Penny Journal* and in various published tours and guides. James Howard Burgess (c.1817–90) of Belfast was a skilled topographical artist who provided 25 views for S.C. Hall's *Ireland: its scenery, character, &c.* (London, 1846).(6) A volume of *Reports of... the Drapers' Company* (London, 1829), contained 9 attractive views of Draperstown and Moneymore, drawn by W.J. Booth in 1827. In 1845 Lord George Hill published his *Facts from Gweedore*, followed by a sequel in 1847. Both contained fascinating plates on County Donegal, drawn by various artists, probably in the early 1840's.(7)

In recent times engravings such as these have often been used to illustrate texts, but usually there has been little attempt to name the artist and engraver involved or to accurately date the picture. In this volume, however, an effort has been made to identify both the artist and engraver responsible for a particular piece of work. This has not been possible in every case and where the full information has not been given this is because it is not available. The title of the book, and the date and place of publication, have been given with each print so that we can establish a date for the particular view.

Brian M. Walker **Belfast, 2004**

References

(1) See Frederick Boase, (ed.) *Modern English biography*, vol. 2 (London, 1965), p. 417.

(2) See Tim Cadogan's introduction to *Lewis's Cork* (Cork, 1998). Extracts of parts of Co. Londonderry have been published by the enterprising Ballinascreen Historical Society. *Lewis's Loughinsolin*, foreword by Seamus Heaney, (Draperstown, 1999).

(3) Angelique Day and Patrick McWilliams, *Ordnance survey memoirs of Ireland*, vols 1–40 (Belfast, 1990–8).

(4) See Patrick McKay, *A dictionary of Ulster place-names* (Belfast, 1999); Gregory Toner (ed.), *Place-names of northern Ireland; vol. 5, Co. Derry; the Moyola Valley* (Belfast, 1996).

(5) See J.H. Andrews, *A paper landscape: the ordnance survey in nineteenth century Ireland* (Oxford, 1993; second edition, Dublin, 2002).

(6) See John Hewitt, *Art in Ulster* (Belfast, 1977). Bio. notes by Theo Snoody.

(7) Lord George Hill, *Facts from Gweedore* (Dublin, 1845); *Hints to Donegal tourists; with a brief notice of Rathlin Island. A sequel to Facts from Gweedore* (Dublin, 1847).

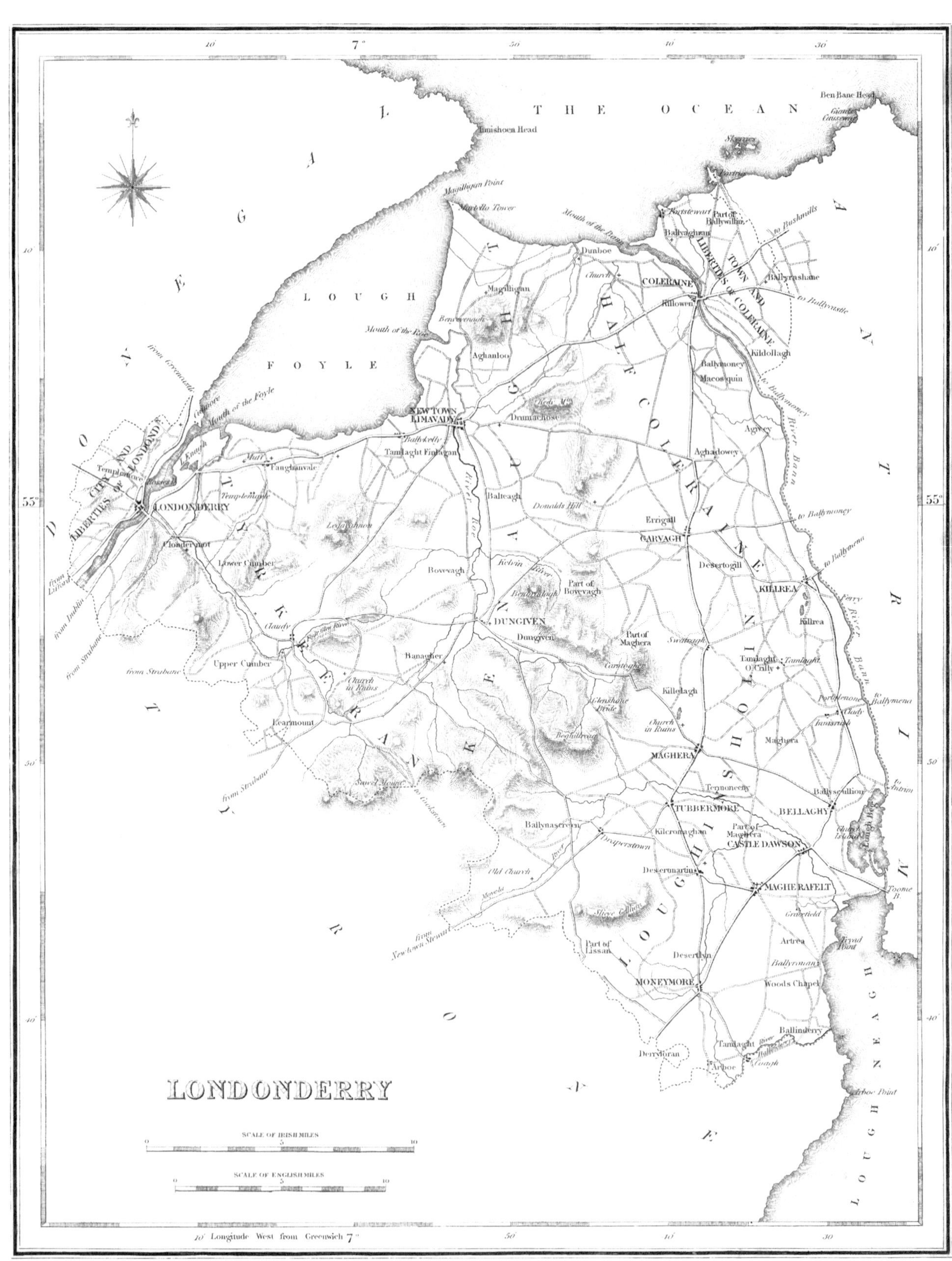

Londonderry. Drawn by R. Creighton and engraved by I. Dower. From Lewis's Atlas, *(London, 1837).*

COUNTY LONDONDERRY

A

TOPOGRAPHICAL DICTIONARY

LONDONDERRY (County of), a maritime county of the province of ULSTER, bounded on the south and south-west by the county of Tyrone; on the west, by that of Donegal; on the north-west, by Lough Foyle; on the north, by the Atlantic Ocean; and on the east, by the county of Antrim. It extends from 54° 37′ to 55° 12′ (N. Lat.), and from 6° 26′ to 7° 18′ (W. Lon.); and comprises an area, according to the Ordnance survey, of 518,423 acres, of which 388,817 are cultivated, 119,202 are mountain waste and bog, and 10,404 are occupied by water. The population, in 1821, was 193,869, and in 1831, 222,012.

The river Foyle appears to have been the Argita, and the Bann the Logia, of Ptolemy; and the intervening territory, constituting the present county of Londonderry, formed, according to this geographer, part of the country of the Darnii or Darini, whose name appears to be perpetuated in the more modern designation of "Derry." The earliest internal evidence represents it as being chiefly the territory of the O'Cathans, O'Catrans or O'Kanes, under the name of Tir Cahan or Cathan-aght, signifying "O'Kane's country:" they were a branch of and, tributary to the O'Nials, and their chief seat was at a place now called the Deer Park, in the vale of the Roe. When their country was reduced to shire ground by Sir John Perrot, in the reign of Elizabeth, it was intended that Coleraine should be the capital; and the county was therefore designated, and long bore the name of, "the county of Coleraine," although it is a singular fact that the ruins of the court-house and gaol then built for the county are at Desertmartin, 15 miles from the proposed capital. Derry was seized by the English towards the close of Elizabeth's reign, for the purpose of checking the power of O'Nial and O'Donnel; and when the earls of Tyrone and Tyrconnel fled the country, in 1607, nearly the whole of six counties in Ulster were confiscated. At this period the southern side of the county appears to have been possessed by the O'Donnels, O'Conors, and O'Murrys: the O'Cahans were not among the attainted septs, and consequently, in the ensuing schemes of plantation, many of them were settled among the native freeholders by Jas. I., though they afterwards forfeited their estates in the subsequent civil war.

King James, conceiving the citizens of London to be the ablest body to undertake the establishment of a Protestant colony in the forfeited territory, directed overtures to be made to the municipal authorities; and on Jan. 28th, 1609, articles of agreement were entered into between the Lords of the Privy Council and the Committees appointed by act of Common Council. On the part of the citizens it was stipulated, that they should expend £20,000 on the plantation; and on the other hand, the Crown was to assign to them entire possession of the county of Coleraine, and the towns of Coleraine and Derry, with extensive lands attached, excepting 60 acres out of every 1000 for church lands and certain portions to be assigned to three native Irish gentlemen. To this extensive grant the king added the woods of Glenconkene and Killetragh, and ordained that the whole should be held with the amplest powers and privileges, such as the patronage of the churches, admiralty jurisdiction on the coasts, the fishery of the two great rivers and all other streams, &c. For the management of this new branch of their affairs the Common Council elected a body of twenty-six, consisting, as at present, of a governor, deputy-governor, and assistants, of whom one-half retire every year, and their places are supplied by a new election. In 1613, this company or court was incorporated by royal charter, under its present style of "The Society of the Governor and Assistants of London of the New Plantation in Ulster, within the Realm of Ireland;" but is commonly known as the "Irish Society," and was invested with all the towns, castles, lordships, manors, lands, and hereditaments given to the city, which were erected by the charter into a distinct county, to be called "the County of Londonderry." The sum of £40,000 having now been expended on the plantation, it was deemed most advantageous to divide the territorial possessions of the Society into twelve equal portions, which were appropriated by lot to each of the twelve chief companies of the city, and so many of the smaller companies joined as made by their total contributions a twelfth of the entire sum. The twelve chief companies were the Mercers, Grocers, Drapers, Fishmongers, Goldsmiths, Skinners, Merchant Tailors, Haberdashers, Salters, Ironmongers, Vintners, and Clothworkers; and in their respective proportions is now included the chief part of the county. The houses and lands in the city of Londonderry and the town of Coleraine, with their woods, fisheries and ferries (except that at the estuary of the Foyle, connecting the county with that of Donegal, which belonged to the Chichesters), not being susceptible of division, were retained by the Society, who were to receive the profits, and account for them to the twelve chief companies. In 1616, information was received by Sir Thomas Philips of Newtown Limavady of a design formed by the Irish to surprise Londonderry and Coleraine, which being communicated to the Irish Government effectual measures were adopted for its prevention. On the communication of the intelligence to the Irish Society instructions were immediately issued by it to the twelve companies to furnish arms and accoutrements to be transmitted by the keeper of Guildhall for the better defence of the plantation, the prompt execution of which preserved the colony and gave new vigour to the exertions to stock it with English and Scotch settlers.

About the same period directions were also issued to the companies to repair the churches, to furnish each of the ministers with a bible, common-prayer book and communion cup, and to send thither a stipulated number of artizans; the trades thus introduced were those of weavers, hat-makers, locksmiths, farriers, tanners, fellmongers, ironmongers, glassblowers, pewterers, fishermen, turners, basketmakers, tallowchandlers, dyers and curriers. The Salters' company erected glass-houses at Magherafelt, and iron-works were opened on the Mercers' proportion near Kilrea which were carried on until timber failed for fuel. Notwithstanding the disbursement of large sums of money, at length amounting to £60,000, continued dissatisfaction was expressed by the Crown at the mode in which the stipulations of the society were fulfilled: in 1632, the whole county was sequestered; and in 1637, the charter was cancelled, and the county seized into the king's hands. Parliament, however, decreed the illegality of these proceedings; Cromwell restored the Society to its former state; and on the Restoration, Chas. II. granted it a new charter, nearly in the same words as that of James, under which its affairs have ever since been conducted. Of the twelve principal companies, all retain their estates except four, viz., the Goldsmiths, Haberdashers, Vintners, and Merchant Tailors, who at various periods disposed of their proportions to private individuals. The Goldsmiths' share was situated mostly within the liberties of Derry, south-east of the Foyle; that of the Haberdashers was around Aghanloo and Bovevagh. The Vintners had Bellaghy, and the Merchant Tailors' proportion was Macosquin. These proportions are now held in perpetuity by the Marquess of Waterford, the Richardsons, the Ponsonbys, the Alexanders, and the heirs of the late Right Hon. Thomas Conolly. Of the estates now belonging to the other eight companies, the Mercers have Kilrea and its neighbourhood; the Grocers, Muff and its dependencies; Moneymore and its rich and improved district belongs to the Drapers; the Fishmongers have Ballykelly; Dungiven belongs to the Skinners; Magherafelt to the Salters; Aghadowey to the Ironmongers; and Killowen, forming part of the borough of Coleraine, to the Clothworkers; all are under lease, except those of the Drapers, Mercers, and Grocers, which are managed by agents, deputed by these respective companies. The first intimation of the intended insurrection in 1641 came from Moneymore, in this county, through Owen O'Conolly, an Irish Protestant, in time to save Dublin, but not to prevent the explosion of the plot in the north. On the first day of the explosion Moneymore was seized by the Irish, and Maghera and Bellaghy, then called Vintners'-town, burned, as were most of the other towns and villages throughout the county. On the termination of the war the county and the city fell under the dominion of the parliament, and Sir Charles Coote and Governor Hunks ruled there with great severity. From the restoration to the revolution the county affords few materials for history; the siege of Londonderry, one of the most striking events of the latter period, more properly belongs to the history of the city.

The county is chiefly in the diocese of Derry, with some portions in those of Armagh and Connor. For the purposes of civil jurisdiction it is divided into the city and liberties of Londonderry, the town and liberties of Coleraine, and the baronies of Coleraine, Tirkeeran, Kenaught, and Loughinsholin. It contains the city of Londonderry; the borough and market-town of Coleraine; the disfranchised borough, market and post. town of Newtown-Limavady; the market and post-towns of Castledawson, Dungiven, Draperstown, Moneymore, Garvagh, Magherafelt, and Maghera; and the post towns of Bellaghy, Kilrea, and Tubbermore. The principal villages are Articlave, Ballykelly, Claudy, Muff, Portstewart (each of which has a penny-post), Ballyronan, Desertmartin, and Swattragh. It sent eight members to the Irish parliament, two for the county, two for the city and two each for the boroughs of Coleraine and Newtown-Limavady. Since the Union it has sent only four to the Imperial parliament, two for the county, one for the city, and one for the borough of Coleraine; those for the city and county are elected in the city of Londonderry. The county constituency as registered up to the October sessions of 1836, consists of 239 £50, 198 £20, and 1402 £10 freeholders; 41 £20 and 412 £10 leaseholders; and 7 £50, and 32 £20 rent-chargers; making a total of 2331 registered electors. Londonderry is included in the north-west circuit: the assizes are held in the city, and quarter sessions are held there and at Coleraine, Newtown-Limavady, and Magherafelt. The county gaol and court-house are in Londonderry, and there are court-houses and bridewells at each of the other sessions towns. The local government is vested in a lieutenant, a vice-lieutenant, 8 deputy-lieutenants, and 61 other magistrates; besides whom there are the usual county officers, including four coroners, one for the city, one for the borough of Coleraine, and two for the county at large. Of its civil jurisdiction it is remarkable that, like the county of Middlesex, its sheriffs are those elected by the citizens of its capital, who serve for the whole, excepting the liberties of Coleraine: the town-clerk of Londonderry, also, is the clerk of the peace for the county at large. There are 19 constabulary police stations, having in the whole a force of a stipendiary magistrate, a sub-inspector, a paymaster, 4 chief officers, 20 constables, 83 men, and 6 horses. The District Lunatic Asylum, and County Infirmary are in the city of Londonderry, and there are dispensaries at Londonderry, Bellaghy,Tamlaght O'Crilly, Port-stewart, Dungiven, Magherafelt, Maghera, Glendermot, Lower-Cumber, Newtown-Limavady, Coleraine, Killowen, Moneymore, Aghadowey, Ballynascreen, and Garvagh, which are supported equally by Grand Jury presentments, and by subscriptions from the Irish Society, the London companies, the landed proprietors, and other private individuals. For the convenience of holding petty sessions, the county is divided into the districts of Coleraine, Garvagh, Innisrush, Maghera, Moneymore, Magherafelt, Kilrea, Inver, city of Londonderry, Newtown-Limavady, Muff, Dungiven, and Clady. The amount of Grand Jury presentments for the county and city, for the year 1835, was £23,996.16.1, of which £1756.12.7 was for the roads, bridges, buildings, &c., of the county at large; £7464.16.3 for the roads, bridges, &c., of the baronies; £8702.11.10 for public buildings, charities, salaries of officers, and incidents; £2066.17.6 for the police; and £4005.17.11 for repayment of advances made by Government. In the military arrangements the county is included in the northern district.

In form the county approaches to an equilateral triangle: its greatest length is from the point of Magilligan, at the mouth of Lough Foyle, nearly southward, to the vicinity of Coagh, a distance of $32\frac{1}{2}$ miles. Although by no means distinguished for picturesque beauty, its surface presents many varieties of form, from the flat alluvial lands along its rivers to the wildest mountains. The latter form its central portion, extending in various chains, covered chiefly with heath, from near the sea-coast to the southern limit. Sawel mountain, in the south, attains an elevation of 2236 feet; Slieve Gallion rises to the height of 1730 feet; Carutogher, near the source of the Roe, 1521 feet; Donald's Hill, east of the same river, 1315 feet; Benyevenagh, forming the termination of that range towards the sea, 1260 feet; and Legavannon, between the Roe and the Faughan, 1289 feet. Even in these wild regions there are secluded vales, called by the inhabitants "slacks," in which are often found charming spots of fertile soil and romantic scenery. The principal of these are, Faughanvale, where there are some romantic waterfalls; Muffglen, which, with the beautiful glen of the Ness, affords mountain passes from the Foyle to the Faughan; Laughermore, between the Roe and the Faughan, which commands various fine prospects, and has in its vicinity numerous traces of ancient forests; Lissane, with some deep romantic glens; Feeny, between the higher parts of the Roe and the Faughan, into which several other glens open, of which the most beautiful is Finglen; the neighbouring slacks of Moneyniceny and Carntogher; that of Ballyness, leading into the wild district of Glenullen; that of Dunmore, between Coleraine and Newtown-Limavady; and that of Druim-na-Gullion, to the north. The most extensive and diversified view in this part of Ireland, is that from the summit of Benyevenagh, near the mouth of the Roe, from which mountain the huge masses of fallen strata form successive terraces descending to the sandy flats bounded by Lough Foyle and the ocean.

The great natural divisions of the profitable lands are, the rich and fertile vales of the Roe, the Faughan, the Foyle (with the liberties of Londonderry), the Moyola, the shores of Lough Neagh, the half valley of the Bann (with the liberties of Coleraine), and the sea coast with the flats of Lough Foyle. The longest of the vales opening from the mountains is that of the Roe, environed by hills appropriated as sheepwalks, and in many places having midway up their declivities a sort of natural terrace, frequently two or three hundred yards in breadth. To the west is the nearly parallel vale of Faughan, which, next to those of the Roe and the Moyola, displays, from Clondermot to the coast of Lough Foyle, one of the most delightful tracts in the county: a considerable portion, however, is occupied by rough though valuable turbaries, while other parts are clothed with natural wood: in the higher part the scenery is frequently romantic, and in other places is improved by round alluvial hills. The vale of the Foyle is highly improved, and comprises the western extremity of the county, in which stands the city of Londonderry. The rich vale of Moyola extends from the eastern side of the mountains of Ballynascreen, towards Lough Neagh, being bounded on the south by Slieve Gallion. The borders of Lough Neagh form a low tract which presents a rich landscape, its surface being composed partly of gentle swells, and its fertility broken only by some extensive bogs. Around Ballinderry are considerable steeps, and at Spring Hill and over the town of Moneymore is a beautiful range of high land: beyond this extends a rich low tract called "the Golden Vale of Ballydawley." Lough Neagh bounds the county for nearly six miles, when the Bann, issuing from it, immediately falls into Lough Beg, the Londonderry shore of which is five miles in extent.

The half valley of the Bann is composed of bleak ridges or tummocks of basalt, with a few more favoured spots near the streams, but accompanied by a series of scattered bogs,

Down Hill. Drawn by J.F. Neale and engraved by T. Higham, published in London, 1821.

bordering the course of the river. These sometimes comprise high and barren swells, with lakes and small bogs intervening. About Tubbermore, Fort William, and Maghaer, however, there is a pleasing and more fertile tract; and the interior of the district bordering on the Bann is greatly enlivened by the woody scenery around Garvagh. The sea coast, formed by the Atlantic for 12 miles from Portrush to Magilligan point, and thence for 16 miles by Lough Foyle, exhibits a succession of varied and interesting scenery. Commencing with Portrush it presents a number of creeks and inlets, of which the most remarkable is Port-Stewart, whence to the mouth of the Bann is a strand of great extent and beauty, succeeded by a range of cliffs rising boldly from the sea, on the summit of one of which is the mansion of Down Hill and Mussenden Temple, built by the Earl of Bristol, Bishop of Derry. From Down Hill to Magilligan Point, a distance of 7 miles, is a strand extending a mile in breadth from the base of the mountains to the water's edge, and on which the whole army of Great Britain might be reviewed. Thence the coast turns nearly due south to the mouth of the Roe, presenting a dreary expanse in which is seen only a deserted house half covered by drifted sand, and a martello tower, after which a varied tract of highly improved land continues to the mouth of Londonderry harbour.

The soil is of great variety. The vale of the Roe chiefly consists of gravelly loams of different degrees of fertility; the levels on the banks of the river are very rich; and though the higher grounds are sometimes intermingled with cold clays, there is scarcely any unproductive land in it. In the vale of Faughan good loams are found in the lowest situations. Bond's glen, which joins it, and rests on a limestone base, is one of the most fertile spots in the county. The valley of the Foyle is also a strong loam below, declining in fertility and depth towards the heights. In the vale of Moyola are levels of the richest quality, but liable to great ravages by floods. In the district bordering on Loughs Neagh and Beg are found sharp gravelly soils of decayed granite, with some moorland, and then extensive swells of sandy loam with intervening flats of great fertility and some bog. Along the sea coast the soil is an intermixture of silicious and calcareous sand, occasionally covered with peat. At the mouth of the Bann these sands form hillocks, kept from shifting by the roots of bentgrass and available only as rabbit warrens; nearly the whole of Magilligan strand is warren, followed by sandy hills covered with bent, and extensive tracts of bog. Beyond Walworth, along the shores of Lough Foyle, the beach is covered with herbage, forming salt marshes greatly esteemed for grazing horses. Lough Foyle is a large gulf, which, communicating with the Atlantic by a very narrow mouth, opens into a fine expanse, extending 15 miles into the country to the city of Londonderry, and being 7 miles across where broadest. Though there are shifting sand banks in some parts, the largest vessel may ride in safety in it in all weathers. The principal part of the mountain soils is based on basalt, generally presenting nothing to the view but bleak knolls rising out of the bog and covered with heath or marshy plants. In some more favoured situations the soil, though poor and loose, produces an herbage greedily depastured by sheep; and in the slacks or glens are found loams of better quality, varying in texture according to the soil of the hills from which they have been deposited.

The fertile soils are chiefly under tillage, in farms varying in size from 2 to 200 acres and averaging eight. Though wheat is cultivated on some of the richest soils, barley is grown to a far more considerable extent, especially in the districts bordering on Lough Neagh, also around Myroe and Coleraine; the other crops most extensively raised are oats, potatoes, and flax; barley is said to pay the summer's rent and flax the winter's. Beans were formerly grown in vast quantities in Aghanloo and in Myroe, and rye in some of the lower districts, but both are now uncommon; four kinds of wheat, red, white, plain and bearded are sown, the produce of which varies from twelve to twenty barrels per acre; of barley, which is all of the four-rowed kind, called bere or Scotch barley, from eight to fourteen barrels of 21 stone (one-half more than the wheat measure); and of oats, of which the brown Poland, lightfoot, blantire and potato oat are commonly sown, from 30 to 70 bushels per acre. Potatoes yield from 200 to 800 bushels per acre. An acre of good flax will produce twelve stooks, each yielding seventy-two pounds of clean scutched flax; but the common produce is one-third less. Turnips are grown by all the gentry and leading farmers, and mangel wurzel is a favourite crop with some; but its cultivation is yet imperfectly understood. The principal artificial grass is clover, to which the annual and perennial ray are sometimes added: these seeds are generally sown as the last crop of a course, but the common farmers seldom sow any, trusting to the powers of the soil and the humidity of the climate to restore the herbage: the prevailing kind is, in marshy situations, the fiorin, or jointed grass, which produces crops of amazing weight and good quality. Of manures, lime, which can be procured in almost every part of the county, is in most extensive use, that of Desertmartin being esteemed the best; the contiguous marl is also used, especially at Cruintballyguillen, or the Leck. In the maritime districts, and from six to ten miles inland, a favourite manure is sea-shells brought by boats from islands in Lough Foyle the shells are chiefly oyster, muscle, and cockle; from 30 to 60 barrels are spread on an acre. Shelly sand is also gathered from the coast and from the shores of the Bann: trenching and throwing the mould on an unturned ridge, and the burning of peat for the ashes, are likewise practised. The breeds of cattle of every kind are much improved by judicious crossing; Derry not being a sheep-feeding county, the attention of the farmers has been less turned to this species of stock; yet some of the gentry have large flocks. Pigs are to be found in almost every house and cottage; they are usually slaughtered at home and the carcasses sent to market for the supply of the provision merchants of Belfast, Londonderry, and Coleraine. Of the horses, one breed is the active, hardy mountain garran, of a bay or sorrel colour and slight make: the Scottish highland horses are likewise in great request, and, together with a cross with the sinewy draught horse, are in common use. A cross with the blood horse has also been introduced. Myroe is famous for good cattle. All the improved agricultural implements are in general use; the advances made in every department of rural economy have been considerably promoted by the exertions of the North West Farming Society, which holds its meetings in Londonderry and receives an annual donation of ten guineas from the Irish Society of London. Among wild fowl, one species is very remarkable, the barnacle, which frequents Lough Foyle in great numbers, and is here much esteemed for the sweetness of its flesh, in like manner as at Wexford and Strangford, though elsewhere rank and unsavoury: this difference arises from its here feeding on the fucus saccharinus. The ancient abundance of timber is evinced both by tradition and public documents, also by the abundance of pine found in all the bogs, of yew at Magilligan, and of fossil oak and fir in the mosses, even in the most exposed situations; but the woods have been wholly demolished by the policy of clearing the country, the lavish waste of fuel, the destruction made by exporting staves (once the staple of the county), and the demand for charcoal for smelting lead and iron. Coal, chiefly from Lancashire, is the principal fuel of the respectable classes in Londonderry and its vicinity. English, Scotch, and Ballycastle coals are used at Coleraine: but almost the universal fuel of the county is turf; in the fertile and thickly inhabited districts many of the bogs are exhausted, and recourse has been had to those of the mountains.

Geologically the county is composed of two great districts, divided into two nearly equal portions by the course of the Roe. The western is the extensive mountain tract reaching from that river to Strabane, in which mica slate predominates in such proportions as to compose nine-tenths of the whole; it is accompanied by primitive limestone in the lower districts, especially in those bordering on the vale of the Roe. On the eastern bank of the same river this system of mountains is succeeded by a range of secondary heights, reposing on and concealing the mica slate, which dips under them eastward. On these is piled a vast area of basalt, forming the basis of almost the entire country between the Roe and the Bann. These basaltic strata dip with the fall of the hills towards the north-east, to meet the opposite dip of the strata on the other side of the Bann, forming the other half of this great basaltic tract. The covering of basalt appears to acquire its greatest thickness on the north, where, as in the cap of Benyevenagh, it is more than 900 feet thick. Between the basalt and the subjacent mica slate are found in close succession many of the most important formations which occupy a great part of the southern and eastern counties of England. Next to the basalt (descending westward towards Lough Foyle and the vale of the Roe, and to the rich lands in the vale of Moyola and its vicinity) is found chalk, in beds of an aggregate thickness of about 200 feet, analogous to the lower beds of the English chalk formation, and therefore approaching in character to white limestone, being used and commonly designated as such. Even in its fossils and organic remains, this chalk is perfectly identified with that of England. Next is seen mulatto, precisely analogous to the green sandstone formations of England: the mulatto rests immediately on a lias limestone, blue and argillaceous, disposed in small beds alternating with slate clay, and distinguished by ammonites, gryphites, and other fossil remains. The lias, in turn, reposes, as in England, on beds of red and variegated marl, containing gypsum, and even distinguished by numerous salt springs; and this marl is underlaid by a thick deposit of red and variegated sandstone, containing clay galls, and in its turn incumbent on the mica slate formation. Sometimes, however, the mulatto and lias are entirely wanting, and the chalk may be seen immediately resting on the sandstone, both of which are constant and continuous. The deep valleys separating the detached eminences of the basalt region afford abundant evidence of their formation in excavations of part of the solid strata by some vast convulsions or operations of nature. North-east of the source of the Roe is a small detached district of mica slate, nearly surrounded by the basaltic ridges of Benbradagh and Cragnashoack, and forming the entire mass of the mountain of Coolcoscrahan. The mountain limestone, which is micaceous and granular, occurs to the most remarkable extent on the north-west side of Carntogher mountain, in Bennady glen, near the old church at Dungiven, at Banagher, near Clady, near Newtown Limavady, and on Slieve Gallion mountain, where it contains crystallised hornblende in abundance. Horn blende slate occurs in Bennady glen, Aglish glen, and the bed of the Roe river near Dungiven, where it is contiguous to the primitive limestone. Porphyry is the fundamental rock on the east side of Slieve Gallion, and one variety resembles sienite, with which it is in connection. Transition trap also occurs on Slieve Gallion.

The transition limestone, intervening in a few places between the primitive formations and the sandstone, is of the same kind as that which occupies so great a portion of the central counties: it is of a smoke grey colour, contains two sorts of terebratulites, and nodules of glassy quartz, which render it dangerous to blast; but being, nevertheless, the best species in the county for manure and all ordinary purposes, it is most extensively quarried. The sandstone extends the entire length of the county, from its northern extremity near Down hill up the eastern side of the Roe, and surrounding Cragnashoack and Carntogher mountains, whence it stretches by the eastern declivity of Slieve Gallion into the county of Tyrone. The upper strata of chalk are characterised by parallel beds of flinty nodules; and, at their junction with the basalt, these flints are found imbedded in the lowest member of the trap deposit: it is curiously affected by intersecting dykes filled with basalt. The only great geological phenomenon exhibited on the sea-coast is the gradual emergence of the chalk from under the trap beds. The basalt is chiefly tabular, with the varieties called greenstone, amygdaloidal wacke, &c. A laminated schist of the mica slate formation is quarried between Derry and Newtown; there is a good quarry of lamellated schist between Bond's glen and Gossaden; gneiss occurs in the quarries of the mica slate near the Faughan river; granite on the northern summit of Slieve Gallion; the finest rock crystals are found in Finglen, Dungiven, Banagher, and in the primitive mountains near Learmount; and steatite is found in the basaltic region. Iron is found disseminated through many of the strata of the county, and in the basalt is sometimes so abundant as to affcct the needle. Ironstone, found in great abundance in Slieve Gallion, was formerly worked, but the undertaking was abandoned on the failure of fuel. The metal is found in a mixed state with manganese; and in the mountain streams mounds of it are observed in the character of yellow ochre. To the abundance of this metal in the peat moss are owing the red colour and weight of the ashes. Coal, copper, and lead have been found in very small quantities.

The staple manufacture is that of linen, of which the raw material is grown here, chiefly from American and Riga seed, though partly from Dutch, which is most esteemed. The flax is spun by the rural population, and the weavers themselves are husbandmen; so that during seed-time and harvest the loom is abandoned. The flax is generally spun from three to four hanks in the pound weight, and the tow yarn is made into sacking for home use. The coarser yarn is carried to Londonderry to be exported to Liverpool for Manchester, and some to Scotland, the finer being disposed of at Coleraine, Newtown, &c. The fabric made in Coleraine is the finest, and all webs of the same texture, wherever manufactured, are called Coleraines. The fabrics of Londonderry are of two kinds, one only twenty-seven inches wide, made of tow yarn, and called Derry wrappers; the other thirty-two inches wide, and made of fine yarn. Considerable quantities of linens are exported unbleached; the coarse chiefly to Liverpool. The white linens are shipped from Londonderry or Coleraine to Liverpool or London. Coarse red pottery is made at Agivey, and at some other places. There are several distilleries and breweries, and numerous corn and flour mills. The coast abounds with all the ordinary kinds of fish, which are taken for home consumption; but the principal fisheries are those of salmon and eels in the Bann, which are superior in extent to any others in Ireland, employing a great number of persons; almost the entire produce of salmon is exported. There are several other considerable fisheries along the sea-coast and in the small rivers; but most of the salmon brought to the provincial markets comes from a distance of several miles, and is much inferior to that of the Bann. The commerce of the county centres in the city of Londonderry and the town of Coleraine, but chiefly the former. At Ballyronan, on Lough Neagh, vessels of sixty tons burden can unlade, and, though the exports are inconsiderable, timber, iron, slates, coal, flax seed, hardware, and groceries are landed in large quantities.

The principal rivers are the Foyle, the Bann, the Roe, and the Faughan. The Foyle, which derives its name from the smoothness of its current, intersects the liberties of the city of Londonderry, in a majestic course north-eastward, having descended from Lifford, where, after the union of several important streams, it first obtains its name: at Culmore, six miles below the city, which it appears formerly to have insulated, it expands into the estuary of Lough Foyle. The Bann, or "White River," so called from the purity of its waters, intersects the liberties of Coleraine, within four miles of its junction with the ocean; but the navigation is greatly obstructed by shallows and a very dangerous bar, where the currents of the fresh water and the tide meet. The Roe, or "Red River," so called from the colour of its waters, receives at Dungiven the Owen-Reagh: hence, in its course directly north, it receives from the mountains on each side the Owen-Beg, the Gelvin-water, the Balteagh river, and the Castle and Curley rivers; and winding through the fertile flat by Newtown-Limavady, it falls into Lough Foyle at Myroe. The flat country bordering the lower part of its course is exposed to sudden and impetuous floods poured down from the surrounding mountains: many acres of the finest lands are with difficulty defended by embankments, and even with this protection the securing of the crop is never a matter of certainty. The deposits brought down by this river form many shifting banks in the Lough, which prevent its mouth from becoming a convenient little port, although there is sufficient depth of water at high tides. The Faughan in its course receives numerous rills and streams from the surrounding heights, and falls into Lough Foyle. The Moyola is a considerable stream descending into Lough Neagh; the principal tributaries of the Bann are the Clady, Agivey, and Macosquin streams. There are no canals connected with the county, but an inland navigation, either by a canal, or lateral cuts along the Bann, is contemplated from Lough Neagh to Coleraine, and a bill is now being applied for to enable the proprietors of the lands round the lake to lower it to a summer level, and thereby render the Baun navigable to Coleraine. The contemplated line of railway from Armagh to Portrush will pass for more than 30 miles through the county, but no steps have yet been taken respecting it, beyond the selection of the line. The roads are numerous and highly important, several very useful lines have been made and others greatly improved solely at the expense of the Drapers' Company; all the other roads are made and kept in repair by Grand Jury presentments. Several new lines of road are contemplated, the principal of which is a mail road from Belfast to Derry, of which that portion from the Pullans to Coleraine is already commenced.

In the original plantation of the county in 1609, and the subsequent years, the English settlers were located in the fertile tracts along the borders of Loughs Foyle and Neagh, and the banks of the Roe and Bann; the Scotch were placed in the higher lands as a kind of military barrier between their more favoured brethren of the south country and the Irish, who, with the exception of a few native freeholders, were removed to the mountain districts. The varieties of religion corresponded with those of country, the English being Protestants of the Established Church; the Scotch, Presbyterians, or other sects of Protestant dissenters; and the Irish, Roman Catholics. This arrangement of severance long prevented, and still in some degree continues to prevent, the amalgamation of the several classes. The Irish, shut up within their secluded mountain ravines, retain many of their peculiarities of language, customs, and religion; those of Glenullin, though near a large Protestant settlement at Garvagh will admit none but members of their own church to reside among them, though in other respects they are on terms of great kindliness with their neighbours of a different creed, except when under the excitation of party animosity. The residences of many respectable gentlemen are in the cottage style, generally ornamented and surrounded with planting and gardens: the habitations of the rural population are of every description, from the slated two-story house of brick or stone, and the long narrow cottage with two or three partitions, to the cabin of dry stone or clay, without even a window. In the districts of Coleraine and Desertmartin, where lime is plentiful, the dwellings of the peasantry are neatly white-washed, and sometimes rough-cast, but in other parts they present a very sombre appearance.

Remains of its ancient inhabitants of every period are scattered over the county. There is a cromlech at Slaght Manus, another at Letter-Shandenny, a third at Slaghtaverty, and others at Bally-na-screen: some had been surrounded by a circle of upright stones. There are remains of sepulchral mounts or tumuli at Mullaghcross, and a vast tumulus is seen at Dovinc, between Newtown-Limavady and Coleraine, besides several of smaller dimensions. Numerous cairns are met with in every quarter, especially on the summits of the mountains. Near Dungiven is a very remarkable sepulchral pillar. Raths or Danish forts are likewise scattered in chains in every direction, each being generally within sight of two others: the most remarkable is that called the Giant's Sconce, anciently commanding the communication between the districts of Newtown and Coleraine. Ditches enclosing spaces of from half a rood to several acres are also discernible contiguous to these forts. There is a curious mound surrounded with a moat on the road from Springhill to Lough Neagh; and another, of larger size, at Dungorkin, on the road from Cumber Clady through Loughermore. Ancient intrenchments of different character are seen at Prospect, and between Gortnagasan and Cathery. Various coins, pins, rings, and forks have been found about a moat near Lough Neagh, and, among other ancient instruments, quern stones have often been discovered. Hatchets made of hard basalt, spears of grey granite, and barbed arrowheads of flint (the last sometimes neatly executed, and vulgarly called elfstones) are very frequently found. Sometimes gold and silver coins, fibulae, and gorgets, with other ornaments, are dug up, but these are rare. There are many artificial caverns, which seem to have been designed for the concealment of goods, or for the refuge of families in case of sudden attack: the sides are built of common land stones without cement, and the roof is composed of flags, or long stones, but the vault is seldom high enough for the passage of a man in a stooping posture; they consist sometimes of different galleries, and the mouth was most usually concealed by a rock or grassy sod.

Besides the remains of monastic institutions in the city of Londonderry, seventeen others appear to have existed within the limits of the county; there are still remains of those situated respectively at Camus, Errigal, Tamlaghtfinlagan, Domnach-Dola, and Dungiven, at the last of which are the most interesting of all the ecclesiastical ruins. Near the old church of Banagher is a monastic building almost entire. There are few castles of Irish erection. Ballyreagh, on a rocky cliff overhanging the sea, is said to have belonged to one of the Mac Quillans; and a castle which stood near the church of Ballyaghran is reported to have been the abode of the chief of that sept. There were several English castles, with bawns and flankers, built by the London companies, one at least in every proportion of allotment, but they are all in ruins except Bellaghy, which is still occupied.

AGHADOWEY, or AGHADOEY, a parish, in the half-barony of COLERAINE, county of LONDONDERRY, and province of ULSTER, 6 miles (S. by W.) from Coleraine, on the road from that place to Dungannon; containing 7634 inhabitants. This parish, which is bounded on the north-east by the river Bann, is $10^3/_4$ miles in length from north-west to south-east; and $4^1/_2$ miles in breadth from north-east to south-west; and, with the extra-parochial grange or liberty of Agivey, which is locally within its limits, and has since the Reformation been attached to it, comprises, according to the Ordnance survey, $18,115^3/_4$ statute acres, of which $1727^3/_4$ are in Agivey, $119^1/_2$ are covered with water, and 16,290 are applotted under the tithe act. Its western extremity is mountainous and barren, but eastward towards the river the soil is fertile; the lands are generally in a high state of cultivation, particularly in the neighbourhood of Keeley, Ballybrittan, Rushbrook, Flowerfield, and Mullamore; in the valley where the Agivey and Aghadowy waters meet, the soil is very rich. Previously to the year 1828, no wheat was grown in this parish; but since that period the system of agriculture has been greatly improved, and, in 1832, Mr. James Hemphill introduced the cultivation of mangel-wurzel and turnips, which has been attended with complete success. There are considerable tracts of bog, but they will soon be exhausted by the large quantities annually consumed in the bleach-greens; and in the western or mountainous parts are large tracts of land which, from the depth of the soil, might easily be brought into cultivation. Ironstone is found in several parts, but is more particularly plentiful in the townland of Bovagh. The greater portion of the parish formed part of the lands granted, in 1609, by Jas. I. to the Irish Society, and is now held under the Ironmongers' Company, of London, by whom, on the expiration of the present leases, the lands will be let, as far as may be practicable, on the English principle: the Mercers' company, the Bishop of Derry, and the Rev. T. Richardson are also proprietors. There are numerous gentlemen's seats, of which the principal are Rushbrook, the residence of J. Knox, Esq.; Landmore, of Geo. Dunbar, Esq.; Flowerfield, of J. Hunter, Esq.; Flowerfield, of Mrs. Hemphill; Keeley, of Andrew Orr, Esq.; Ballydivitt, of T. Bennett, Esq.; Mullamore, of A. Barklie, Esq.; Moneycarrie, of J. McCleery, Esq.; Meath Park, of J. Wilson, Esq.; Bovagh, of R. Hezlett, Esq.; and Killeague, of Mrs. Wilson. Previously to 1730 the parish was for the greater part unenclosed and uncultivated; but three streams of water which intersect it attracted the attention of some spirited individuals engaged in the linen trade, which at that time was coming into notice, and had obtained the sanction of some legislative enactments for its encouragement and support. Of these, the first that settled here with a view to the introduction of that trade were Mr. J. Orr, of Ballybrittan, and Mr. J. Blair of Ballydivitt, who, in 1744, established some bleach-greens; since that time the number has greatly increased, and there are at present not less than eleven in the parish, of which ten are in full operation. The quantity of linen bleached and finished here, in 1833, amounted to 126,000 pieces, almost exclusively for the English market; they are chiefly purchased in the brown state in the markets of Coleraine, Ballymoney, Strabane, and Londonderry, and are generally known in England as "Coleraines," by which name all linens of a similar kind, wherever made, are now called, from the early celebrity which that town acquired for linens of a certain width and quality. In addition to the bleaching and finishing, Messrs. A. and G. Barklie have recently introduced the manufacture of linens, and have already 800 looms employed. Coarse kinds of earthenware, bricks, and water pipes, are manufactured in considerable quantities; and when the navigation of the river Bann is opened, there is every probability that this place will increase in importance.

The living is a rectory, in the diocese of Derry, constituting the corps of the prebend of Aghadowy in the cathedral church of that see, and in the patronage of the Bishop the tithes amount to £500. The church, situated in a fertile vale near the centre of the parish, and rebuilt in 1797, is a small neat edifice with a handsome tower, formerly surmounted by a lofty octagonal spire, erected at the expense of the late Earl of Bristol (when bishop of Derry), but which was destroyed by lightning in 1826; the tower, being but slightly injured, was afterwards embattled and crowned with pinnacles: the Ecclesiastical Commissioners have lately granted £183 for the repair of the church. The late Board of First Fruits granted £100 towards the erection of a glebe-house, in 1789; and in 1794 the present house, called Blackheath, was built by the late Sir Harvey Bruce, Bart, as a glebe-house for the parish. It is a handsome residence; over the mantel-piece in the drawing-room is an elegant sculpture, representing Socrates discovering his pupil Alcibiades in the haunts of dissipation, which was brought from Italy by Lord Bristol, and presented to Sir H. Bruce. The glebe lands comprise 403 statute acres, exclusively of a glebe of 121 acres in Agivey; and the gross value of the prebend, as returned by His Majesty's Commissioners on Ecclesiastical Revenues, is £880 per annum. In the R. C. divisions this parish forms part of the union or district of Killowen, or Coleraine, and contains a small chapel at Mullaghinch. There are places of worship for Presbyterians of the Synod of Ulster (of the first class), Seceders in connection with the Associate Synod (of the second class), and Covenanters, situated respectively at Aghadowy, Ringsend, Ballylintagh, and Killeague. There are five schools, situated respectively at Mullaghinch, Droghead, Collins, Drumstaple, and Killeague, supported by the Ironmongers' Company; two free schools at Gorran and Callyrammer, and two schools situated at Blackheath and Ballynakelly, of which the former, for females only, is supported by the rector's lady, and the latter is aided by an annual donation from Mr. Knox. About 530 boys and 350 girls are taught in these schools; and there is a private school of about 16 boys and 20 girls. A religious establishment was founded here, in the 7th century, by St. Goarcus, as a cell to the priory or abbey founded by him at Agivey, the latter of which became a grange to the abbey of St. Mary-de-la-Fouta, or Mecasquin, in 1172. A very splendid lachrymatory or double patera of pure gold, of exquisite workmanship and in good preservation, was found at Mullaghinch in 1832, and is now in the possession of Alexander Barklie, Esq. In the townland of Crevilla is a large druidical altar, called by the country people the "Grey Stane;" and on the mountains above Rushbrook is a copious chalybeate spring, powerfully impregnated with iron and sulphur held in solution by carbonic acid gas.

AGHANLOO, or AGHANLOE, a parish, in the barony of KENAUGHT, county of LONDONDERRY, and province of ULSTER, 2 miles (N.) from Newtown-Limavady; containing 2159 inhabitants. It comprises, according to the Ordnance survey, 8251¼ statute acres, of which 50¾ acres are under water. On the plantation of Ulster in the reign of Jas. I., the lands of this parish and several others were allotted to the Haberdashers' Company, of London, who selected this as the head of their territory, and built a bawn and castle for its defence, in 1619, which was called Bally Castle, or "the Castle of the Town," and placed under the custody of Sir Robt. McLellan, who had a garrison of 80 able men and arms for its protection. In the war of 1641 the castle was besieged by the insurgents, headed by Capt. 0. Hagan, but was bravely defended by Capt. Philips, its governor, till May in the following year, when it was relieved by the united Derry and Strabane troops, under the command of Col. Mervyn, and the assailants put to flight; but in the contentions which afterwards ensued it was destroyed, and has ever since been in ruins. The lands are of variable quality; in the district bordering on the Roe the soil is fertile, being principally composed of gravel, with a mixture of clay, and produces abundant crops of wheat, oats, &c.; towards the mountains it is a stiff marl, with a substratum of white limestone, and produces excellent crops of flax and oats. The mountain of Benyevenagh, consisting entirely of basalt, and rising to the height of 1260 feet above the level of Lough Foyle, which washes its base, affords excellent pasturage, and is cultivated on the western side nearly to its summit. Limestone abounds, and is found ranging immediately under the basalt throughout the whole length of the parish. The living is a rectory, in the diocese of Derry, and in the patronage of the Bishop: the tithes amount to £315. The church, a small neat edifice in the early English style, was erected in 1826, by aid of a grant from the late Board of First Fruits; it has a lofty square tower crowned with pinnacles, and is situated about a quarter of a mile to the south of the ruins of the old church. Divine service is also performed in two school-houses, in distant parts of the parish, alternately once every Sunday, in summer, and twice in winter. The glebe-house, nearly adjoining the church, is a handsome residence; the glebe comprises 32a. 1r. l9p. of excellent land. In the R. C. divisions the parish is included partly in the union or district of Magilligan, and partly in that of Newtown-Limavady. There are schools at Lisnagrib, Stradragh, and Ballycarton, in which are about 140 boys and 90 girls; and there is also a private school of about 11 boys and 7 girls. The parochial school, supported by the rector, is at present discontinued, in consequence of the erection of a new school-house now in progress at the expense of the Marquess of Waterford. A portion of the south wall of the old church is still remaining; it was destroyed by the insurgents in 1641, and was rebuilt from the produce of forfeited impropriations, by order of Wm. III. The Rev. G. V. Sampson, author of a "Map and Memoir of the County of Derry," was rector of this parish, and his statistical survey is dated from the glebe of Aghanloo.

AGHERTON, or BALLYAGHRAN, a parish, in the liberties of COLERAINE, county of LONDONDERRY, and province of ULSTER, 3 miles (N. N. W.) from Coleraine; containing, with the town of Portstewart, 2746 inhabitants. This parish occupies the whole of the promontory between the Bann and the Atlantic, comprising, according to the Ordnance survey, 3896¾ statute acres, of which 3709 are applotted under the tithe act, and valued at £2831 per annum. With the exception of about 320 acres, the whole is arable; there is a small portion of unenclosed land, part of which is light and sandy, and chiefly a rabbit warren, and part affords excellent pasture. The cultivation of wheat was introduced by Mr. Orr, in 1829, and great quantities are now annually raised. Similar success attended the cultivation of barley, potatoes, mangel-wurzel, and turnips; and the agriculture of the parish is at present in a very flourishing state. Iron-ore is found in great quantities, and might be worked to great advantage, but no works have yet been established. There are several gentlemen's seats, the principal of which are Cromore, an elegant mansion, the residence of J. Cromie, Esq. the principal proprietor in the parish, who has recently planted several acres with forest and other trees; Flowerfield, of S. Orr, Esq.; O'Hara Castle, of H. O'Hara, Esq.; Low Rock, of Miss McManus; and Black Rock, of T. Bennett, Esq. There are also several villas and handsome bathing lodges at Portstewart, a pleasant and well-attended watering-place. A small manufacture of linen and linen yarn is carried on, and many of the inhabitants are employed in the fisheries, particularly in the salmon fishery on the river Bann. Of late, great quantities of salmon have been taken along the whole coast, by means of a newly invented net; and the sea fishery is continued for a long time after that on the river is by law compelled to cease. The Bann, which is the only outlet from Lough Neagh, discharges itself into the Atlantic at the western point of the parish; it appears to have changed its course, and now passes close under the point of Down Hill, the celebrated mansion erected by the Earl of Bristol, when Bishop of Derry.

The living is a rectory, in the diocese of Connor, united by charter of Jas. I., in 1609, to the rectory of Ardclinis, together constituting the union of Agherton, and the corps of the treasurership in the cathedral church of St. Saviour, Connor, in the patronage of the Bishop. The tithes amount to £240; and the tithes of the union, including glebe, amount to £470, constituting the gross income of the treasurership, to which no duty is annexed. The church, a small edifice, was erected in 1826, at an expense of £960, of which £100 was raised by subscription, £800 was a loan from the late Board of First Fruits, and £60 was given by John Cromie, Esq., who also paid the interest on £700 of the loan until the debt was cancelled in 1833. Divine service is also performed by the curate every Sunday in the school-house at Portstewart. The glebe-house, a handsome residence close adjoining the church, was built in 1806, for which the Board granted a gift of £250 and a loan of £500; the glebe comprises 20 acres of profitable land, valued at £80 per annum. In the R. C. divisions the parish forms part of the union or district of Coleraine. There are places of worship for Presbyterians and Wesleyan Methodists, the former in connection with the Synod of Ulster and of the third class. There is a male free school, and a female and two infants' schools are supported by Mrs. Cromie, who has built a large school-room for one of the latter: 275 children are taught in these schools; and there are four private schools, in which are about 130 children, and four Sunday schools. Mark Kerr O'Neill, Esq., in 1814, bequeathed £40 per ann. to the poor. There are some remains of the ancient castle of Mac Quillan on the glebe land adjoining the church. Near them are the gabled walls of the old church, still tolerably entire; and in the adjoining field is an extensive cave formed of uncemented walls covered with large flat stones, one of the largest and most perfect yet known in this part of the country there are also several other caves in the parish. In the townland of Carnanee is a very fine triangular fort, called Craig-an-Ariff; it is defended by fosses and breastworks, and is the only fort so constructed in this part of Ireland; within the enclosure are two cairns or tumuli. Dr. Adam Clarke, whose father kept a school for several years in the old parish church, received the rudiments of his education here; and in the latter part of his life spent much of his time in the summer at Portstewart, where during his stay in 1830, he built a handsome house, and erected in the gardens of Mr. Cromie a curious astronomical and geographical dial, which is still preserved there. – See PORTSTEWART.

AGIVEY, a grange, or extra-parochial district, locally in the parish of AGHADOWY, half-barony of COLERAINE, county of LONDONDERRY, and province of ULSTER, 6 miles (S. S. E.) from Coleraine; containing 938 inhabitants. This place appears to have been the site of a religious establishment, by some called a priory and by others an abbey, the foundation of which, about the beginning of the seventh century, is attributed to St. Goarcus, who afterwards founded a cell at Agha. Dubthaigh, now Aghadowy. This establishment subsequently became dependent on the abbey of St. Mary-de-la-Fonta, or Mecasquin, which was founded in the year 1172, and to which this district became a grange. There are still some slight remains of the ancient religious house, with an extensive cemetery, in which are some tombs of the ancient family of the Cannings, ancestors of the present Lord Garvagh. The liberty is situated on the western bank of the river Bann, and on the road from Newtown-Limavady to Ballymoney, which is continued over the river by a light and handsome bridge of wood, of 6 arches 203 feet in span, erected in 1834 at the joint expense of the counties of Londonderry and Antrim. It comprises, according to the Ordnance survey, 1727$^{3}/_{4}$ statute acres, the whole of which is free from tithe or parochial assessment, and forms part of the estates of the Ironmongers' Company, of London. The land is fertile, but being divided into small holdings in the occupation of tenants without capital to expend on its Improvement, has been greatly neglected, and no regular system of agriculture has been adopted; there is a small tract of bog, which is now nearly worked out for fuel. Potters' clay of good quality is found here in great abundance; and a considerable manufacture of coarse earthenware, bricks, and water pipes is carried on for the supply of the neighbourhood. Iron-stone is found near the Aghadowy water, and there are also some indications of coal. A fair is held on Nov. 12th, under a charter granted to the monks of Coleraine at a very early period, and is chiefly for the sale of cattle and pigs. There is neither church nor any place of worship in the district; the inhabitants attend divine service at the several places of worship in Aghadowy.

ARBOE, or ARDBOE, a parish, partly in the barony of

LOUGHINSHOLIN, county of LONDONDERRY, but chiefly in the barony of DUNGANNON, county of TYRONE, and province of ULSTER, 5 miles (E. N. E.) from Stewartstown; containing 8148 inhabitants. A monastery was founded here by St. Colman, son of Aidhe, and surnamed Mucaidhe, whose reliques were long preserved in it: it was destroyed in 1166, by Rory Makang Makillmory Omorna, but there are still some remains. The parish is situated on the shore of Lough Neagh, by which it is bounded on the east, and comprises, according to the Ordnance survey, 33,504 statute acres, of which 21,000 form part of Lough Neagh, and 56 are in small islands. The greater portion is under tillage, and there are some tracts of good meadow, about 50 acres of woodland, and 1000 acres of bog. The system of agriculture is improved; the soil is fertile, and the lands generally in a high state of cultivation. There are several large and handsome houses, the principal of which is Elogh, the residence of Mrs. Mackay. The living is a rectory, in the diocese of Armagh, and in the patronage of the Provost and Fellows of Trinity College Dublin: the tithes amount to £507.13.10½. The church, a neat small edifice, was erected in the reign of William and Mary, on a site two miles westward from the ruins of the ancient abbey. The glebe-house is a handsome building; and the glebe comprises 212 acres. The R. C. parish is co-extensive with that of the Established Church; the chapel, a spacious and handsome edifice, is situated at New Arboe; and there are two altars in the open air, where divine service is performed alternately once every Sunday. There is a place of worship for Presbyterians in connection with the Seceding synod. There are four public schools, in which about 320 boys and 240 girls are taught; and there are also five private schools, in which are about 140 boys and 50 girls, and five Sunday schools. On the western shore of Lough Neagh are the ruins of the ancient abbey; which form an interesting and picturesque feature; and the remains of an old church, of which the walls are standing. Near them is an ancient ornamented stone cross in good preservation.

BALLINDERRY, or BALLYDERRY, a parish, partly in the barony of DUNGANNON, county of TYRONE, but chiefly in the barony of LOUGHINSHOLIN, county of LONDONDERRY, and province of ULSTER, 7 miles (S. E. by E.) from Moneymore; containing 3163 inhabitants. This parish is situated on the Ballinderry river, which here separates the above-named baronies and counties, and falls into the north-western portion of Lough Neagh. It comprises, according to the Ordnance survey, 8177 statute acres, of which 2268½ are in the county of Tyrone, and 5908½ are in Londonderry; 2978 acres form a portion of Lough Neagh. The greater part belongs to the Salters' Company, of London; part belongs to the see of Derry; and some of the lands are held under Cromwellian debentures, and are the only lands in the county of Londonderry, west of the river Bann, that are held by that tenure. A castle was built by the Salters' Company at Salterstown, in 1615, soon after they had obtained the grant of those lands from Jas. I.; and in the insurrection of 1641 it was surprised by Sir Phelim O'Nial, who put all the inmates to death, with the exception of the keeper, who, with his wife and family, effected their escape to Carrickfergus, where, taking refuge in the church, they were finally starved to death. It continued for some time in the possession of the insurgents, who, being ultimately driven from their post, destroyed it, together with the church adjoining. Nearly the whole of the land is arable and under an excellent system of cultivation; a valuable tract of bog produces excellent fuel, and there is no wasteland. There are several large and well-built houses in the parish; but the only seat is Ballyronan, that of J. Gaussen, Esq. The inhabitants combine with agricultural pursuits the weaving of linen and cotton cloth; and at Ballyronan an extensive distillery has been lately established by Messrs. Gaussen, situated on the shore of Lough Neagh, close to the little port of Ballyronan. The living is a rectory, in the diocese of Armagh, and in the patronage of the Lord-Primate: the tithes amount to £192.6.2. The church, a large edifice in the later English style of architecture, was erected in 1707. The glebe-house, nearly adjoining, was built at an expense of £980, of which £100 was a gift from the late Board of First Fruits, in 1795: the glebe comprises 413 acres of well-cultivated arable land. The R. C. parish is co-extensive with that of the Established Church; there is a chapel at Ballylifford, and at Derryaghrin is an altar in the open air. Near the church is a place of worship for Wesleyan Methodists. The parochial school, in which are about 40 boys and 20 girls, is aided by a donation of £10 per annum from the rector; and there are three Sunday schools, one of which is held in the R. C. chapel, and three daily pay schools, in which are about 80 children. The ruins of the castle at Salterstown, situated on the margin of the lake, present a picturesque and interesting appearance, but are fast mouldering away. Adjoining the bridge over the river are the remains of an ancient iron forge, erected by the Salters' Company in 1626, but which soon after fell into disuse. At Salterstown, near the site of the old church and close to the shore of Lough Neagh, is a chalybeate spring, which has been found efficacious in cutaneous disorders, and was formerly much resorted to; but having become mixed with other water, its efficacy is greatly diminished. At Ballyronan is a large ancient fortress in good preservation.

BALLYKELLY, a village, in the parish of TAMLAGHT-FINLAGAN, barony of KENAUGHT, county of LONDONDERRY, and province of ULSTER, 3 miles (W. by S.) from Newtownlimavady; containing 290 inhabitants. This place, with the lands around it, was granted by Jas. I., on the plantation of Ulster, to the Fishmongers' Company of London, who, in 1619, erected a large and handsome castle, the custody of which was entrusted to James Higgins, Esq., who had a garrison of 40 able men, with arms for its defence. The estate was held under lease from the company, by the Hamiltons and Beresfords, from the year 1628 till the death of Geo. III., when it reverted to the company, who immediately commenced improvements on an extensive scale. The village is situated on the road from Londonderry to Coleraine, and contains 67 houses, of which the greater number are handsomely built. The proprietors have built in it several very neat cottages; a large and handsome meeting-house, in the Grecian style of architecture, for Presbyterians in connection with the Synod of Ulster; an excellent dispensary, with a very good house for a resident surgeon; and large and substantial school-rooms, with residences for the master and mistress; and various other improvements are in progress in and around the village. Nearly adjoining are several large and handsome houses, the principal of which arc Walworth, the residence of the Rev. G. V. Sampson; Walworth Cottage, of Major Stirling; Drummond, of A. Sampson, Esq.; and Finlagan, of the Rev. O. McCausland. Walworth was built by the Beresfords in 1705, and occupied by that family till the death of Geo. III.; the woods around it contain some of the finest timber in the county, and arc among the most extensive in the north of Ireland. Corn stores have been built; and a market for grain is occasionally held. A penny post from Londonderry to this place has been established. Close to the village is the parish church of Tamlaght-Finlagan, a small but handsome edifice, with a large square tower surmounted by a lofty octagonal spire; and here is a Presbyterian meeting-house, a spacious and handsome edifice, of the first class. Near the church are the ruins of Walworth castle, erected by the company in 1619; and adjoining are the ruins of a church, built by the Hamilton family in 1629. – See TAMLAGHT-FINLAGAN.

BALLYNASCREEN, a parish, in the barony of LOUGHINSHOLIN, county of LONDONDERRY, and province of ULSTER; containing, with the market and post-town of Draperstown, 7854 inhabitants.This appears to have been a place of importance at a very early period; frequent notice of it occurs in the Trias Thaumaturga and other ancient records, though it is neither mentioned in the Monasticon nor in the Visitation of 1622, which include every other parish in the neighbourhood. The original church, the ruins of which are situated in a romantic and sequestered glen among the mountains, is said to have been founded by St Patrick, and subsequently conscrecated by St Columb as a parochial church. The parish is intersected by the river Moyola, which has its sources amidst the mountain regions of Slieve Gullion, Moneymeeney, and Slieve Dovin, which extend into the county of Tyrone, where they meet the Munterloney range. It comprises, according to the Ordnance Survey, 32,492 statute acres, of which about 200 acres are mountain, waste and bog. Part of the parish belongs to the Drapers' Company, of London, part to the representative of the Skinners' Company, and part to the see of Derry. The soil is various: around Draperstown and on the banks of the Moyola it is a deep gravel and sand, and in an excellent state of cultivation, producing good crops of wheat, flax, oats, and potatoes, and some barley, but on the higher grounds the chief crops are flax, oats, and potatoes. The freestone is of superior quality and is extensively worked for building. Manganese has been found in detached nodules in several of the mountain streams: and Boate, in his natural History, states that gold has been also discovered here. Derrynoyd Lodge is the residence of the Rt. Hon. Judge Torrens. The inhabitants are principally employed in agriculture, with which they combine the weaving of linen and dealing in cattle, great numbers of which are bred on the mountains and exported to England and Scotland.

The living is a rectory, in the diocese of Derry, and in the patronage of the Bishop: the tithes amount to £623.1.6$^1/_2$. The church, a large handsome edifice in the early English style, is situated at Draperstown, and was erected in 1760, principally through means of the Earl of Bristol, then Bishop of Derry; and the tower and a handsome octagonal spire were added in 1792, aided by contributions from Sir Wm. Rowley, Bart., and the Drapers' Company, the latter of whom are proprietors of the estate and contributed £50. The glebe-house, a handsome residence, is situated on a glebe of 161a.3r.12p; and there is another glebe in the townland of Bancran, containing 750a.1r.7p, much of which is mountain and pasture land. The R. C. parish is co-extensive with that of the Established Church; there are chapels at Moneymeeny and Straw. Two male and female schools are supported by the rector; two, situated at Black Hill and Carnamony, are supported by the Drapers' Company; and there are seven schools, situated respectively at Draperstown, Derrynoyd, Brackragh-Dysart, Drumard, Labby, Altyaskey, and Straw, under the National Board. In these schools are about 700 boys and 520 girls; and there are also two private schools, in which are about 100 children; and five Sunday schools. The ruins of the old church are highly interesting. There are numerous relics of antiquity, particularly cromlechs, of which there were formerly five within the limits of the parish. – See DRAPERSTOWN.

BALLYRASHANE, or ST. JOHN'S-TOWN, a parish, partly in the barony of LOWER DUNLUCE, county of ANTRIM, but chiefly in the north-east liberties of COLERAINE, county of LONDONDERRY, and province of ULSTER, 3 miles (N. E.) from Coleraine; containing 2851 inhabitants. This parish is situated on the road from Coleraine to Ballycastle, and comprises, according to the Ordnance survey, 6360$^3/_4$ statute acres, of which 2689 are in the county of Antrim, and the remainder in the county of Londonderry. The greater portion of the land is fertile and in a high state of cultivation; wheat and barley have been introduced since the year 1829, and are raised with great success. There are detached portions of bog, affording a good supply of fuel. Vast quantities of basalt are raised; and in a geological point of view the parish is very interesting, containing beautiful specimens of amorphous, columnar, and divaricated basalt, which arc found here in all their varieties, accompanied with chalcedony, opal, zeolite, and other fossils; it abounds

BAL

also with botanical specimens of considerable interest. Brookhall, the seat of S. Boyce, Esq., is in this parish. The inhabitants are principally employed in the weaving of linen cloth; and there are some paper-mills for brown and fancy papers, affording employment to about 30 persons. The living is a rectory, in the diocese of Connor, and in the patronage of the Bishop: the tithes amount to £350. The church is a plain small edifice, in the later English style, erected by aid of a grant of £900 from the late Board of First Fruits, in 1826. The glebe-house, nearly adjoining it, was built in 1828: there is no glebe. In the R. C. divisions the parish forms part of the union or district of Coleraine. There are two places of worship for Presbyterians in connection with the Synod of Ulster; one at Kirkstown of the first class, and the other at Ballywatt of the third class. The male and female parochial schools at Lisnarick are supported by the rector, who also contributes annually to the support of a school at Ballyrack; at Ballyvelton is also a school, and there are two private pay schools and two Sunday schools. At Revellagh are the ruins of a castle and fort. There are also some extensive artificial caverns at Ballyvarten, Island Effick, and Ballynock; the first has four rooms or cells, 5 feet high and $2\frac{1}{2}$ feet wide, having the sides formed of unhewn stones and the roof of large flat stones.

BALLYRONAN, or PORTBALLYRON, a village, in the district of Wood's-chapel, barony of LOUGHINSHOLIN, county of LONDONDERRY, and province of ULSTER, 3 miles (S. E.) from Magherafelt, on the western shore of Lough Neagh. This village was founded by the late D. Gaussen, who, in 1788, built a forge here for manufacturing spades, &c., and soon afterwards erected stores, which led to the building of quays and the formation of a port, which has greatly benefited the surrounding country. A large distillery was erected in 1824, and a brewery in 1830, by Messrs. Gaussen and Sons. Vessels of about 50 tons burden ply regularly between this port and Belfast and Newry, exporting wheat fruit spirits, ale, and freestone, and bringing back barley, timber, slate, iron, wine, groceries, &c. This village is well situated for trade, as, besides being on Lough Neagh, several roads diverge from it, and the projected railroad from Coleraine to Armagh will pass near it. It is on the estate of the Salters' Company, of London, which is held by the Marquess of Londonderry and Sir Robert Bateson, Bart., under a lease which will expire about 1852, when the company intend to make extensive improvements. Here is a public school, principally supported by the lessees of the estate, Mrs. Gaussen, sen., and D. Gaussen, Esq., one of the proprietors of the village. Near it are the ruins of Salterstown castle and a cromlech.

BALLYSCULLION, a parish, partly in the barony of UPPER TOOME, county of ANTRIM, but chiefly in that of LOUGHINSHOLIN, county of LONDONDERRY, and province of ULSTER; containing, with the post-town of Bellaghy, 6453 inhabitants. This parish, which is intersected by the roads leading respectively from Castle-Dawson to Portglenone, and from Maghera to Bellaghy, comprises, according to the Ordnance survey, $12,750\frac{1}{4}$ statute acres, of which $10,617\frac{1}{4}$ are in the county of Londonderry, 2406 are part of Lough Beg, and $72\frac{3}{4}$ part of the river Bann, which here forms the boundary of the parish, barony, and county. On the plantation of Ulster, these lands were granted by Jas. I. to the Irish Society, and by them transferred to the Vintners' Company of London, who founded the castle and town of Bellaghy, described under its own head. At a very early period a monastery was founded on an island in Lough Beg, about two miles from the shore, then called Ynis Teda, but now Church island, from the parish church having been subsequently erected there: this establishment continued to flourish till the dissolution, and some of the lands which belonged to it are still tithe-free. Two townlands in the parish belong to the see of Derry, and the remainder has been leased in perpetuity by the Vintners' Company to the Marquess of Lothian, the Earl of Clancarty, Lord Strafford, and Sir Thomas Pakenham. There are from 400 to 450 acres of bog, part of which in summer affords coarse pasturage for cattle; a portion of it lying remote from the Bann is of a blackish colour, and capable of cultivation for rye and potatoes; the other part, which from its white colour is called "flour bog,' is quite incapable of cultivation till it has been cut away for fuel, when the subsoil appears, varying from 5 to 10 feet in depth. The land is fertile, and under the auspices of the North-West Agricultural Society, of which a branch has been established here, is generally in an excellent state of cultivation; mangel-wurzel, rape, turnips, and other green crops, are being introduced with success. There are indications of coal in several parts, particularly on the Castle-Dawson estate; but there is no prospect of their being explored or worked while the extensive bogs afford so plentiful a supply of fuel. Of the numerous seats the principal are Castle-Dawson, the seat of the Right Hon. G. R. Dawson; Bellaghy Castle, the residence of J. Hill, Esq.; Bellaghy House, of H. B. Hunter, Esq.; Fairview, of R. Henry, Esq.; and Rowensgift, of A. Leckey, Esq. The splendid palace built here by the Earl of Bristol, when Bishop of Derry, one of the most magnificent in the country, was scarcely finished at his Lordship's decease, and was soon after taken down and the materials sold: the only entire portion that has been preserved is the beautiful portico, which was purchased by Dr. Alexander, Bishop of Down and Connor, who presented it to the parish of St. George, Belfast, as an ornament to that church. A small portion of the domestics' apartments and a fragment of one of the picture galleries are all that remain. There are some extensive cotton-mills at Castle-Dawson, also flour, corn, and flax-mills; and about a mile above the town is a small bleach-green. Fairs for cattle, sheep, and pigs are held at Bellaghy on the first Monday in every month; and a manorial court is held monthly, for the recovery of debts not exceeding £2.

The living is a rectory, in the diocese of Derry, and in the patronage of the Bishop: the tithes amount to £350. The church, situated in Bellaghy, is a large and handsome edifice, erected in 1794 on the site of a former church built in 1625: it is in the early English style, with a lofty and beautiful octagonal spire erected at the expense of the Earl of Bristol, and is about to be enlarged by the addition of a north aisle. There is a chapel at Castle-Dawson belonging to the Dawson family, by whom it was built and endowed; it is open to the inhabitants. The glebe-house is about a quarter of a mile from the town on a glebe comprising 70 acres; and there is also a glebe of 84 acres at Moneystachan, in the parish of Tamlaght-O'Crilly, all arable land. In the R. C. divisions this parish comprehends the grange of Ballyscullion, in the diocese of Connor, in which union are two chapels, one at Bellaghy and the other in the grange. At Ballaghy are places of worship for Presbyterians in connection with the Synod of Ulster, Methodists, and Seceders. There is a male and female parochial school, aided by annual donations from the rector and the proprietors of the Bellaghy estate, who built the school-house; and there are five other schools, which afford instruction to about 300 boys and 240 girls; also three private schools, in which are about 100 boys and 20 girls. Here is a dispensary conducted on the most approved plan; and the proprietors of the Bellaghy estate annually distribute blankets and clothes among the poor. The ruins of the old church on Ynis Teda, or Church island, are extensive and highly interesting; and close to them a square tower surmounted by a lofty octangular spire of hewn freestone was erected by the Earl of Bristol, which is a beautiful object in the landscape. A large mis-shapen stone, called Clogh O'Neill, is pointed out as an object of interest; and not far distant is a rock basin, or holy stone, to which numbers annually resort in the hope of deriving benefit from the efficacy of the water in healing diseases.

BALLYWILLIN, or MILLTOWN, a parish, partly in the barony of LOWER DUNLUCE, county of ANTRIM, but chiefly in the North-East liberties of COLERAINE, county of LONDONDERRY, and province of ULSTER, $3^1/_2$ miles (N. by E.) from Coleraine, on the road to Portrush; containing 2219 inhabitants. This parish is bounded on the north by the Atlantic ocean, and comprises, according to the Ordnance survey, $4673^1/_4$ statute acres, of which 1617 are in the county of Antrim about 300 are sand and 150 bog; the remainder is arable and pasture. The entire district abounds with fossils and minerals of great variety, and with features of high geological interest. The soil, though various, is generally good; and the lands are in an excellent state of cultivation, particularly where not exposed to the drifting of the sand, which accumulates on the coast near Portrush. There is no waste land, except the sand hills near Portrush, which, from the constant blowing of the north and north-west winds, have overspread a large tract of excellent land, which it has been found impossible to reclaim. Much of the bog has been exhausted and brought under cultivation, and there is now barely sufficient for the supply of fuel. There are vast quantities of ironstone; in some places the ore is found nearly in a metallic state, and in nodules of stone used for making the roads have been found nuclei of almost pure metal. Limestone is very abundant, but is not worked; the extensive quarries in the adjoining parish of Dunluce being held under a lease which prohibits the opening of any other upon the estate. Basalt in every variety is found here in a confused mixture of amorphous basalt with veins of red ochre, chert, soap-stone, and zeolite. In other parts there are magnificent columnar masses, the prisms of which are more perfect and more beautiful than those of the Causeway. These columns form part of a bold ridge of hills lying north and south, and displaying some of the finest features of basaltic formation in the island. Beardiville, the seat of Sir F. Macnaghten, Bart., a spacious and handsome mansion, is pleasantly situated and surrounded with extensive and thriving plantations; and at Portrush are several elegant lodges and pleasing villas, which are occupied by their respective proprietors during the bathing season, and one of which belongs to the Bishop of Derry. The Skerries, a cluster of islands about a mile from the shore, and containing, according to the Ordnance survey, 24a. 1r. 9p., belong to this parish. Behind the middle of the largest of them a vessel may ride well sheltered in from to 7 fathoms of water, and on good holding ground.

The living is a rectory, in the diocese of Connor, and in the patronage of the Bishop: it was formerly an appendage to the chancellorship of that see, under a grant by Jas. I., at which time a vicarage was instituted; but it again became a rectory under the provisions of Dr. Mants act on the death of Dr. Trail in 1831. The tithes amount to £263. The church is an ancient, spacious, and handsome edifice, in the early English style, and is said to be the only one in the diocese or county, built prior to the Reformation, in which divine service is now performed; it has neither tower nor spire, but being situated on an eminence it is visible at the distance of several leagues at sea. There is a glebe-house, for the erection of which the late Board of First Fruits, in 1828, gave £450 and lent £140. In the R. C. divisions this parish forms part of the union or district of Coleraine. There is a place of worship at Magherabuoy for Presbyterians in connection with the Synod of Ulster, and of the second class, and at Portrush is one for Wesleyan Methodists. The male and female school at Portrush is aided by an annual donation from Miss Rice; the school-house was erected in 1832 by Dr. Adam Clarke. A male and female school is aided by an annual donation from Mr. Lyle. In these schools are about 80 boys and 60 girls; and there are also a pay school, in which are about 40 boys and 10 girls, and a Sunday school. Here are the remains of Ballyreagh, or "the Royal Castle," situated on a promontory having a bold facade of rock rising to the height of 296 feet, the base of which is washed by the Atlantic. Dunmull, originally a druidical circle, afterwards a Danish fort, and now a pasture for sheep, is one of the most curious and extensive vestiges of antiquity in the country; and about half a mile to the north-west of the church are the remains of a druidical circle and altar, with an extensive and well-arranged cave; there is also a druidical altar near Beardiville, in a very perfect state. Fine impressions of the cornua ammonis are found in the chert at Portrush; the cornua and the echenite are found also in the limestone, and every variety of the zeolite and opal in the basaltic or trap formation, with chalcedony, strontium, agate, rock tallow, and veins of fullers' earth.

BALTEAGH, or BALLYDAIGH, a parish, in the barony of KENAUGHT, county of LONDONDERRY, and province of ULSTER, 2 miles (S. E.) from Newtownlimavady; containing 3326 inhabitants. This parish, which is situated on the Balteagh water and bounded on the west by the river Roe, is intersected by the roads leading respectively from Dungiven and Garvagh to Newtownlimavady, and by the road from Coleraine to Londonderry. It comprises, according to the Ordnance survey, 11,505$^3/_4$ statute acres, and, except a small portion belonging to the see of Derry, is the property of the Marquess of Waterford, being part of the grant made by Jas. I. to the Haberdashers' Company of London, who have long since alienated it in perpetuity. About one-fourth part of the land forms a portion of the mountains of Cedy and Donaldshill, which latter is the highest ground in the parish, and, according to the Ordnance survey, has an elevation of 1315 feet above the sea at low water. Much of the mountainous land affords excellent pasture for cattle, and might easily be reclaimed; and the remainder, extending from the bases of these mountains towards the river Roe, is rich and fertile, and in a good state of cultivation, producing abundant crops. In the front of the Cedy mountain is a large quarry of white limestone, which is there topped by the lofty mountains of basalt extending on the east to Coleraine, on the south-east to Garvagh, and on the north-east to Magilligan. In the bed of the Balteagh water, freestone, calcareous sand-stone, and thin layers of coal are found alternating. The principal seats are Ballyquin House, the residence of Capt. Tedlie, and Drumagoscar, of the Rev. R. Henderson. The weaving of linen is carried on in some of the farm-houses and there are a flour and two oatmeal-mills, and two flax-mills in the parish. The living is a rectory, in the diocese of Derry, and in the patronage of the Bishop: the tithes amount to £373.18.6. The church, a small edifice with a square tower crowned with pinnacles, was erected in 1815, on a site near the ruins of the old church at the base of Donaldshill, at an expense of £700, a gift from the late Board of First Fruits, which also granted a loan of £277 for its repair in 1828. The glebe-house, situated about a quarter of a mile to the north of it, is a good residence; the glebe comprises 135a. 0r. 33p., lying on both sides of the Balteagh water. In the R. C. divisions this parish forms part of the union or district of Newtownlimavady, and contains a chapel. There is a place of worship at Lislane for Presbyterians in connection with the Synod of Ulster, of the second class. The parochial schools are at Ardmore: there are other schools at Terrydrummood and Carrick, aided by the rector and W. Campbell, Esq.; and the Marquess of Waterford is about to establish schools at Lisbane and Drumsurn. The number of children at present taught in these schools is, on the average, 250, of which about one-third are girls: there are also four Sunday schools (one of which is held in the Presbyterian meeting-house), and a private school in which about 30 children are educated. There are remains of an extensive cromlech; and the walls of the ancient church form an interesting ruin. There are sulphureous and chalybeate springs in several parts of the parish. Numerous fossils are imbedded in the limestone of Cedy, particularly belemnites, trilobites, and dendrites.

BANAGHER, a parish, partly in the barony of TIRKEERAN, but chiefly in that of KENAUGHT, county of LONDONDERRY, and province of ULSTER, 2 miles (W. by S.) from Dungiven; containing 4086 inhabitants. This parish, which for extent is the second in the county, is situated on the road from Toome to Londonderry, and is nine miles in length from east to west and sevenmiles in breadth from north to south. It contains 27 townlands, of which 16 are in the barony of Tirkeeran and 11 in that of Kenaught, and comprises, according to the Ordnance survey, 32,475 statute acres, of which 17,748$^1/_4$ are in the latter barony. The apparent decrease in its population, since 1821, is attributable to the separation of nine townlands, which, together with nine from the parishes of Upper and Lower Cumber, were taken, in 1831, to form the district curacy of Learmount. The early history of this place is involved in great obscurity; by some writers it is said that St. Patrick, when he crossed the Foyle, visited it and founded the church, the ruins of which are still remaining, and on a stone is inscribed, in modern capitals, "This church was built in the year of God 474." The style of the building is. evidently of a much later period, and corresponds with a local tradition that the church was built by St. O'Heney, and with the style of the tomb erected to his memory in the adjoining cemetery. It is also said that a monastery, of which St. O'Heney was abbot, formerly existed here; but though there are, near the church, the remains of a small square building of more recent erection and evidently used for domestic purposes, which is called the abbey, no mention occurs in historic records of any religious establishment, nor are there any monastic lands in the parish, except such as belonged to the abbey of Dungiven.

The parish is divided among several proprietors; seven townlands belong to the see of Derry, six to the Skinners' and three to the Fishmongers' Companies; ten are freeholds, of which nine pay a chief rent to the Skinners' and one to the Fishmongers' Companies; and one, on which are the church, glebe-house, and parochial schools, belongs to the rector. The land in many places is well drained and in a good state of cultivation, but not less than 13,432 acres are mountain land, though affording good pasturage; and there are 546 acres of flow bog, which is being rapidly reclaimed and brought into cultivation. In the mountains, particularly in Finglen, are found very large and beautiful specimens of rock crystals, or Irish diamonds, generally truncated pentagonal prisms, with facets often of the clearest lustre, and sometimes of the colour and brilliancy of the beryl. These crystals vary, however, in colour and lustre, and are found of all sizes. The largest ever discovered was found in Finglen water, in 1796; it weighs 84½ lb., and is in the possession of Michael Ross, Esq., of Banagher Cottage; it is called the Dungiven Crystal, and has been noticed by several writers as an object of admiration. Freestone is found in great quantities, and is of a bright fawn colour and very durable, as appears from the old churches of Banagher and Dungiven; limestone is also abundant. There are several handsome seats in the parish, and most of them are embosomed in rich and flourishing plantations; the principal are Ashpark, the residence of J. Stevenson, Esq.; Knockan, of I. Stevenson, Esq.; Drumcovatt, now occupied as a farm-house; Banagher Cottage, the residence of Michael Ross, Esq.; Kilcreen, of I. Beresford, Esq.; and Straid Lodge, of the Rev. S. Hunter. There is a large bleach-green at Knockan, where 8000 pieces of linen are annually bleached and finished for the English markets; some linen cloth is also woven by the farmers in their own houses, but the greater number of the inhabitants are employed its agriculture.

The living is a rectory, in the diocese of Derry, episcopally united to the vicarage of Dungiven, which two parishes form the union of Banagher, in the patronage of Robert Ogilby, Esq., as lessee under the Skinners' Company: the tithes amount to £650, and the gross value of the benefice, including tithe and glebe, is £1201. There is a church in each of the parishes: the church of Banagher, a large and handsome edifice, with a tower surmounted by a beautiful octagonal spire, is situated on elevated ground about a mile west of the old church, and was built in 1782; the spire was added at the expense of the Earl of Bristol, then Bishop of Derry. The glebe-house, nearly adjoining the church, is a large and handsome residence, built in 1819 by the Rev. Alexander Ross, the present incumbent, at an expense of £2350, upon the glebe townland of Rallagh, which comprises 422a. 0r. 39p. of arable land. The Ecclesiastical Commissioners, in their report for 1831, have recommended the dissolution of the union, and that each parish shall become a separate benefice on the next avoidance. In the R. C. divisions this parish is the head of a union or district, which comprises also the parishes of Bovevagh and Learmount, and contains three chapels, one at Feeny, one at Altinure in the mountain district, and one at Foreglen. There is a place of worship at Ballyhenedein for Presbyterians in connection with the Synod of Ulster, of the second class; it is a handsome building, in the Grecian style of architecture, erected in 1825 at the expense of the Fishmongers' Company. There are male and female parochial schools at Ballagh, aided by an annual donation from the rector; the school-house is a large and handsome building, erected by subscription. At Tyrglassen is a male and female school, supported by the Fishmongers' Company; and at Fincarn is a male and female school supported by R. Ogilby, Esq. In these schools are about 120 boys and 100 girls; and there are also three private schools, in which are about 200 children, and three Sunday schools, one of which at Tyrglassen is supported by the Fishmongers' Company.

The ruins of the old church are situated on the summit of a sandy ridge on the south side of the river Owenreagh, in a retired and beautiful valley, and are very interesting; they consist of the church and a small square building, sometimes called the abbey. The church consisted of a nave and chancel, but the partition wall, the arch, and the eastern gable have disappeared; the side walls and the west front are remaining and tolerably entire; the nave and chancel appear each to have been lighted by a very narrow lancet window on the south side, ornamented externally with curious circular mouldings; the only entrance appears to have been from the west, through a square-headed doorway with a bold architrave, and on one of the stones on the north side is the inscription in modern capitals before noticed. There are also the ruins of an ancient church at Straid, said by the country people to have been the second founded by St. Patrick in this part of the kingdom; but the style of the building is of much less remote antiquity. There are also the foundations of a third church in the townland of Templemoile, but no part of the building is remaining, nor is there any history or tradition of it extant. On the glebe is a curious vitrified fort, on which the Midsummer fires are made; and near the church is an extensive artificial cave. In the cemetery of the old church is a curious monument to the memory of St. O'Heney, the supposed founder of the church and of the small building near it which is called the abbey; it is of a square form, with sharp pointed gables and a roof of stone; and on the western side is an effigy of the saint in tolerable preservation. Here is a very curious ancient cross, with the fragments of a second, which, with three others, marked out the consecrated ground around this venerable pile.

BELLAGHY, a village and post-town, in the parish of BALLYSCULLION, barony of LOUGHINSHOLIN, county of LONDONDERRY, and province of ULSTER, 9½ miles (S.) from Kilrea, and 100¼ (N.) from Dublin: the population is returned with the parish. This place became the head of a district granted in the reign of Jas. I. to the Vintners' Company, of London, who, in 1619, founded the village, and erected a strong and spacious castle, the custody of which they entrusted to Baptist Jones, Esq., who had a well-armed garrison of 76 men for its defence. In the war of 1641 the castle was besieged and taken by a party of insurgents under the command of one of the Mac Donnells, and in the following year burned to the ground. It occupied a gentle eminence on the north-west side of the village, but no portion of it is remaining; the very site has been cultivated as gardens, and the only traces are some of the arched cellars beneath the roots of some large trees. The village is situated on the western shore of Lough Beg, and on the roads leading respectively from Castle Dawson to Portglenone and from Kilrea to Toome; it consists of one long street intersected at right angles by two shorter streets; the houses are generally small, but well built; and the environs are remarkably pleasant, and are embellished with gentlemen's seats, of which the principal near the village are Bellaghy Castle, the residence of J. Hill, Esq., and Bellaghy House, of H. B. Hunter, Esq. Fairs are held on the first Monday in every month, for the sale of cattle, sheep, and pigs, and are well attended. A court for the Vintners' manor is held once every month, for the recovery of debts under £2: its jurisdiction extends over the parishes of Ballyscullion, Kilrea, Tamlaght-OCrilly, Termoneeny, Maghera, Desertmartin, Kileronaghan, Magherafelt, and Killelagh. Adjoining the village is the parish church of Ballyscullion, a large and handsome building; and at a short distance is a small R. C. chapel. Here is also a place of worship for Wesleyan Methodists; and a meeting-house is now being built for Presbyterians in connection with the Synod of Ulster. The parochial school for boys and girls, a large and handsome building, was erected at the joint expense of the Marquess of Lothian, Earl of Clancarty, Lord Strafford, and the Hon. T. Pakenham, G.C.B., proprietors of the estate by purchase from the Vintners' Company, who have also endowed it with £5 per annum, and a like sum is granted by the rector: and there is a school for girls, supported by subscription, also a school built and supported by the Methodists. – See BALLYSCULLION.

BOVEVAGH, a parish, in the barony of KENAUGHT, county of LONDONDERRY, and province of ULSTER, 2 miles (N.) from Dungiven; containing 5552 inhabitants. At this place, anciently called Boith-Medhbha, a monastery was founded in 557 by St. Columb, of which Aidan, nephew of St. Patrick, was the first abbot. This establishment was situated on the western bank of the river Roe, and continued to flourish for some years, but was plundered and destroyed by the Danes, and was never afterwards rebuilt. The parish is intersected by two roads, one on each side of the river, leading from Dungiven to Newtownlimavady and, according to the Ordnance survey, comprises 18,596 statute acres. The land is generally fertile, but the soil is very variable, passing through all the gradations from light sand to stiff clay and marl: on the banks of the river it is gravelly and remarkably productive. The system of agriculture is greatly improved; there is scarcely any mountain or wasteland, and the bogs are mostly worked out and reclaimed. The geological features of the parish are highly interesting: the strata are laid open to view in the river and the several streams; the most valuable of those hitherto worked is the freestone, which is found in several parts, and of which the principal quarry is at Ballyhargan. From this quarry was procured the stone used in building the palace of Ballyscullion, the magnificent portico of which was removed to St. George's church, at Belfast; the stone found here is easily worked, but hardens by exposure to the air, and is of very good colour. Indications of manganese are also observable, and the beautiful pebbles called Dungiven crystals are frequently found. The weaving of linen cloth is carried on in many of the farm-houses and cottages. There are several seats, the principal of which are Streth House, the residence of Mrs. Edwards; Ballyhargan, of W. Osborne, Esq.; Ardenariff, of W. Douglas, Esq.; and Camnish House, of the Rev. Mr. Kidd.

The living is a rectory, in the diocese of Derry, and in the patronage of the Bishop: the tithes amount to £580. The church is a large and handsome edifice, in the later English style, with a lofty square tower crowned with pinnacles; it was erected in 1823, by aid of a gift of £300 from the late Board of First Fruits, and is situated on the west bank of the Roe, about a quarter of a mile from the site of the old church, which had fallen to decay some years previously. The glebe-house, a large and well-built residence, is situated on the east bank of the river: the glebe comprises 79 acres of fertile land. In the R. C. divisions this parish forms part of the union or district of Banagher, and contains two chapels, one at Derrylane, where service is performed every alternate Sunday, and the other at Ballymoney. There is a place of worship at Camnish for Presbyterians in connection with the Synod of Ulster, of the second class. The male and female parochial school at Burnfoot is aided by an annual donation from the rector, and was endowed with half an acre of land by Mr. Edwards; the school-house, a good building of stone, was erected at an expense of £110, of which £50 was granted from the lord-lieutenant's fund, and the remainder raised by subscription. At Drumneesy is a male and female school, aided by the rector, who also contributes to the support of an infants' school at Bovevagh in these schools are about 260 children; and there are six private schools, in which are about 280 children, and five Sunday schools. Near the old church is an artificial cave, 82 yards in length, with several galleries branching from it in different directions. About a mile north-east of the church is an upright stone, near which, according to tradition, a battle was fought, but which may probably be part of a cromlech, as there are other stones and vestiges of a druidical circle near the spot.

CASTLE-DAWSON, or DAWSON'S-BRIDGE, a market and post-town, partly in the parish of BALLYSCULLION, but chiefly in that of MAGHERAFELT, barony of LOUGHINSHOLIN, county of LONDONDERRY, and province of ULSTER, 28 miles (N. W.) from Belfast, and 97 (N.) from Dublin; containing 674 inhabitants. This place derives its name from its proprietors, the Dawson family. On the plantation of Ulster, the eight townlands of Mayola were granted by Jas. I. to Sir Thomas Philips, whose sons sold them, in 1633, to Thomas Dawson, Esq., from whom they have descended to the Right Hon. G. R. Dawson. The town appears to have assumed its present form and name in the year 1710, during the proprietorship of Joshua Dawson, Esq., chief secretary for Ireland, and for many years member of parliament for the borough of Wicklow. It is delightfully situated on the two sides of the Mayola, over which is a handsome stone arch, erected by the Dawson family, and from this circumstance the town derived its former name of Dawson's Bridge: it consists of two principal and some smaller streets, containing, in 1831, 129 houses, many of which are large and well built. Here are extensive cotton twist mills, built in 1803, and furnishing employment to about 100 persons in the buildings and about 800 in the adjoining parishes. Near the town are large flour and oatmeal-mills; and in several places in the neighbourhood are manufactories of coarse earthenware, bricks, &c., and a bleach-green in which 800 pieces of linen are annually prepared for the London market. The market is on Saturday, and is well supplied with every kind of provisions; and in the season great quantities of grain, pork, and butter are purchased here, principally for the Belfast merchants: the market-house and grain stores are extensive and well built. Fairs are held on the last Saturday in each month, for the sale of linen cloth, yarn, cattle, pigs, sheep, and pedlery. The eight townlands of Mayola were, by letters patent, in 1712, erected into the manor of Castle-Dawson, with etensive privileges; and a manorial court is held monthly by the seneschal, in which debts to the amount of £20 are recoverable. Petty sessions are held every alternate week; and there is a constabulary police station. The soil in every part of the neighbourhood is fertile, and under an excellent system of cultivation. Coal is found, but no attempt has been made to work it, the seams being too thin to pay the expense, while turf is abundant. Nearly adjoining the town is The House, the residence of the Right Hon. G. R. Dawson, situated in a beautiful demesne, in which is an ancient avenue three miles in length, opening to a magnificent view of Lough Neagh, to which it extends. On an eminence close adjoining the town stands a beautiful and lofty obelisk, erected by the Earl of Bristol, to commemorate the virtues and benevolence of the Dawson family. There are several other handsome houses in the town and neighbourhood, the principal of which are Fairview, the seat of R. Henry, Esq.; Rowens Gift, of Capt. Crofton; Millbrook, of A. Spotswood, Esq.; Mount Aeriel, of S. J. Cassidy, Esq.; with those of Capt. Bouverie, W. Graves, Esq., and others. The church is small, but very neat; it stands on the western side of the Mayola, in the parish of Ballyscullion. The former edifice was built in 1710, by Joshua Dawson, Esq., and having fallen into ruin some years since, the present structure was erected by the Right Hon. G. R. Dawson, by whom it has been beautifully ornamented; on a brass tablet in an ancient carved oak frame is inscribed the genealogy of the Dawson family; it has also a beautiful window of stained glass. There is a large meeting-house for Presbyterians in connection with the Synod of Ulster, of the second class. A school for boys and girls is supported by subscriptions; and at Hill Head is a school supported by the London Hibernian Society. Of the castle built by Thomas Dawson, Esq., who was deputy-commissary in the reign of Chas. I., and which stood in the demesne near the church, little now remains, but the foundations of the walls and terraces are still traceable. The castle built by Joshua Dawson, Esq., in the year 1713, is now in ruins; and The House, built in 1768 by Arthur Dawson, Esq., who was member of parliament for the county of Londonderry, and chief baron of the exchequer, is now the family mansion. The present proprietor has made some extensive plantations around it and on other parts of his estate which flourish luxuriantly, and greatly embellish the surrounding scenery: Shillgray wood is very ancient, and contains some remarkbly fine oak and beech trees. Ancient urns, ornaments of gold, spears, celts, and other relics have been found here. In the neighbourhood are some bogs, 30 feet deep, in which four separate layers of timber are imbedded: the lowest is principally oak, in a very sound and perfect state; the next chiefly yew, the third fir, and the uppermost birch, hazel, hawthorn, &c. Nuts, acorns, and the cones of fir are frequently found in these bogs, in very perfect condition. – See BALLYSCULLION and MAGHERAFELT.

CLAUDY, a village, in the parish of UPPER CUMBER, barony of TIRKERAN, county of LONDONDERRY, and province of ULSTER, 71/2 miles (E. N. E.) from Londonderry; containing 180 inhabitants. It is situated on the road from Belfast to Londonderry, to the latter of which it has a penny post. Eight fairs are held for cattle, horses, and pigs; a constabulary police force has been stationed in the village, and petty sessions are held on the first Friday in every month. In the vicinity are some handsome seats and extensive woods and plantations, which are described in the article on the parish; and there are some large bleach-greens, not now in use. In the village are a R. C. chapel, a place of worship for Presbyterians in connection with the Synod of Ulster, and a national school.

COLERAINE, a sea-port, borough, market and post-town, and a parish, in the barony or district called the town and liberties of COLERAINE, county of LONDONDERRY, and province of ULSTER, $24^{1}/_{2}$ miles (E.N.E.) from Londonderry, and $118^{1}/_{4}$ (N.) from Dublin; containing 7646 inhabitants, of which number, 1978 are in the parish of Killowen, and 5668 in the town. This place derives its present name from Cuil-Rathuin, descriptive of the numerous forts in the vicinity, and is by some writers identified with the Rath-mor-Muighe-line, the royal seat of the kings of Dalnaruidhe. The original town, now called Killowen, on the western bank of the river Bann, and which subsequently became the chief or shire town of the county of Coleraine, is of very remote antiquity; and in 540 had a priory of Canons Regular, of which St. Carbreus, a disciple of St. Finian, and first bishop of Coleraine, was abbot. This establishment continued to flourish till the year 930, when Ardmedius, or Armedacius, was put to death by the Danes; it was, together with several other churches, plundered in 1171 by Manus Mac Dunleve, since which period no notice of it occurs till the year 1213, when, with the exception of the church, it was destroyed to furnish materials for a castle which was erected here by Thomas Mac Uchtry and the Gaels of Ulster. The county of Coleraine is described as having extended from the river Bann, on the east, to Lough Foyle on the west, and as having formed part of the possessions of O'Cahan, from whose partici pation in the rebellion of the Earl of Tyrone, in the reign of Elizabeth, it became, with the whole province of Ulster, forfeited to the crown. Jas. I., in 1613, granted this district to a number of London merchants, who were in that year incorporated by charter, under the designation of the "Governor and Assistants of the New Plantation in Ulster," and from that period the name of the county was changed into Londonderry. The Governor and Assistants, generally called the Irish Society, were by their charter bound to build the town of Coleraine, to people it, to enclose it with a wall, and to establish a market, within seven years from the date of their charter, by which were granted to them the entire abbey of St. Mary, its site, and the lands belonging to it, together with the old town, now Killowen, and all its appurtenances. But this condition appears to have been very much neglected, for Pynnar, in his first survey, in 1619, says, "that part of the town which is unbuilt is so dirty that no man is able to go into it, especially what is called, and should be, the market-place." The same writer, in his second survey, dated 1625, says, – "The town of Coleraine is in the same state as at the last survey; only three houses are added, which are built by private individuals, the society allowing them £20 a piece. The walls and ramparts are built of sods; they do begin to decay, on account of their narrowness; the bulwarks are exceedingly little, and the town is so poorly inhabited that there are not men enough to man tile sixth part of the wall." So unpromising was the condition of this settlement that, in addition to the sum of £20, large portions of land were allotted for each tenement, and long leases at nominal rents were offered to all who would undertake to build houses.

A conspiracy of the natives having been formed to seize the place, in 1615, military stores were sent hither from London; and by a vote of the common council, a citadel was built for its defence in the following year; it was a strong fortress, commanding the ferry, and was kept in repair and well garrisoned by the Irish Society, till the erection of the bridge in 1716. The bridge, which was wholly of wood, was so much injured by floods that it fell in 1739; and in 1743 a new bridge was built, with pillars and buttresses of stone, towards the erection of which the Irish Society gave the timber and £2050 in money; in 1806 it was widened, at the expense of the county, by transverse beams supporting a foot-path of four feet on each side. The growth of the place was exceedingly slow, and so little had its trade advanced that, in 1633, the customs of the port, for the half year ending on Lady-day in that year, amounted only to £18.9.8$^1/_2$. On the breaking out of the war in 1641, the town was attacked by a body of 1000 insurgents, but was vigorously defended by the garrison and inhabitants, amounting to 200, who defeated the assailants. It was taken by Gen. Monk for the parliament, in 1648, but was afterwards given up to Sir C. Coote. On the advance of the forces of Jas. II. into the north, in order to repress the Protestant party, Mount-Alexander, Rawdon, and other leaders, stationed themselves with a force of about 4000 men at Coleraine, which they fortified and kept possession of with a view to prevent the Irish from passing the Bann. They were here joined by Lord Blaney with his party from Armagh; and though for a time they repulsed the enemy, yet the Irish, after a successful skirmish, passed the river in boats, and the party stationed here finding the place no longer tenable, fled by various routes to Derry, in order to take possession of it, before the Irish should cut them off from their last place of refuge. The subsequent history of the town consists of little more than a succession of disputes in the corporation, and between that body and the Irish Society, relative to their respective rights, privileges, and possessions: the Society enclosed the quay and made the port duty free, in 1741.

The town, which is the second in the county in importance, and is rapidly increasing, is situated on the east bank of the river Bann, about three miles from its influx into the sea, and is connected by a handsome bridge with the village of Killowen, or Waterside, a considerable suburb on the opposite bank of the river. It is large and handsomely built, consisting of five principal streets, a spacious square called the Diamond, and several smaller streets; the houses in the Diamond, New-row, Church-street, and Bridge-street. are large and well-built, especially those of later erection; in the Diamond and in Church-street are some ancient houses of timber cage-work, said to have been framed in London and sent over by the Irish Society to be erected here. A Board of Commissioners has been appointed under the act of the 9th of Geo. IV., for lighting and cleansing the town, which is paved at the expense of the county; and the inhabitants are supplied with excellent water from numerous springs at the outlets of the town and from pumps. It is a very great thoroughfare, and is the principal passage over tile river Bann, connecting the counties of Antrim and Derry, and opening a communication with all the ports on the north and north-western coasts. The neighbourhood is remarkable for the pleasing diversity of its scenery, enlivened by the fine stream of the Bann, and embellished with the grounds of some handsome seats. On the west side of the river, immediately below Killowen, is Jackson Hall, the residence of Mrs. Maxwell, an elegant mansion situated in extensive grounds tastefully laid out; and there are various others, among which are Down Hill, built by the Earl of Bristol,

Coleraine. Part of 6 inch O.S. map of Co.Londonderry, sheet 7, published 1833 (reproduced at 140%).

when Bishop of Derry, and now the property and residence of Sir James R. Bruce, Bart.; Somerset, the residence of the Rev. Thomas Richardson; Knockintern, of Hugh Lyle, Esq.; Ballysally, of W. Gait, Esq.; Castleroe, of Lieut.-Col. Cairnes; Mill-burn House, of Stewart C. Bruce, Esq.; Cromore, of J. M. Cromore, Esq.; and Ballyness, of Capt. Hannay. The air is extremely salubrious, and during the prevalence of typhus fever in 1817, and of the cholera in 1832, the number of deaths in proportion to the population was very small. The town is abundantly supplied with all the necessaries and luxuries of life at a moderate charge, which renders it desirable as a place of residence for persons of limited income. There is a public library, supported by annual subscriptions of a guinea; also a subscription news-room, and an amateur concert, which is held weekly.

This place has long been celebrated for its trade in the finer linens, known as "Coleraines," but at what time it was first established here is not precisely known. The first bleach-green ever known in this part of the country was established at Ballybrittan, by Mr. John Orr, in 1734, for the bleaching of fine 7-8th and 4-4th linens. That gentleman having succeeded in establishing a very lucrative trade, other bleach-greens were soon afterwards formed at Gortin, Ballydivitt, Macosquin, Drumcroom, Muilamore, Keeley, Aghadowey, Rusbrook, Collans, Mullycarrie, Island Effrick, Castle Roe, Green-field, and other places. The quantity now bleached annually exceeds 200,000 pieces; they are of the finest quality, and four-fifths of them are sent to the English markets. These linens are woven at the farm-houses throughout the country; the webs, when finished, are brought to market in the brown state, and sold to the bleachers, who assemble on their stands every Saturday from 10 till 11 o'clock, during which hour more than 1000 webs are generally purchased. This is one of the very few towns of which the market has not been materially injured by the recent changes that have taken place in the linen trade. The bleachers of the neighbourhood also attend the markets of Ballymoney, Dungannon, Fintona, Stewartstown, Armagh, Newtownstewart, Strabane, and Derry, for the purchase of brown webs; but the best markets in Ireland for these goods are Coleraine and Ballymoney. At Mullamore is a large establishment for the preparation of warps and yarn for linen webs, commenced in 1832, by Alexander Barklie, Esq.; there are at present more than 800 looms in constant operation; the weaving is not done on the premises, but is given out as task work to men who weave it at their own houses. The only manufactures carried on are those of linen, cotton, hard and soft soap, bleaching salts, leather, and paper. A brewery and malt-house was originally established by Messrs I. and C. Gait, in 1770, and after passing through various hands was purchased by Messrs. O'Kane and Mitchell, the present proprietors, who annually consume 200 tons of malt in the production of 2000 barrels of strong and common ale.

The town, from its situation on the river Bann, only four miles from the Atlantic, enjoys important advantages for commerce, but at present its trade is limited. Its chief imports are timber, iron, barilla, ashes, coal, and salt; and its exports are linen cloth, pork, butter, salmon, wheat, barley, oats, potatoes, and whiskey, and since the construction of the harbour of Portrush, there has been a considerable trade in live stock, poultry, eggs, and fruit. The number of vessels trading annually to the port, including the outer harbour of Portrush, is about 160, having an aggregate burden of about 13,000 tons. From the 1st of September, 1831, to the 31st of August, 1832, 36,888 sacks (or 5533 tons 4 cwt.), of grain and 3491 pigs were shipped from this place. During the following year, the quantity of grain decreased to 27,132 sacks, the cause of which may be attributed to the establishment of markets at Garvagh, Bushmills, and Ballymoney; the number of pigs shipped during the latter period increased to 6340, notwithstanding the establishment of those markets. The quantity of butter exported varies considerably; since the passing of the recent act it has decreased from 11,000 to 9000 firkins, from the same cause. The port immediately adjoins the town; the entrance to the river is obstructed by a bar of shifting sand, over which vessels drawing more than five feet of water at neap tides, or nine feet at spring tides, cannot pass; the current of the tide runs past the mouth of the river, and the rise in Lough Foyle is nearly twice as great as in the Bann. During winter the navigation of the river is in a manner stopped, the spring tides occurring too early and too late, before and after daylight,and a heavy swell of the sea generally setting in from October till April. To remedy this inconvenience, a new harbour was constructed at Portrush, about $4^1/_2$ miles distant from thetown, atanexpenseof £16,225.17.11, raised under an act of parliament in shares of £100 each: the entrance is 27 feet deep at low water of spring tides, and vessels drawing 17 feet can enter and ride in perfect safety. A steam-boat, built for this station, commenced plying between Portrush and Liverpool in August 1835; and another has since been established from the port to Glasgow, each of which makes a passage every week. There is a custom-house with the usual officers; and there are bonding stores and a timber-yard. An extensive and lucrative salmon fishery is carried on at Crannagh, on the Bann, under lease from the Irish Society; there is but one season during the year, beginning in May and ending on the 12th of August. The quantity taken is generally about 190 tons the whole of which is packed in ice and conveyed by smacks and steam-boats to Liverpool and other distant markets, where they are in high estimation for their size and flavour. There is also another salmon fishery on the Bann, at a part called the Cutts, where the river makes a rapid fall of 12 feet over a ledge of rocks which the fish cannot ascend, except when there is a strong fresh in the river, and where a weir has been placed to intercept them; about 80 tons are annually taken here; both stations belong to the same Company. There is also an eel fishery, which commences in September, when the fish are returning from Lough Neagh and the rivers, to the sea; they are taken by means of pales and wattling, constructed so as to converge in the direction of the current, and having a net attached; this fishery is worth £800 per annum. Great quantities of eels are taken and sold fresh in the neighbouring markets, or salted for winter use.

The market is on Saturday, and is well supplied with provisions of all kinds. The grain market was first established in 1819, since which time it has rapidly increased: it is held on Monday, Wednesday, and Friday, and on an average 3000 tons of grain, principally oats, are annually sold, of which the greater part is sent to Liverpool, and some to London, Bristol, and Glasgow. An additional market for pork and butter is held on Wednesday. The market-place is situated on the eastern side of the town, on ground belonging to the corporation, by whom it was built at an expense of £2744, and to whom belong the tolls, customs, pickage, and stallage, amounting to about £300 per annum: it is commodiously fitted up, with separate apartments for the sale of butter, pork, and meal, sheds for tallow, hides, and flax, stores and offices for provision merchants, keepers' houses and every accommodation; and was opened on the 25th of March, 1830. There are fairs on the 12th of May, 5th of July, and 1st of November; the principal is on the 12th of May, for black cattle, horses, and sheep. A branch of the Northern Banking Company, one of the Belfast Banking Company, and one of the Provincial Bank of Ireland have been established here.

The inhabitants received a charter of incorporation from Jas. I., in 1613, by which the government was vested in a portreeve, free burgesses, and commonalty, and by another charter granted in the same year, which latter is the governing charter, in a mayor, recorder, chamberlain, coroner, twelve aldermen (including the mayor), and 24 principal burgesses, assisted by a townclerk, prothonotary, serjeants-at-mace, and other officers. The mayor is elected by the common council from the body of aldermen, on the 1st of October, and is sworn into office on the 25th of March following. The aldermen are elected from the burgesses, and the burgesses from the freemen, though in general the burgess is made a freeman to qualify him for election: the freedom is obtained only by gift of the corporation. The mayor, recorder, and four of the senior aldermen are justices of the peace within the borough and liberties; and the county magistrates, of whom, by virtue of his office, the mayor is always senior and sits on the right hand of the judge at the assizes, have concurrent jurisdiction. The corporation hold courts of record for the recovery of debts and the determination of pleas to any amount within the town and liberties, of which, according to their charter, the jurisdiction extends to the distance of three miles in every direction from the centre of the town; they are also empowered to hold courts of session for the borough, but do not exercise that privilege. Previously to the Union, the borough returned two members to the Irish parliament; the right of election was vested in the mayor, aldermen, and burgesses alone, but by the decision of a parliamentary committee it was declared to be vested also in the freemen. Since the Union it has returned one member to the Imperial parliament; and since the passing of the act of the 2nd of William IV., cap. 88, the right of election is in the corporation, freemen, and £10 householders. A new boundary has been drawn round the borough. The number of electors is 214, of whom 26 are burgesses and freemen, whose rights are reserved for life, 184 £10 householders, and 4 occupiers of houses and lands of the yearly value of £10; of these, 185 polled at the late election for the borough, in 1835: the mayor is the returning officer. The quarter sessions for the county are held here in April and October; the assistant barrister presides with the magistrates, for the trial of offences against persons and property, and alone in civil actions not exceeding £20. By the original grant each of the twelve proprietors of the county was empowered to hold a manorial court, but the business of these courts is generally transferred to the quarter sessions. Petty sessions are held on alternate Thursdays. The town-hall is situated in the centre of the square called the Diamond; it was originally erected in 1743, and has been more than once enlarged, and is now undergoing a thorough repair at the expense of the corporation: it is a lofty square building surmounted by a cupola, in which a clock was placed in 1830, at the expense of the Marquess of Waterford: the hall contains courts for the quarter sessions, apartments for transacting the corporation business and the election of members, a news-room, library, ballast-office, and a savings' bank.

The borough comprises, independently of several others within its liberties, the parishes of Coleraine and Killowen (described under its own head), the former comprising the town on the eastern side, and the latter the suburb of that name on the western side, of the Bann, The parish contains, according to the Ordnance survey, 4846 statute acres. The living is a rectory, in the diocese of Connor, and in the patronage of the Irish Society: the tithes amount to £450: the glebe-house was built by aid of a loan of £692 and a gift of £92, in 1828, from the late Board of First Fruits: the glebe comprises 45 acres. The church, a large plain edifice, was erected in the year 1614, by the Irish Society, and in 1684 a south aisle was added to it, at the expense of the corporation; a very handsome spire was built at the expense of the Society in 1719, but it stood for a short time only. The church contains many ancient and some very elegant monuments, and the Ecclesiastical Commissioners have recently granted £282.19.6 towards its repair. In the R. C. divisions this place is partly in the diocese of Connor, and partly in that of Derry, and forms part of the union or district of Killowen or Coleraine; the chapel is a spacious and handsome edifice, situated at Killowen. There are two places of worship for Presbyterians in connection with the Synod of Ulster, one of the first class, and one of the second class; one for Seceders, of the first class, and one each for Independents and Methodists. A school for the gratuitous instruction of 130 boys and 130 girls was founded and endowed, in 1705, by the Irish Society, but from mismanagement it fell into disuse about the year 1739, and was altogether discontinued till 1820, when a new school, with houses for the master and mistress, was built by the Society, who, in 1828, transferred their interest in it to trustees chosen from the most respectable inhabitants of the town, since which time it has been productive of the greatest benefit; the salaries of the master and mistress are paid by the Society. There is a very excellent female work school, where the children are taught sewing and other domestic accomplishments, which is supported by Miss Rippingham, by whom it was established many years since; there are also, at Killowen, a school which was founded and endowed by the late Mr. Kyle, and a parochial school held in the old church and supported by the Clothworkers' Company. There are also four other schools, two of which, situated respectively at Gateside and Ballyclaber, are under the National Board; and seven pay and four Sunday schools. A dispensary is supported in the usual way. A loan fund was established in 1764, for lending two guineas each to industrious workmen, to be repaid by monthly instalments of 3s. 6d.; out of this establishment arose a poor-house fund, which was laid out in fitting up a house for the reception of old and decayed inhabitants: it was supported by subscription and the earnings of the inmates, who were employed in the spinning of cotton. This establishment was discontinued in the year 1790, and the house was given to a few poor aged persons, who occupied it rent-free till 1803, when a portion of it was fitted up as a private dwelling, and the rent paid to the actuary of the loan fund. It was subsequently rebuilt, at an expense of £800, by the Marquess of Waterford, who presented it to the town, and in 1830 it was opened for the reception of the poor, who are maintained and clothed by subscription and annual donations from the Marquess of Waterford and the Irish Society, and a bequest of £20 per annum by the late Griffin Curtis, Esq. The house will accommodate 40 persons. A mendicity society was also formed here in 1825; the committee, who are subscribers of £1.1 per annum, meet every Tuesday, when claims for relief are examined, and two members appointed to administer relief to the poor at their own dwellings.

The priory of St. John, or Kil-Eoin, from which the suburb on the western side of the Bann, now Killowen, took its name, has altogether disappeared; a part of that establishment formed the old parish church, on the site of which another was subsequently erected, the remains of which have been converted into a schoolroom. Not far distant was the monastery for Canons Regular, founded by Carbreus in 540, and the site of the castle which was built on the ruins is now occupied by Jackson Hall. In sinking for foundations in the part of the town of Coleraine which occupies the site of the ancient abbey of St. Mary, stone coffins, human bones, and other relics of antiquity, together with foundations of some of the conventual buildings, are frequently discovered. One mile south of the town is Mount Sandel, one of the largest and most perfect raths in the kingdom; it is 200 feet high, surrounded by a deep dry fosse, and encircled near its summit by a magnificent terrace; in the centre is a deep oblong cavity, called the Giant's Grave, formed apparently for the purpose of concealment. There is also a very high and perfect rath a little west of the Cranagh; another close to the church of Killowen; and a very curious fort near Ballysally. This place has been celebrated from the earliest annals of Irish history, and has produced many eminent lawyers, senators, and divines: among the latter was Dr. John Vesey, born here in March, 1632, and successively Archdeacon of Armagh, Dean of Cork, Bishop of Limerick. and Archbishop of Tuam. From this last dignity he was driven by the harsh conduct of Lord Tyrconnell, and remained in London in great poverty till he was restored to his see, on the accession of William III.; he was three times after his restoration made Lord-Justice of Ireland, and died in 1716, aged 84. John Abernethy, an eminent Presbyterian divine, was born here in 1680. Coleraine has given title to many noblemen; the last was that of baron to the family of Hanger.

CUMBER, LOWER, a parish, in the barony of TIRKEERAN, county of LONDONDERRY, and province of ULSTER, 6 miles (S. E. by S.) from Londonderry, on the road to Dungiven; containing 4584 inhabitants. This parish was separated from the original parish of Cumber in 1794, when this portion of it, comprising, according to the Ordnance survey, 14,909 statute acres, was constituted a parish of itself. The land under cultivation is very fertile, particularly that portion which lies in the vale of the Faughan; good pasturage is obtained on the mountains, which compose about one-third of its surface. Several mountain streams run through the parish, of which the Buratallaght is the most interesting; on this water is a beautiful cascade, called the Neiss, which falls over a ridge of clay-slate nearly 80 feet. Considerable portions of the parish are the property of some of the London chartered companies, by whom great improvements have been effected, In the vale of the Faughan, which extends through the parish and is pleasingly wooded, stand several elegant houses, surrounded by grounds of singular beauty. The inhabitants combine with their agricultural pursuits the weaving of linen cloth; and there is an extensive bleach-green, where 16,000 pieces are annually finished, principally for the English market. There are several handsome bridges both of wood and stone, and between the Oaks and Oaks Lodge is a suspension bridge, which, as seen from the road, has a very pleasing effect. The principal residences are the Oaks, that of Acheson Lyle, Esq.; Oaks Lodge, of Hugh Lyle, Esq.; the Cross, of James Smith, Esq.; and the Glebe-house, of the Rev. Wm. Hayden.

The living is a rectory, in the diocese of Derry, and in the patronage of the Bishop: the tithes amount to £560. The glebe-house was erected in 1800, by a gift of £100 from the late Board of First Fruits: the glebe comprises 106 acres, of which about 30 are uncultivated. The church is a convenient and substantial edifice, built in 1795, by aid of a gift of £500 from the Board. The rector has every fifth presentation to the perpetual cure of Learmount, a district formed out of the original parish of Cumber, in 1831. In the R. C. divisions the parish is partly in the union or district of Glendermot, and partly in that of Cumber Claudy; the chapel, which belongs to the former, is a small edifice, situated at Mullaghbuoy, in the mountain district. The Presbyterians have a large meeting-house at Breakfield, in connection with the Synod of Ulster, of the first class. The male and female parochial schools at Aughill are supported by the rector; and there are large schools at Ervey, Tamnamore, and Ballinamore; the first was built and is supported by the Grocers' Company. The remains of antiquity are numerous; at Slaght Manus is a very large cromlech, the table stone of which is 10 feet long, and is supported by four pillars; and at Mullaghbuoy are the remains of another, but less perfect. In the townland of Listress is a large artificial cave, with five chambers, all built of field stones, covered with broad flagstones, over which is a covering of earth two feet thick.

CUMBER, UPPER, a parish, partly in the barony of STRABANE, county of TYRONE, but chiefly in that of TIRKEERAN, county of DERRY, and province of ULSTER, 7½ miles (N. E.) from Londonderry; containing, with Claudy (which has a daily penny post), 5430 inhabitants. The early history of this parish cannot be satisfactorily traced, further than that St. Patrick, having crossed the Foyle, founded several churches in this district, one of which occupied the site of the present church of Cumber. The original name is variously written by early historians; the present is modern, and acquired since the taxation of Pope Nicholas in 1291. At the Reformation the rectory belonged to the abbey of Derry, and was given by Jas. I. to the bishop, as part of the abbey lands. In 1622, it appears, by the Ulster Visitation book, to have been held with Banagher. The ancient parish of Cumber was the most extensive in the diocese, until 1794, when it was divided into Upper and Lower Cumber, by order in council: the parish of Upper Cumber, according to the Ordnance survey, comprising 26,202¼ statute acres, of which 23,072¾ are in Derry, and 3129½ in Tyrone; the latter form a hilly district amid the Mounterloney mountains. In some parts, particularly on the Walworth estate, and on that of Learmout, the land, though hilly, is well cultivated; the extensive bogs are being worked out, and brought into cultivation. The inhabitants combine the weaving of linen cloth, with agricultural pursuits; there are several commodious and excellent bleach-greens on the Faughan water, none of which, however, are now at work. The southern parts of the parish consist chiefly of mountains, the principal of which is Sawel, the highest in the county, being 2236 feet above the level of the sea; its summit, is on the boundary between two counties. These mountains afford excellent pasturage on every side; and the rivers Faughan, Glenrandle, and Dungorthin have their sources in them. There are large woods and much valuable timber in the demesne of Park-Learmont; and the plantations of Cumber, Alla, and Kilcatton greatly embellish the surrounding scenery. There are several large and elegant houses, of which the principal are Learmont, the seat of Barre Beresford, Esq.; Cumber House, of John H. Browne, Esq.; Kilcatton Hall, of Alexander Ogilby, Esq.; and Alla, of the Rev. Francis Brownlow.

The living is a rectory, in the diocese of Derry, and forms the corps of a prebend in the cathedral of Derry, in the patronage of the Bishop: the tithes amount to £740. The glebe, situated in Glenrandle, half a mile from the church, consists of the townlands of Alla, Gilky Hill, and Tullentraim, containing 1508 statute acres. The church is a large modern edifice, with a small bell turret on the western gable, erected in 1757, on the site of an ancient building. In 1831, eight townlands were separated from the parish, to form part of the new district or parish of Learmont, and the rector of Upper Cumber has the alternate presentation to that perpetual cure. In the R. C. divisions the parish is partly included in the union or district of Banagher, and partly forms the head of a district, comprising also a part of that of Lower Cumber; there are chapels at Claudy and Gortscreagan. The Presbyterians have a meeting-house at Claudy, in connection with the Synod of Ulster. The parochial school, situated on the glebe lands of Alla, is well built and convenient; it is supported by the trustees of Erasmus Smith's charity, and is under the management of the rector, who has endowed it with two acres of land. Male and female schools were built and are supported by the Fishmongers' Company; and they have also excellent male and female schools at Gortilca and Killycor. There are also schools at Ballyarton, Craig, Kilcatton, and Claudy. A female school at Claudy is principally supported by Lady Catherine Brownlow, who likewise contributes to some others. A female work school at Cumber was built and is supported by Mrs. Browne and other ladies of the parish. A male and female school at Learmont is principally supported by the Beresford family. There are also Sunday schools and a private day school. At Mulderg is a large dispensary, built and supported by the Fishmongers' Company. There are the remains of a druidical altar at Baltibrecan; and at Altaghoney were discovered, in the summer of 1835, three stone coffins, each covered with three flag stones, and in each an urn containing ashes, calcined bones, &c. The graves were two feet deep in the gravel, where 8 feet of bog had been cut off the surface; and near the coffins were two idols, carved out of solid oak, which, with the urns, are now in good preservation, in the museum of Alex. Ogilby, Esq., of Kilcatton, who has also a good collection of landscapes, groups, &c. more than 200 of which are from his own pencil.

CURRAN, a village, in the detached portion of the parish of MAGHERA, barony of LOUGHINSHOLIN, county of LONDONDERRY, and province of ULSTER, 3 miles (N. E.)

from Maghera; containing 34 houses and 174 inhabitants. This village is situated on the road from Tobbermore to Castledawson, and on the river Moyola, which is here crossed by a handsome bridge. Fairs are held on June 23rd and November 22nd, for cattle and pigs; and there is a large flour-mill in the village. Here are a male and female school under the National Board. The land around the village, except on the banks of the Moyola, is poor; there are large and valuable bogs extending hence to Tobbermore. – See MAGHERA.

DESERTLYN, or DYSERTLYN, a parish, in the barony of LOUGHINSHOLIN, county of LONDONDERRY, and province of ULSTER, on the road from Dublin to Coleraine; containing, with part of the post-town of Moneymore, 3318 inhabitants. It comprises, according to the Ordnance survey, 5561 statute acres, of which 4977 are applotted under the tithe act and valued at £3243 per annum. There are several bogs, and the soil is variable but generally good and well cultivated. The linen manufacture is connected with agriculture, and affords occasional occupation to the inhabitants. Coal and freestone are visible in several places, but the seams of coal are too thin to pay the expense of working, while turf is cheap. Limestone is also abundant and extensively worked. The principal seats are those of the Hon. and Rev. J. P. Hewitt, Rowley Miller, Esq., and James Smyth, Esq.

The living is a rectory, in the diocese of Armagh, and in the gift of the Lord-Primate: the tithes amount to £230.15.4$^{1}/_{2}$. The glebe-house was built in 1831, on a glebe of 200 acres. The church, which was built at Moneymore, in 1766, by aid of a gift of £424 from the late Board of First Fruits, is disused; and a beautiful church, in the Norman style of architecture, was erected by the Drapers' Company, in 1832, at an expense of £6000. In the R. C. divisions the parish is partly in the union or district of Lissan, and partly in that of Ardtrea. There is a place of worship for Baptists. In addition to the parochial schools, a large and handsome school-house at Larrycormick was erected and is chiefly supported by the Drapers' Company; there are two others within the parish. They afford instruction to about 320 children, exclusively of those in the Sunday school at Moneymore. The parish contains several raths, and a remarkable cairn on the top of Slieve Gallion. – See MONEYMORE.

DESERTMARTIN, a parish, in the barony of LOUGHINSHOLIN, county of LONDONDERRY, and province of ULSTER, 2 miles (W.) from Magherafelt, on the road from Armagh to Coleraine, containing 4934 inhabitants, of which number, 257 are in the village, This parish comprises, according to the Ordnance survey, 9580 statute acres, of which 6952 are applotted under the tithe act. Within its limits is Lough Insholin,which gives name to the barony; it contains several islands, and is nearly dry in summer. The soil is every where good, and the system of agriculture improved; the lands are chiefly in tillage, producing abundant crops; there are some valuable tracts of bog. A great portion of the mountain of Slieve Gallion, is within the parish; notwithstanding its great height, it affords excellent pasturage nearly to its summit. Limestone abounds, and some very valuable quarries are worked for building and for agricultural purposes. Freestone of excellent quality is also quarried for building; and numerous thin seams of coal have been discovered, but not of sufficient depth to pay the expense of working them. Dromore House is the residence of the Hon. and Rev. A. W. Pomeroy. The inhabitants combine with their agricultural pursuits the spinning of flax and the weaving of linen to some extent in the farm-houses. The village contains about 40 houses, most of which are well built, and, though small, it is remarkably clean and has a very neat and pleasing appearance. Fairs were formerly held here, but they have been for some time discontinued.

The living is a rectory, in the diocese of Derry, and in the patronage of the Bishop: the tithes amount to £400. The glebe comprises 326a. 1r. l7p., of which, 105 are not cultivated; there is also another glebe belonging to the parish, called the townland of Lisgorgan, situated in Tamlaght-O'Crilly, and containing 179 acres. The church is a small edifice with a square tower, erected by aid of a loan of £800 from the late Board of First Fruits, in 1820; and is situated on the glebe, about a mile from the village. The R. C. parish is co-extensive with that of the Established Church; there are two chapels, situated respectively at Munsterlin and Cullion. There is a place of worship at Lecumpher for Presbyterians in connection with the Seceding Synod, and of the second class. The parochial school is chiefly supported by the rector, who also gives a house rent-free both to the master and mistress; the school-house, a handsome slated building, was erected in 1820. There are schools at Inniscarran and Cranny, founded and supported by the Drapers' Company, also three under the National Board, In these about 500 boys and 370 girls receive gratuitous instruction; and there are also a pay school, in which are about 30 boys and 20 girls, and five Sunday schools. Some remains of the old church exist on the bank of a small river near the village; and on the opposite bank are the remains of a fort, evidently raised to defend the pass of the river; a portion of the old church was taken down in 1820, to supply materials for building the parochial school-house.

DESERTOGHILL, a parish, in the barony of COLERAINE, county of LONDONDERRY, and province of ULSTER, 1 mile (S. E.) from Garvagh; containing 4701 inhabitants, This parish is intersected by the road from Dublin to Coleraine, and according to the Ordnance survey contains 11,469$^{1}/_{2}$ statute acres, of which about 6309 are arable, 2867 pasture, and 2293 bog, or wasteland. The soil, though thin, is tolerably well cultivated, and produces abundant crops. The inhabitants combine with their agricultural pursuits the weaving of linen cloth in their own houses. The living is a rectory, in the diocese of Derry, and in the patronage of the Bishop: the tithes amount to £290.

The glebe-house is a small old building on the glebe townland of Meettigan, in the parish of Errigal, which comprises 370 acres, 30 of which are on the southern side of the river, in the parish of Desertoghill, besides a plot of seven acres contiguous to the ruins of the old church. The present church is a large edifice, in the ancient style of English architecture, built in 1784, partly at the expense of Dr. Hervey, afterwards Earl of Bristol, and the Ecclesiastical Commissioners have recently granted £227.4.1 for its repair; it stands in the townland of Moyletra, one mile south of the old church. In the R. C. divisions the parish is the head of a union or district, also called Kilrea, comprising the parishes of Desertoghill. Tamlaght O'Crilly, and Kilrea, and containing three chapels, one here and two in Tamlaght O'Crilly. A large and handsome meeting-house is now being built at Moneydig for Presbyterians in connection with the Synod of Ulster. The parochial school at Ballyagan is supported by the rector; there are two schools under the Mercers' Company, two under the Ironmongers' Company, one under the National Board, and four others, also a private school. St. Columbkill here founded an abbey, which afterwards became parochial, but the old church, though now a picturesque ruin, does not bear evidence of such remote antiquity as some others in the neighbourhood; in 1622 it was one of the very few in the county that were in perfect repair. Not far distant from the old church is a small fortress; and in an adjoining field is an artificial cave of considerable extent, having three chambers or galleries. A curious stone, wherein are two small and rude founts, considered by the peasantry to be the impress of the knees of St. Columbkill while praying, stands in the churchyard. Half a mile above Garvagh is a curious encampment, called the Bonny Fort; and not far distant is a smaller one, called Roughfort: both appear to have been constructed to protect the mountain pass.

DRAPERSTOWN, or CROSS of BALLYNASCREEN, a market and post-town, in the parish of BALLYNASCREEN, barony of LOUGHINSHOLIN, county of LONDONDERRY, and province of ULSTER, 30 miles (S. E. by S.) from Londonderry, and 101 (N. by W.) from Dublin, on the road from Newtown-Stewart to Tubbermore; containing 412 inhabitants. In 1818, its name was changed from Cross to Draperstown, in consequence of its principally belonging to the Drapers' Company, under whose auspices a spacious market-house, hotel, and dispensary for their tenants,with surgeon's residence, are being built, chiefly in the Elizabethan style, and of freestone. The market is on Wednesday; and a fair for general farming stock is held on the first Friday in each month, and was established in 1792. The post-office is under Tubbermore, from which it is three miles distant; and here is a constabulary police station. The parochial church and school are situated in the town, and there is a general dispensary. – See BALLYNASCREEN.

DRUMACHOSE, a parish, in the barony of KENAUGHT, county of LONDONDERRY, and province of ULSTER, on the river Roe, and on the road from Londonderry to Coleraine; containing, with the market and post-town of Newtown-Limavady, 5280 inhabitants. The greater part of this parish formed a portion of the grant made to the Haberdashers' Company, in the reign of Jas. I.; part of it was given by the same monarch to Sir T. Phillips, upon which he built a castle, and founded the town of Newtown-Limavady; and part was confirmed to the see of Derry, In the war of 1641 it was the scene of much calamitous hostility, and the inhabitants were at length driven to seek an asylum in Derry, under protection of Col. Mervyn, who finally routed the Irish. In 1688 the town was besieged, and the inhabitants again retired to Derry; and on the retreat of the army of James in 1689, it was wasted with fire and sword. The parish, according to the Ordnance survey, comprises 11,683 statute acres (including 243. under water), of which 11,082 are applotted under the tithe act, and valued at £6032 per ann. Part of the land is very fertile and extremely well cultivated, particularly around Fruit Hill, Streeve, and other neighbouring places, and that portion towards the banks of the Roe is rich gravelly loam, well sheltered. On the mountain range of Cedy, the eastern limit of the parish, at the very summit, are about 1100 acres of mountain pasture. Here is abundance of excellent freestone and limestone, both of which are extensively worked, and there are indications of coal in several parts. The inhabitants combine the weaving of linen cloth with agricultural pursuits. There are two distilleries and a brewery, and two bleach-greens, one only of which is in full operation; there are also several corn, flour, and flax-mills. The scenery in various parts is highly interesting, the woods and plantations are thriving, and the country is ornamented with many handsome houses, of which the principal are Fruit Hill, the residence of Marcus McCausland, Esq.; Streeve Hill, of Marcus Gage, Esq.; Roe House, of W. Moody, Esq.; the Lodge, of R. Conn, Esq; Bridge House, of D. Cather, Esq.; and the glebe-house, of the Rev. J. Olpherts. The living is a rectory, in the diocese of Derry, and in the patronage of the Bishop; the tithes amount to £424.12.$3^3/_4$. The glebe-house was erected in 1816 on a glebe of $6^1/_2$ acres purchased by the late Board of First Fruits; the glebe, of which the greater part is at Gortygarn, 2 miles distant, comprises 112a. 2r. 15p. of arable land. The church, a handsome Grecian structure with a square tower, was erected, in 1750, upon the site of a former edifice at Newtown; and a north aisle was added in 1825 by aid of a loan of £200 from the late Board. In the R. C. divisions the parish is the head of a union or district, called Newtown-Limavady, comprising the parishes of Drumachose, Balteagh, Tamlaghtfinlagan, and parts of Aghanloo and Bovevagh, and containing three chapels, of which one is at Roe-mills, in this parish. There are places of worship for Presbyterians in connection with the Synod of Ulster, the Seceding Synod, and the Remonstrant Synod, all of the second class; and also for Covenanters, original Burghers, and Wesleyan Methodists. About 360 children are

Draperstown. Drawn by W.J. Booth, 1827, and engraved by T.W. Baynes. From Reports of... the Drapers' company *(London, 1829).*

taught in eight public schools, of which one is supported by Erasmus Smith's trustees and endowed with three acres of glebe, one chiefly by the rector, a female school built and supported by Mrs. McCausland, a female work school built and supported by Mrs. Olpherts, and a school supported by Mr. McCausland: there are also seven private and four Sunday schools. Near Fruit Hill are the extensive and beautiful ruins of the ancient church; and at the Dog-Leap is the site of the ancient castle of the powerful sept of O'Cahan.

DUNBOE, or DRUMBOE, a parish, in the barony of COLERAINE, county of LONDONDERRY, and province of ULSTER, 5 miles (W. by N.) from Coleraine; containing 5018 inhabitants. This appears to have been a very important district from an early period, for, even in the 5th century, we find it mentioned under the name of Le Bendrigi, which seems to have comprised the northern parts of the present barony of Coleraine; and it is stated that St. Patrick founded the old church here. The parish comprises, according to the Ordnance survey, 14,811$^1/_4$ statute acres, of which 14,576 are applotted under the tithe act, and valued at £5796 per ann. On the south and west it is composed of basaltic mountains, which afford good pasturage, and on the opposite sides it is washed by the ocean and the river Bann, towards which latter the surface gradually descends, and the sands at its mouth formed the most extensive rabbit warrens in the kingdom, until the decline in the price of the fur, when the warrens were mostly destroyed, and the land brought into cultivation. Numerous streams descend from the mountains, fertilizing the meadows through which they pass. Near Articlave and Downhill the land is good and under an excellent system of cultivation. Downhill, the splendid residence of Sir Jas. R. Bruce, Bart., occupies an elevated point of land between the Bann and Foyle, opening in full view on the Atlantic ocean; was erected by the late Earl of Bristol, Bishop of Derry, and is built in the Italian style, of hewn freestone; the pilasters are extremely chaste and beautiful. The interior is finished in the most costly manner, the saloons being adorned with marble statues, and the halls and galleries with statuary and paintings of the most celebrated ancient and modern masters. In the glens, the plantations are extensive, beautifully laid out, and ornamented with rustic buildings and bridges. On the lawn stands a unique and beautiful mausoleum, erected by the bishop to the memory of his brother, who was ambassador to the court of Spain, exhibiting a full-length statue of him, beneath an elevated canopy. The living is a rectory, forming the corps of the archdeaconry of Derry, and in the patronage of the Bishop: the tithes amount to £480. The glebe-house is a commodious residence, occupied by the Rev. Archdeacon Monsell; there are four glebes, containing together 550 statute acres, 382 of which are cultivated land,

Down Hill. Drawn by J.F. Neale and engraved by F.R. Hay, published in London, 1821.

the remainder being hilly and affording good pasturage for cattle. The church is a large and handsome edifice, situated at Articlave, for the repair of which the Ecclesiastical Commissioners have recently granted £230; it was erected on a new site in 1691, the old church having been destroyed by King James's army, on its retreat from Derry. In the R. C. divisions the parish forms part of the union of Killowen. In the village of Articlave is a meeting-house for Presbyterians, in connection with the Synod of Ulster, and at Ballinrees is one in connection with the Seceding Synod, both of the second class. The parochial schools, situated at Articlave, are supported by the archdeacon; there are also schools at Downhill, built by Sir J. R. Bruce, and supported by him and Lady Bruce. Schools are maintained in other parts of the parish, together affording instruction to more than 500 children. There are also two private and eight Sunday schools. The parish belongs partly to Sir J. R. Bruce, and partly to the Clothworkers' Company; the latter contribute £15 per ann. to the poor on their own estate. Not far from Downhill are the ruins of the ancient abbey of Duncruthin, which became the parish church previously to 1291: and in the western part of the parish stands a great fort, called the Giant's Sconce, occupying the summit of a lofty isolated hill of basalt, strongly fortified by nature.

DUNGIVEN, a market and post-town, and a parish, in the barony of KENAUGHT, county of DERRY, and province of ULSTER, 16 miles (E. S. E.) from Londonderry, and 138$^1/_4$ (N. N. W.) from Dublin; containing 3565 inhabitants, of which number, 1162 are in the town. This place was a seat of the O'Cahans, and was called Dun-y-even, or Doon-yeven; and here, on the summit of a rock, on the eastern bank of the Roe, Domnach O'Cahan, or O'Cathan, founded, in 1100, an abbey for Augustinian canons, which, being shortly afterwards polluted by a cruel massacre, lay for a long time in ruins, but was restored with much solemnity by the Archbishop of Armagh, and flourished till the dissolution, after which the lands were granted to the Irish Society, and are now in the possession of the Skinners Company. It is situated on the road between Londonderry and Dublin, and on the banks of the river Roe; and comprises, according to the Ordnance survey, 30,367$^1/_2$ statute acres, one-third of which is mountain, everywhere affording excellent pasturage. The land around the town is fertile and well cultivated; even the mountain Benbradagh, 1,530 feet above the level of the sea, is chiefly under tillage; and Carntogher, Moneyneiney, Carn, and other mountains, all very high, afford turbary and sufficient pasturage for vast herds of cattle: grouse and other game abound in the higher parts. The town is in a vale, near the junction of the Owen-reagh and the Owen-beg, which descend in nearly parallel lines from Glenfin and Cairnaban, with the Roe, here crossed by a handsome bridge of freestone: it consists of one long street, intersected by two shorter; some of the houses

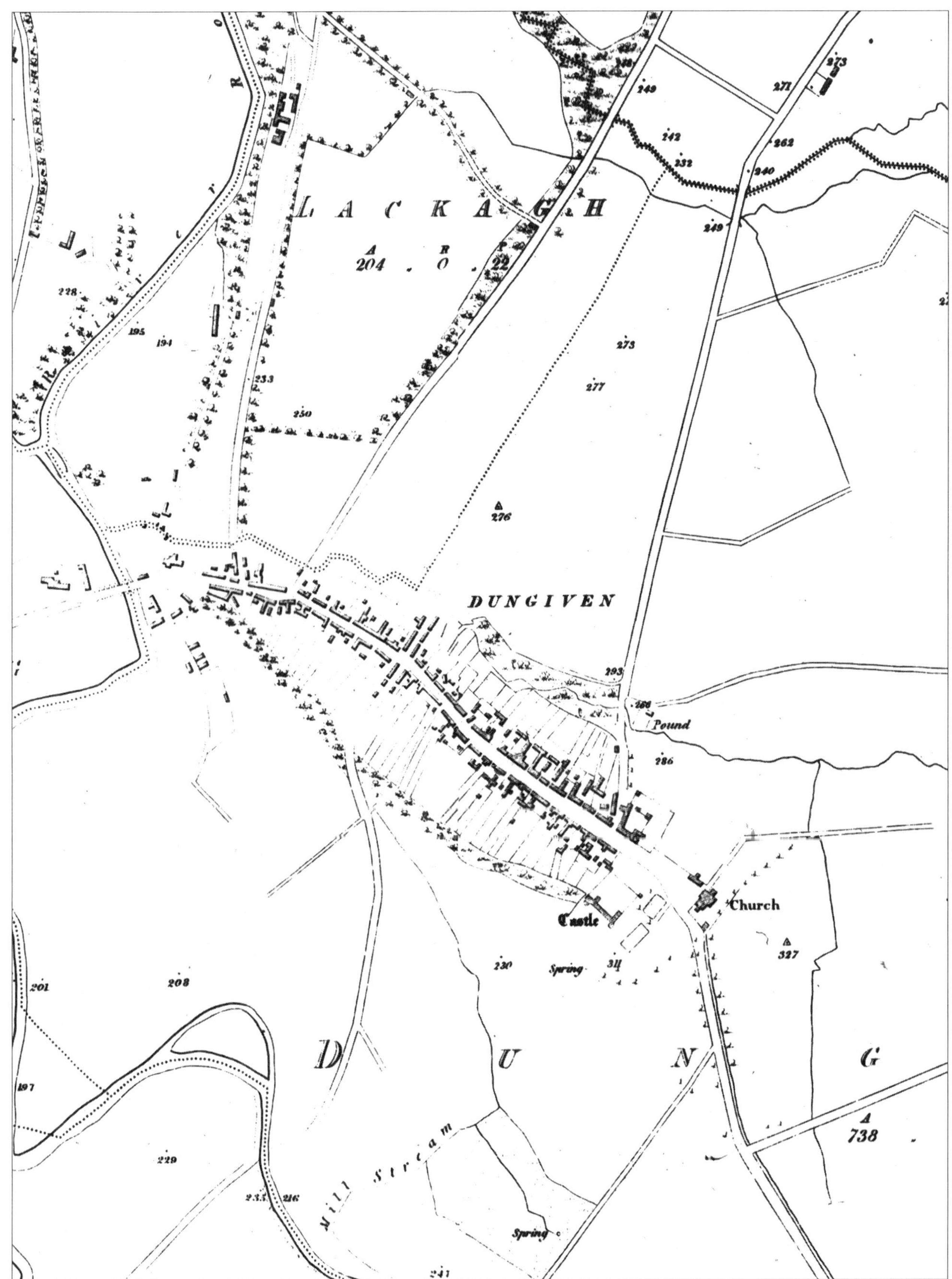

Dungiven. Part of 6 inch O.S. map of Co.Londonderry, sheet 24/25, published 1833 (reproduced at 140%).

are well built, but the greater number are low and only thatched. Formerly there were four extensive bleach-greens; they are now unemployed, and the manufacture is limited to a small quantity woven by the inhabitants in their own houses. A large market is held every Tuesday; the market-house is extensive, and there are stores for grain, &c.; considerable fairs are held on the second Tuesday in each month, except May and October, when they take place on the 25th. A court for the manor of Pellipar is held in the court-house at Dungiven, every third Thursday, for the recovery of debts under 40s.; its jurisdiction extends into the parishes of Dungiven, Banagher, Ballynascreen, and Upper and Lower Cumber. Petty sessions are likewise held monthly in the court-house. Here is a constabulary police station; adjoining the market-house is the barrack store. The gentlemen's residences are Pellipar House, that of R. Ogilby, Esq.; the Cottage, of R. Leslie Ogilby, Esq.; and Roe Lodge, of M. King, Esq.

The living is a vicarage, in the diocese of Derry, and in the patronage of the impropriator. Robert Ogilby, Esq., lessee of the manor of Pellipar under the Skinners Company, to whom the entire tithes, amounting to £480.14.8, are payable; it is usually held in connection with Banagher. The glebe townland of Tirmeal comprises 654a.2r.17p, of which 89 are mountain and bog. The church is a commodious cruciform edifice of hewn freestone, built in 1817 (on the site of a former one erected in 1711), at a cost of £1460, of which £1200 was a loan from the late Board of First Fruits. In the R. C. divisions this parish is the head of a union or district, comprising Dungiven and parts of Banagher and Bovevagh; the chapel is a large building in the town. At Scriggan is a Presbyterian meeting-house, in connection with the Synod of Ulster; and one is in course of erection at Dungiven, in connection with the Seceding Synod. The male and female parochial schools are situated on the glebe of Tirmeal, and are aided by the vicar, who also contributes principally to the support of a school at Gortnacross; a school at Ballymacallion is endowed with an acre of land by the Marquess of Waterford; and in the town are a school built and supported by R. Ogilby, Esq., and a female work school supported by the vicar and his lady. In these schools about 190 boys and 90 girls are taught; and there are five private schools, in which are about 200 boys and 80 girls, and four Sunday schools. An excellent dispensary is supported in the usual manner. The interesting remains of the abbey church occupy a remarkably picturesque situation, on a rock 200 feet in perpendicular height above the river Roe; they consist of the side walls of the nave and chancel, which are nearly entire, with the gable of the latter, in which, within a circular arch resting on corbels and cylindrical pillars, are two narrow lancet-shaped windows, with a niche on each side and a square-headed window above. The nave is separated from the chancel by a lofty circular arch, and has on the north side a low doorway of corresponding style; it was lighted by a window ornamented with tracery, in good preservation. Under a beautifully ornamented arch in the chancel is an altar-tomb, bearing a recumbent effigy of an armed warrior, said to be one of the O'Cahans; the stones in front are ornamented with figures of armed knights, sculptured in relief, in niches. The remains of the abbey have from time to time been removed, and the capitals, pillars, mullions, &c., may be seen in the churchyard, forming boundaries round the graves or head-stones. Adjoining the town are extensive ruins of a castle and bawn, built in 1618, by the Skinners' Company. A lofty stone stands near the old church, set up as the record of an ecclesiastical assembly held here in 590, at which St. Columbkill was present. Near the river Roe is Tubber-Phadrig, or St. Patrick's fountain; and a single stone, in the bed of the river, exists, around which the people assemble on certain days. There are many raths or forts in different parts of the parish: celts of stone and bronze, spear-heads, and Roman coins and other antiquities have been discovered, and are in the possession of R. L. Ogilby and M. Ross, Esqrs.

Dungiven Abbey. Drawn by Andrew Nicholl and engraved by Branston and Wright. From The Dublin Penny Journal, *vol.1, 1833.*

ERRIGAL, or ARRIGLE, a parish, in the barony of COLERAINE, county of LONDONDERRY, and province of ULSTER; containing, with the post-town of Garvagh (which is described under its own head), 5401 inhabitants. A monastery was founded here by St. Columb in 589, which flourished until the ninth century, when it was plundered and destroyed by the Danes, The parish is bounded on the south by the Agivey water, and comprises, according to the Ordnance survey, 19,625¼ statute acres, of which 18,113 are applotted under the tithe act and valued at £5163 per ann.; about 7500 acres are arable, 5500 pasture, 100 woodland, and the remainder bog and mountain; the latter affording good pasturage to large herds of cattle. The vale of Glenullen, and all the lands around Garvagh and on the banks of the Agivey water, are fertile, and even many of the more elevated lands produce excellent crops, though agriculture has been but little improved. The mountain range consists principally of the eastern slopes of Ballyness and Donald's hill, extending to the boundary of the barony, and are exclusively basalt, but everywhere produce sweet herbage. The inhabitants unite with agriculture the weaving of linen cloth. There are several handsome houses in the parish, the principal of which are Garvagh, the seat of Lord Garvagh, adjoining which is the picturesque vale of Glenullen; Ballintemple, of Mrs. Arthur Heyland; Woodbank, of Capt. Orr; Garvagh Cottage, of Capt. Crossley; and Meetigan glebe-house, of the Rev. W. Smith. The living is a rectory, in the diocese of Derry, and in the patronage of the Bishop: the tithes amount to £353, of which £300 are payable to the rector, the percentage to the landlord being about £53. The glebe-house, a small old building, is delightfully situated near the top of Glenullen; the glebe comprises about 254 acres. The church is a low plain building, adjoining the town of Garvagh, to the repairs of which the Ecclesiastical Commissioners have recently made a grant of £201. In the R. C. divisions this parish is the head of a union or district, comprising also parts of Desertog hill and Balteagh, and containing two chapels, one at Ballerin, and the other in Glenullen. There are places of worship in Garvagh for Presbyterians in connection with the Synod of Ulster and the Seceding Synod, and for Separatists from the Seceding Synod, also one for Wesleyan Methodists. There are parochial and five other public schools, some of which are aided by donations from Lord Garvagh, R. McCausland, Esq., Mrs. Heyland, the rector, and the Ironmongers' Company; they afford instruction to about 400 children. A school founded by Dr. Adam Clarke is supported by the Wesleyan Methodists; and about 120 children are educated in four private schools. Here are numerous forts, particularly in Glenullen, evidently constructed to protect the pass into the mountains. The old church at Ballintemple is a very interesting ruin. The Rev. G. V. Sampson, author of the Map and Memoir of Londonderry, and the Statistical Survey of the same county, was rector of this parish, and died at the glebe-house; he was buried at Aghanloo.

FAUGHANVALE, a parish, in the barony of TIRKERAN, county of LONDONDERRY, and province of ULSTER, 8 miles (S. E.) from Londonderry, on the mail coach road to Coleraine; containing 6218 inhabitants. This parish, which is bounded on the north by Lough Foyle, comprises, according to the Ordnance survey, 18,582¼ statute acres, the greater portion of which was granted in 1609, by Jas. I., to the Grocers' Company of London, who in 1619 erected a strong and handsome castle, surrounded by a bawn, in which they placed a powerful garrison, In the war of 1641 this castle sustained a siege for several months, and resolutely held out against the parliamentarians till the garrison was relieved; it was again besieged and finally taken and dismantled by the parliament; the ruins were standing till 1823, when they were removed, and the present glebe-house erected on the site. Of the remainder of the parish, part is held in perpetuity equally by Lesley Alexander, Esq., and the heirs of the late Sir Wm. Ponsonby, who pay a chief rent of £200 per ann. to the Goldsmiths' Company; part belongs to Major Scott, part to the see of Derry, and a few of the native townlands in the Grocers' proportion to the Marquess of Londonderry. The land is generally fertile, especially round the villages of Faughanvale and Muff, and the system of agriculture has been greatly improved under the auspices of the North West Agricultural Society, and the gentry resident in the district. Many thousand acres of bog and waste land have been reclaimed and brought into profitable cultivation; the lands are well drained and fenced, and there are extensive and flourishing plantations, exclusively of the ancient oak woods of Walworth, which are principally in this parish. At Creggan and Tullynee are quarries of excellent slate, but they are only partially worked, and principally for flags and tombstones. The principal seats are Willsborough, that of Major Scott; Foyle Park, of Lesley Alexander, Esq.; Campsey, of J. Quin, Esq.; Creggan, of T. Major, Esq.; Coolafeeney, of T. Lecky, Esq.; Muff House, of the Rev. J. Christie; and Tullybrisland, of T. Major, Esq. A manorial court, in which debts not exceeding 40s. are recoverable, is held at Muff for that part of the parish which belongs to the Grocers' Company. The living is a rectory and perpetual curacy, in the diocese of Derry; the rectory forming part of the union of Templemore and of the corps of the deanery of Derry, and the curacy in the patronage of the Dean, The tithes amount to £700, payable to the dean, and the glebe comprises 1035 statute acres. The curacy was instituted in 1823; the stipend is £92.6.2, of which £69.4.7½ is paid by the dean, and £23.1.6½ from Primate Boulter's fund. The glebe-house, with a glebe of 10 acres, was given to the curate by the Grocers' Company. The church, a spacious and handsome edifice, with a square tower crowned with pinnacles, was built in 1821, by a loan of £1000 from the late Board of First Fruits, near the ruins of a former church built by the Grocers' Company in 1626, in the village of Muff, and about three miles distant from the ruins of the ancient parish church. The R. C. parish is coextensive with that of the Established church; the chapel is at Creggan. At Tullinee there is a place of worship for Presbyterians in connection with the Synod of Ulster, of the second class. About 370 children are taught in six public schools, of which the parochial school at Muff is supported by a grant of £30 per ann. from the trustees of Erasmus

Smith's charity, and annual donations from the Grocers' Company and the rector; the school-house, adjoining the church, a large and handsome edifice, was erected in 1814. A school at Graceteel is under the Fishmongers' Company, who pay the whole charges for children of cottiers and one-half for those of farmers on their estate; two are aided by the Marquess of Londonderry and Major Scott; and an agricultural school is supported by shareholders and subscribers, and by the labour of the scholars on the farm. There are also three private schools, in which are about 150 children, and three Sunday schools. A valuable donation of sacramental plate and furniture for the altar and pulpit was bequeathed to the church, in 1665, by Bishop Wild, who also left £5 for the poor.

GARVAGH, a market and post-town, in the parish of ERRIGAL, barony of COLERAINE, county of LONDONDERRY, and province of ULSTER, 8 miles (S.) from Coleraine, and $110^1/_2$ (N. by W.) from Dublin, on the road from Armagh to Coleraine: the population is returned with the parish. It appears to have been a place of some importance soon after the plantation of Ulster. In 1641, Col. Rowley raised a regiment of foot and marched into the town for its protection. After keeping possession of it for some time, he was attacked by a party of forces commanded by Sir Phelim O'Nial, who, making themselves masters of the place, put the Colonel and many of the inhabitants to death, burnt the town, and plundered the country to the very gates of Coleraine. The town consists of one long spacious street intersected at right angles by two smaller streets; many of the houses are large and handsomely built, and the whole has an appearance of great respectability. Adjoining it is Garvagh House, the seat of Lord Garvagh, a spacious mansion with a well-planted demesne and an extensive park; and there are several other gentlemen's seats, which are noticed in the article on the parish. The trade of the place is considerable, and with the town owes its prosperity to the Canning family. The market is on Friday and is well supplied; and on the third Friday in every month a fair is held for the sale of brown linen, horses, cattle, sheep, and pigs, each of which is numerously attended. Petty sessions are held in a court-house on the last Monday of every month. Adjoining the town is the parish church, a small neat edifice; and there is a meeting-house for Presbyterians in connection with the Synod of Ulster, of the second class, built in 1746, rebuilt in 1790, and enlarged in 1830; another in connection with the Seceding Synod, and a third for Separatists from that synod.

GLENDERMOT, or CLONDERMOT, a parish, in the barony of TIRKEERAN, county of LONDONDERRY, and province of ULSTER; containing with the town of Waterside, which is one of the suburbs of Londonderry, 10,338 inhabitants. This parish, which is separated from the city of Londonderry by the river Foyle, over which is a fine wooden bridge, 1068 feet long, comprises 22,495 acres, of which 987 are water. A religious house is said to have been founded here by St. Patrick, which was probably the church of Kil Ard, of which the foundations are still traceable. St. Columbkill founded a monastery here in 588, at the place which still bears his name; and Ailid O'Dermit founded a nunnery at Rossnagalliagh, in 879, of which some traces remain. The founder of the extensive building, of which the ruins are on Lough Enagh, is unknown; it probably belonged to the Knights Hospitallers, and was afterwards a chapel of ease to Clondermot, and as such was confirmed to the Dean of Derry in 1609, under the name of Annagh. In the Earl of Tyrone's rebellion the church of St. Columb and the parish church were destroyed; the former was not rebuilt, but some of its ruins are visible. The soil in the northern portion of the parish is rich and well cultivated, but there is a considerable quantity of moorland in the southern part. Quarries of slate and blue limestone exist. At Ardmore is a bleach-green, the first established in this part of the country, where 25,000 pieces of linen are finished annually; there is also one at the Oaks, and a large distillery at Waterside. The water for the supply of the city of Londonderry is obtained from an elevated spot near Prehen, and conveyed in cast-iron pipes over the bridge across the Foyle into the city. Besides that bridge, there is a handsome one over the Faughan, near Enagh; another on the Coleraine road, a little lower down, and a third at Drumahoe. The Bishop's, the Goldsmiths', and the Grocers' manors extend over parts of this parish, but no manorial courts are held. The principal seats are Prehen, the residence of Col. Knox; Beech Hill, of Conolly Skipton, Esq.; Ashbrook, of W. H. Ashe, Esq.; Ardmore, of J. A. Smith, Esq.; Larchmount, of C. McClelland, Esq.; Lisdillon, of W. J. Smith, Esq.; Berryburn, of Capt. Reynolds; Ardkill, of R. Stephenson, Esq.; Bellevue, of the Rev. J. D. Maughan; Bonds Hill, of J. Murray, Esq.; St. Columbs, of G. Hill, Esq.; Glendermot glebe, of the Rev. A. G. Cary; Caw, of A. Harvey, Esq.; Lower Caw, of J. Alexander, Esq.; and Coolkeragh, of R. Young, Esq. The living is a perpetual curacy, in the diocese of Derry, and in the gift of the Dean of Derry; the rectory was united by patent in 1609, to Templemore and Faughanvale, the three forming the union of Templemore and the corps of the deanery of Derry, which is in the patronage of the Crown; the Ecclesiastical Commissioners recommend the dissolution of the union. The tithes amount to £920.11.8, and the perpetual curate is paid by the dean. The church is a large handsome building, in the Grecian style, erected in 1753, and for the repairs of which the Ecclesiastical Commissioners have recently granted £509. The glebe-house is situated on a glebe of 12 acres, purchased by the late Board of First Fruits in 1824, and is occupied by the perpetual curate. The rector's glebe comprises 407 acres, and the deanery lands in Clouder mot consist of 1284 acres. In the R. C. divisions the parish is united to part of Lower Cumber; there is a small neat chapel at Curryneirin. At Altnagelirn are two meeting-houses for Presbyterians in connection with the Synod of Ulster, one of the first, the other of the third, class; and at Drumahoe is one connected with the Seceding Synod. There are parochial schools at Clondermot, on the glebe, and at the new church, aided by the dean; there are also schools at Salem, Ardmore, Lisdillon, and Drumahoe; the Grocers' Company have built and maintain a school at Gortnessey; a school at Prehen is supported by Col. Knox and the perpetual curate; there is a national school at Curryneirin, and female work schools at Ardmore and Bellevue; also four Sunday schools. Col. Mitchelburne, who was a native of this place, and many of the other defenders of Londonderry, are interred in the burial-ground of Clondermot, in which are considerable remains of the old church.

KILCRONAGHAN, a parish, in the barony of LOUGHINSHOLIN, county of DERRY, and province of ULSTER; containing, with the post-town of Tubbermore, 4186 inhabitants. It comprises, according to the Ordnance survey, 7992$^3/_4$ statute acres, of which 7409 are applotted under the tithe act, and includes some of the richest portions of the valley of the Mayola, the principal part of which is pasture; there are also above 500 acres of mountain land in pasture. Great quantities of reddish limestone and much valuable freestone are quarried, some of which is exported from Portballyronan: there are also some thin seams of coal. The principal seats are Fort William, the residence of J. Stevenson, Esq., and the glebe-house, of the Rev. J. T. Paul. The living is a rectory, in the diocese of Derry, and in the patronage of the Bishop: the tithes amount to £350. The church is a small edifice, rebuilt in 1816; near the communion table is a beautiful niche in the Norman style, which was part of the ancient edifice: the Ecclesiastical Commissioners lately granted £132 for the repair of this church. The glebe-house, which adjoins it, stands on a glebe of three acres, besides which there is a glebe of 234 acres of arable land, about two miles from the church. In the R. C. divisions this parish forms part of the union or district of Desartmartin, and has a chapel at Keenaght. There is a meeting-house for Presbyterian at Tubbermore: it was built in 1728, and is of the second class, in connection with the Synod of Ulster. There is also a meeting-house for Independents in the town. About 480 children are educated in seven public schools, and there are six Sunday schools. Dr. Adam Clarke, the celebrated biblicist, was born at Moybeg, in this parish. – See TUBBERMORE.

KILDOLLAGH, or KILDALLOCK, a parish, partly in the barony of UPPER DUNLUCE, county of ANTRIM, but chiefly in the North-West Liberties of COLERAINE, county of LONDONDERRY, and province of ULSTER, 2 miles (S. E.) from Coleraine, on the river Bann; containing 982 inhabitants. According to the Ordnance survey it comprises 2006 statute acres, of which 1984 are in Londonderry: the land is fertile and well drained, fenced, and cultivated. It is a rectory, in the diocese of Connor, forming part of the union of Rasharkin. About 40 children are educated in a private school, and there is a Sunday school. Near the village of Loughans are the ruins of the ancient church; also the foundations of the castle of McQuillan, where a sanguinary battle was fought, in 1534, between the rival septs of O'Kane and McQuillan. Not far distant is a lofty fort, containing a large cave.

KILLELAGH, or KILLELA, a parish, in the barony of LOUGHINSHOLIN, county of LONDONDERRY, and province of ULSTER, 2 miles (N.) from Maghera on the river Clody; containing 3045 inhabitants, This parish comprises, according to the Ordnance survey, 10,270 statute acres, of which more than half is good mountain pasture and the remainder under tillage; the substratum is basalt, and the soil generally thin and cold, but the lands have been lately improved by a judicious use of lime; there is a sufficient tract of turbary for fuel, but no waste land. On its eastern boundary is Carntogher mountain, rising 1521 feet above the level of the sea. In the mountain district the inhabitants are principally native Irish, and in the plains, of Scottish extraction. Five townlands are in the manor of Maghera and belong to the see of Derry, three in the manor of Kilrea belong to the Mercers' Company, and four in the manor of Bellaghy to the Vintners' Company, of London. The parish was formerly united to Maghera, but in 1794 was separated from it and now forms a distinct benefice. The living is a rectory, in the diocese of Derry, and in the patronage of the Bishop: the tithes amount to £197.7.4. The church is a small plain edifice without tower or spire, towards the erection of which the late Board of First Fruits gave £500, in 1808, and in 1810 £100 towards the erection of the glebe-house; the glebe comprises 272 acres, constituting the townland of Gortinure, of which 70 acres are under cultivation. In the R. C divisions it forms part of the union or district of Maghera; the chapel is a small ancient building. About 60 children are taught in three public schools, of which the parochial schools are supported by the rector, and a school at Tirhew is aided by Mr. Holmes; and there are two private schools, in which are about 30 children. In the townland of Tirnony is a perfect cromlech, and near it an artificial cave formed of field stones and covered with flags. In the southern part of the parish are the ruins of a very ancient church, which was destroyed in the rebellion of the Earl of Tyrone, and subsequently rebuilt.

KILLOWEN, or ST. JOHN'S CHURCH, a parish, in the barony of COLERAINE, county of LONDONDERRY, and province of ULSTER, forming part of the suburbs of Coleraine, and containing 2906 inhabitants. This parish, which is included within the present borough of Coleraine, is situated on the western bank of the river Bann, and is connected with the town, on the opposite side, by a fine wooden bridge of considerable length. That part of the parish which is more especially the suburb consists of one long street, called Captain street, forming a continuation of Bridge street, Coleraine. It contains many small houses, nearly the whole of which are held by various tenures under the Clothworkers' Company, of London, who obtained a lease of the parish from the Irish Society, to whom it had been granted by Jas. I. in 1609. A small trade is carried on, chiefly in the manufacture of calicoes and ginghams; and fairs are held on May 12th and July 5th. The parish comprises, according to the Ordnance survey, 1796 statute acres, of which 1714 are applotted under the tithe act, and valued at £2243 per annum: the lands are chiefly under tillage, the soil is fertile, and the system of agriculture greatly improved. Jackson's Hall, the seat of Mrs. Maxwell, occupies the site of an ancient castle, erected, in 1213, by Mac Ughtry, who in that year destroyed the abbey founded on the spot by St. Carbreus, in 540.

The living is a rectory, in the diocese of Derry, and in the patronage of the Bishop: the tithes amount to £160. The original parish church, which was part of a priory founded in 1080, was, in 1830, converted into a school-house; and a small neat church, without either tower or spire, was built at an expense of £1000, towards which £300 was given by the Clothworkers' Company, £100 by Bishop Knox, £50 by the Irish Society, and £170 as a gift and £380 as a loan by the late Board of First Fruits. The glebe-house, towards the erection of which the same Board granted a loan of £80, was built in 1822: the glebe comprises 30 acres. In the R. C. divisions the parish is the head of a union or district called Killowen, or Coleraine, comprising also the parishes of Dunboe, Macosquin, and Aghadowy, and containing three chapels, situated respectively at Killowen, Dunboe, and Aghadowy. There is a place of worship for Presbyterians in connection with the Seceding Synod. About 250 children are educated in four public schools, of which the parochial schools are assisted by a gift of £25 per annum from the Clothworkers' Company, and a donation from the rector; and a school at Laurel Hill was founded and endowed with £50 per annum by the late R. Kyle, Esq., in 1830. There are also a private school, in which are about 50 children, and three Sunday schools. Remains of some fine encampments or forts may be seen at Cranagh Hill and Ballycavin, and one of smaller dimensions near the church. On the confines of the parish, near Camus, are two strongly impregnated springs, one chalybeate, the other holding pure sulphur in solution.

KILREA, a market and post-town, and a parish, partly in the barony of COLERAINE, but chiefly in that of LOUGHINSHOLIN, county of LONDONDERRY, and province of ULSTER, 28 miles (S. E.) from Londonderry, and 110 (N.) from Dublin, on the roads leading respectively from Coleraine to Portglenone and Castle Dawson, and from Garvagh to Ballymoney; containing 4262 inhabitants, of which number, 973 are in the town. This place is situated on the western shore of the river Bann, over which is a substantial stone bridge of seven arches, forming a communication between this neighbourhood and the county of Antrim, with which there is a great intercourse. The town, which has a sub-post-office to Portglenone, is near the river, in that part of the parish which is within the barony of Loughinsholin, and consists of a square and four principal streets, comprising 237 houses, of which about 12 are slated, and the remainder thatched. The inhabitants are supplied with water from a public fountain in the south-eastern angle of the square. A spacious and commodious hotel, and a handsome residence for their agent have recently been erected by the Mercers' Company, of London, who are proprietors of the town and surrounding district. Their estate of which this town may be considered the head, comprehends 41 townlands, of which 9 are in this parish, 9 in Desertoghill, 11 in Maghera, 5 in Tamlaght O'Crilly, 4 in Aghadowy, and 3 in Killylagh, together comprising an area of 21,060 statute acres, of which nearly one-fourth part is bog and rocky ground. The spinning of yarn and weaving of linen are carried on generally throughout the district; and the river is navigable for lighters from Belfast and Newry, through Lough Neagh, to Portna, about a quarter of a mile distant from the town. The market is on Wednesday; a flax and linen market is held every alternate market day; and fairs for cattle and horses are held on the second Wednesday in every month. A large and handsome market house is now in progress of erection on the north side of the square, at the expense of the Mercers' Company, who have also built a barrack in Bridge-street for the constabulary police. Manorial courts are held occasionally, and petty sessions on the first Monday in every month.

The parish extends along the western banks of the river Bann more than six miles, and comprises, according to the Ordnance survey, 6314$^1/_2$ statute acres, of which 3486 are applotted under the tithe act, and 138$^1/_2$ are in the Bann. The soil, though varying in different parts, is generally light, resting upon a substratum of basalt, which in many places rises above the surface, and of which detached blocks of various sizes are scattered in the wildest confusion. There is neither limestone nor stone for building in the parish; nor is there any timber or plantation in the neighbourhood; but many of the leases having expired, the Mercers' Company have already commenced some extensive and valuable improvements. The land is principally under tillage, producing tolerably good crops; the system of agriculture, though better than formerly, is still capable of farther improvement; there is an extensive tract of bog, affording an abundant supply of fuel. The line of road between this place and the county of Antrim is now being changed, which will greatly increase the facility of travelling. The living is a rectory, in the diocese of Derry, and in the patronage of the Bishop: the tithes amount to £258.9.3. The glebe-house, situated near the church on a glebe of three acres, was built in 1774; and there is a glebe in the parish of Tamlaght O'Crilly, comprising, 351 acres. The church is a small and very ancient edifice, with a bell turret on the western gable; arrangements are in progress for the erection of a larger at the expense of the Mercers' Company. In the R. C. divisions the parish forms part of the union or district of Desertoghill, called also Kilrea. There is a place of worship for Presbyterians in connection with the Synod of Ulster, of the third class; and a small congregation of Seceders assemble in a temporary building. About 550 children are taught in five public schools, of which the parochial school is supported by subscriptions, aided by the rector; one by the trustees of Erasmus Smith's charity, for which the Mercers' Company erected a handsome stone building, in 1813, at an expense of £700; and two others by the same company. There are also three private schools, in which are about 140 children. The company support 22 schools on their estate, in which together about 1000 children are gratuitously instructed and supplied with books. There are some picturesque remains of the ancient castle of Movanagher, about $1^1/_2$ mile to the north of the present town: during the parliamentary war it was garrisoned for the king, but shortly after fell into the hands of the parliamentarians, by whom, after being repeatedly taken and retaken, it was finally dismantled in 1649. The ford at Portoneil, and the ferry across the Bann, were in the same war scenes of much slaughter; and in 1688 they were severely contested and alternately in the possession of both parties.

LEARMONT, an ecclesiastical district, partly in the barony of TIRKEERAN, county of LONDONDERRY, and partly in that of STRABANE, county of TYRONE, and province of ULSTER, 5 miles (W.) from Dungiven, on the road to Omagh; containing 4411 inhabitants. It was formed in 1831, under the 7th and 8th of Geo. IV., by separating nine townlands from Banagher, eight from Upper Cumber, and one from Lower Cumber, the whole of which are in Londonderry, except Stranagalvally, which is in Tyrone. Much of the land is very good and under an excellent system of cultivation, and the wasteland is being reclaimed under the liberah encouragement of Barre Beresford, Esq., proprietor of the chief portion of this district. Sawel mountain, on the verge of the two counties, rises to the height of 2236 feet above the level of the sea; near it are the precipitous rocks called the Eagle's Nest. Blue limestone is burnt here for manure, and manganese and lead ore are found, also iron ore almost in a metallic state. The village of Learmont, or Park, is situated on the Faughan water, near the base of Sawel mountain, and has been much improved lately by its proprietor. The principal seat is Learmont, the elegant residence of Barre Beresford, Esq., which he is enlarging and finishing in the Elizabethan or Tudor style. Around it is an extensive demesne, containing large and valuable timber, and ornamented with baths and groups of statues. Here is also Kilcreen, the residence of J. C. Beresford, Esq.; Straid Lodge, of the Rev. J. Hunter; and Tamna, the shooting-lodge of Hugh Lyle, Esq. The living is a perpetual curacy, in the diocese of Derry, and in the alternate patronage of the Rectors of Banagher and Upper Cumber, except the fifth turn, which devolves on the Rector of Lower Cumber. The curate's income is £85 per annum, which is paid by the three rectors. The late Bishop Knox proposed to make this district a parish of itself, the tithes of which exceed £300 per ann., in which case Mr. Beresford proposed to exchange land planted and improved for a glebe. The church, a small neat edifice, was built in 1831, at an expense of £750, of which £400 was given by the late Board of First Fruits, £100 by the late Bishop Knox, £100 by B. Beresford, Esq., £50 by the Irish Society, £25 by the Skinners' Company, £25 by Robt. Ogilby, Esq., and the rest by various individuals. In the R. C. divisions it forms part of the union or district of Banagher, and has a chapel at Altenure. There is a school at Park, to which Mr. Beresford allows £5 per annum and a house, and three other public schools, in which about 260 children are educated; there are also three private schools, in which about 150 are educated, and a Sunday school.

LISSAN, or LISANE, a parish, partly in the barony of DUNGANNON, county of TYRONE, and partly in that of LOUGHINSHOLIN, county of LONDONDERRY, and province of ULSTER, 3 miles (N. by E.) from Cookstown, on the road to Moneymore and on that from Omagh to Belfast; containing 6163 inhabitants. This parish, which is bounded on the north by the mountain of Slieve Gallion, comprises, according to the Ordnance survey, $24{,}684^1/_2$ statute acres, including $147^3/_4$ in Lough Fea, and of which $12{,}917^1/_2$ are in the county of Tyrone. The greater portion is in the manor of Ardtrea, belonging to the see of Armagh, and part is in the manor of Moneymore and the property of the Drapers' Company of London. In the war of 1641, the castle, which at that time was the property of the Staples family, to whom it was granted on the plantation of Ulster, was seized by Nial O'Quin for Sir Phelim O'Nial, who plundered the house of Sir Thomas Staples while rendezvousing at Moneymore castle, and compelled the men employed in his iron-works on the Lissan water to make pikes and pike-heads from the stores of their master. The land is mountainous and boggy; about one-third is under tillage and produces excellent crops, and the remainder affords good pasture; the system of agriculture is improved, and much of the bog is of valuable quality; limestone abounds and is extensively quarried for agricultural uses. The mountain of Slieve Gallion has an elevation of 1730 feet above the level of the sea; the surrounding scenery is strongly diversified and in some parts very picturesque. The principal seats are Lissan Park, the residence of Sir Thos. Staples, Bart., a noble mansion in an extensive demesne embellished with thriving plantations, an artificial sheet of water with cascades, and a picturesque bridge, built by the celebrated Ducart; Muff House, of the Rev. J. Molesworth Staples; and Crieve, of W. Maygill, Esq. The linen manufacture is carried on to a great extent by the whole of the population, who combine it with agricultural pursuits. The living is a rectory, in the diocese of Armagh, and in the patronage of the Lord-Primate: the tithes amount to £500. The glebe-house was built at an expense of £1313.14.5, of which £100 was a gift and £650 a loan from the late Board of First Fruits, in 1807, and the remainder was paid by the incumbent; the glebe comprises $87^1/_4$ statute acres, valued at £67.10 per annum. The church is a plain and very ancient structure, with an east window of stained glass. In the R. C. divisions the parish is the head of a union or district, comprising also part of the parish of Desertlyn; the chapel is a neat edifice. About 400 children are taught in five public schools, of which the parochial school, for which a house was built by the Rev. J. M. Staples, at an expense of £500, and a school at Grouse Lodge, for which a house was built by Mrs. Wright, who endowed it with an acre of land, are supported under the trustees of Erasmus Smith's charity; a school at Crevagh was built and is supported by Sir T. Staples, Bart., and one at Donaghbreaghy is aided by the Drapers' Company. There are also a private school, in which are about 30 children, and four Sunday schools.

LONDONDERRY, a city and port, in the parish of TEMPLEMORE, and county of LONDONDERRY (of which it is the chief town), and province of ULSTER, 69¾ miles (N. W. by W.) from Belfast, and 118½ (N. N. W.) from Dublin; containing 10,130 inhabitants.

It was originally and is still popularly called Derry, from the Irish Doire, which signifies literally "a place of oaks," but is likewise used to express "a thick wood." By the ancient Irish it was also designated Doire-Calgaich, or Derry-Calgach, "the oak wood of Calgach;" and Adamnan, abbot of Iona in the 7th century, in the life of his predecessor, St. Columbkill, invariably calls it Roboretum Calgagi. About the end of the 10th century, the name Derry-Calgach gave place to Derry-Columbkill, from an abbey for canons regular of the order of St. Augustine founded here by that saint; but when the place grew into importance above every other Derry, the distinguishing epithet was rejected: the English prefix, London, was imposed in 1613, on the incorporation of the Irish Society by charter of Jas. I., and was for a long time retained by the colonists, but has likewise fallen into popular disuse. The city appears to be indebted for its origin to the abbey founded by St. Columbkill, according to the best authorities in 546, and said to have been the first of the religious houses instituted by that saint; but the exact period of its foundation and its early history are involved in much obscurity. In 783 and 812 the abbey and the town were destroyed by fire; at the latter period, according to the Annals of Munster, the Danes heightened the horrors of the conflagration by a massacre of the clergy and students. The place must have been speedily restored, as, in 832, the Danes were driven with great slaughter from the siege of Derry by Niall Caille, King of Ireland, and Murchadh, Prince of Aileach In 983, the shrine of St. Columbkill was carried away by the Danes, by whom the place was also thrice devastated about the close of the 10th century: in 1095 the abbey was consumed by fire. In 1100, Murtagh O'Brien arrived with a large fleet of foreign vessels and attacked Derry, but was defeated with great slaughter by the son of Mac Loughlin, prince of Aileach. Ardgar, prince of Aileach, was slain in an assault upon Derry in 1124; but on the 30th of March, 1135, the town with its churches was destroyed by fire, in revenge, as some state, of his death: it also sustained a similar calamity in 1149.

In 1158, Flahertagh O'Brolchain, abbot of the Augustine monastery, was raised to the episcopacy and appointed supreme superintendent of all the abbeys under the rule of St. Columb, by a synodical decree of the Irish clergy assembled at Brigh-mac-Taidhg, in the north of Meath. O'Brolchain immediately commenced preparations for the erection of a new church on a larger scale; and in 1162 he removed more than 80 houses adjacent to the abbey church, and enclosed the abbey with a circular wall. In 1164 Temple More, or "the great church," was built, and the original abbey church was thenceforward distinguished as Duv Regles, or "the Black Church:" the new edifice was 240 feet long, and was one of the most splendid ecclesiastical structures erected in Ireland prior to the settlement of the Anglo-Normans; its site was near the Black Church, outside the present city wall, and is now chiefly occupied by the Roman Catholic chapel and cemetery; both edifices were entirely demolished by Sir Henry Docwra, governor of Derry, in 1600, and the materials used in the erection of the extensive works constructed at that period; but the belfry or round tower of the cathedral served till after the celebrated siege, and has given name to a lane called the Long Tower. In 1166 a considerable part of the town was burned by Rory O'Morna; and in 1195 the abbey was plundered by an English force, which was afterwards intercepted and destroyed at Armagh. In 1197, a large body of English forces having set out from the castle of Kill-Sanctain on a predatory excursion, came to Derry and plundered several churches, but were overtaken by Flahertach O'Maoldoraidh, lord of Tyrone and Tyrconnell, and some of the northern Hy-Niall, and a battle ensued on the shore of the adjoining parish of Faughanvale, in which the English were defeated with great slaughter. In this year Sir John De Courcy came with a large army and remained five nights; and in the following year also, having made an incursion into Tyrone to plunder the churches, he arrived at this place, and during his stay plundered Ennishowen and all the adjacent country; while thus engaged he received intelligence of the defeat of the English at Larne by Hugh Boy O'Nial, which caused him to quit Derry. In 1203 the town was much damaged by fire; and in 1211 it was plundered by Thomas Mac Uchtry and the sons of Randal Mac Donnell, who came hither with a fleet of 76 ships, and afterwards passed into Ennishowen and laid waste the whole peninsula. This Thomas and Rory Mac Randal again plundered the town in 1213, carrying away from the cathedral to Coleraine all the jewellery of the people of Derry and of the north of Ireland. A Cistercian nunnery was founded on the south side of the city in 1218, as recorded in the registry of the Honour of Richmond; but from the Annals of the Four Masters it appears that a religious establishment of this kind existed here prior to that period. Nial O'Nial plundered the town in 1222; and, in 1261, sixteen of the most distinguished of the clergy of Tyrone were slain here by Conor O'Nial and the Kinel-Owen or men of Tyrone. In 1274 a Dominican abbey was founded on the north side of the city, of which even the site cannot now be accurately traced.

Edw. II. granted the town to Richard de Burgo, Earl of Ulster, in 1311; but from this period till the reign of Elizabeth, prior to which the English exercised no settled dominion in Derry, no event of importance connected with the place is recorded. In 1565, Edward Randolph arrived in the Foyle with seven companies of foot and one troop of horse, to repress Shane O'Nial, Earl of Tyrone, who had renounced his allegiance to the English crown; and a sanguinary engagement taking place on the plains of Muff, the Irish chieftain was signally defeated. An encampment was then formed by the English near the city; but in a sally against some of O'Nial's forces, who had ostentatiously paraded before it, the English general was slain by a party who had concealed themselves in an adjoining wood, and the command of the garrison was given to Col. St. Lo. The English converted the cathedral into an arsenal, and on the 24th of April, 1566, the gunpowder blew up by accident with so much damage as to render the place untenable; the foot embarked for Dublin, to which city also the horse returned, passing through Tyrconnell and Connaught to avoid O'Nial. In 1599 it was again determined to fortify Derry, a measure long deemed essential in order to divide and check the power of O'Nial and O'Donell, the accomplishment of which object was favoured by its situation and the friendship of O'Dogherty of Ennishowen. With that view Sir Henry Docwra, in 1600, entered the Foyle with a British force of 4000 foot and 200 horse, and landed at Culmore, at the mouth of the river, where he erected a fort. He soon obtained possession of the city, and constructed fortifications and other works for its defence and improvement, pulling down the abbey, cathedral, and other ecclesiastical buildings for the sake of the materials. On the termination of the war at the commencement of 1603, the garrison was reduced to 100 horse and 150 foot under the governor, and 200 foot under Capt. Hansard; and at Culmore were left 20 men. Sir Henry now directed his attention to the improvement of the place with so much zeal as to entitle him to be regarded as the founder of the modern city. A number of English colonists settled here on his invitation; he obtained grants of markets and fairs, and, in 1604, a charter of incorporation with ample privileges. But in 1608, after the flight and forfeiture of O'Nial and O'Donell, the growing prosperity of the new city was checked by the insurrection of Sir Cahir O'Dogherty, the young chief of Ennishowen, who took both Culmore fort and Derry, at the latter of which Sir George Paulet (to whom Sir Henry Docwra had alienated all his interests) and his men were slain; as many of the inhabitants as could escape fled, and the town was plundered and burned.

A large part of Ulster having escheated to the Crown on the attainder of the above-named earls, proposals of colonization were made to the city of London, in which this place is described as "the late ruinated city of Derry, which may be made by land almost impregnable." In accepting the offers of the Crown the city agreed to erect 200 houses here, and leave room for 300 more; 4000 acres contiguous to the city were to be annexed to it in perpetuity, exclusively of bog and barren mountain, which were to be added as waste; convenient sites were allowed for the houses of the bishop and dean; the liberties were to extend three miles or 3000 Irish paces in every direction from the centre of the city; and the London undertakers were to have the neighbouring fort of Culmore, with the lands attached, on condition of maintaining in it a competent ward of officers and men. In 1613 the inhabitants, having surrendered their former charter, were re-incorporated, and the name of the city was altered to Londonderry. The natives having conspired to take the town by surprise, a supply of arms was sent from London in 1615; an additional sum of £5000 was ordered for completing the walls; and, that it might not in future be peopled with Irish, the Society issued directions that a certain number of children from Christ's Hospital, and others, should be sent hither as apprentices and servants, and prohibited the inhabitants from taking Irish apprentices. Leases of most of the houses were granted for thirty one years, and to each was allotted a portion of land according to the rent, with ground for gardens and orchards; 300 acres were assigned for the support of a free school; and of the 4000 acres the Society allotted to the houses or granted to the mayor 3217, including a parcel of 1500 acres which were set apart to support the magistracy of the city, and which subsequently became a source of contention between the Society, the corporation, and the bishop. In 1618 we find the fortifications completed, at an expense of £8357; but notwithstanding the adoption of these and other measures of improvement, the increase of houses and inhabitants was very slow, and the operations of the Society were made the ground of various representations to the Crown respecting the non-fulfilment of the conditions of planting. In 1622, commissioners were appointed to enquire into the affairs of the plantation, to whom the mayor and corporation presented a petition complaining of many grievances resulting from the conduct of the Society, one of the chief of which was the non-erection of the specified number of houses: this enquiry led to several sequestrations of the city and liberties until 1628, and for some time the rents were paid to the Crown.

In the rebellion of 1641 the English and Scottish settlers received a considerable supply of arms and ammunition from London, and having secured themselves within the walls, successfully defended the city from the attacks of the rebels under Sir Phelim O'Nial. In 1643 the inhabitants of Londonderry and Coleraine sent letters to the lords-justices urging their impoverished condition and praying for relief. Sir John Vaughan, the governor, having died this year, Sir Robert Stewart was appointed to the command of the garrison, of which five companies aided in his defeat of Owen O'Nial at Clones, on the 13th of June. Towards the close of the year the parliament having taken the covenant, the London adventurers sent over an agent with letters desiring that it should be taken within their plantation; but in the year following the mayor was ordered by the lord-

Londonderry. Part of 6 inch O.S. map of Co.Down, sheet 20, published 1833 (reproduced at 140%).

lieutenant and council to publish a proclamation against it. Col. Audley Mervin, who had been appointed governor by the Marquess of Ormonde, was nevertheless obliged from expediency to take the covenant: in 1645 he was displaced by the parliament, and was succeeded by Lord Folliott. Sir C. Coote, the parliamentary general, having, in 1648, treacherously seized upon the person of Sir Robert Hamilton, forced him to surrender Culmore fort, by which the parliamentarians became masters of all the forts of Ulster, except Charlemont. The Marquess of Ormonde having failed in his attempts to induce Sir C. Coote to join the king's cause, the latter was blocked up in Derry by the royalists; and soon after the city and Culmore fort were regularly besieged by Sir Robert Stewart, who was subsequently joined by Sir G. Monroe and Lord Montgomery with their respective forces, and Chas. II. was proclaimed with great solemnity before the camp of Derry. The decapitation of the late king having excited general horror among the majority of the people of the north, they rose in arms and soon obtained possession of all the towns and places of strength in that quarter, except Derry and Culmore, which, after a siege of four months, and when the garrison, consisting of 800 foot and 180 horse, was reduced to the greatest extremities, were relieved by Owen Roe O'Nial, to whom Sir C. Coote had promised a reward of £5000 for this service; and by the defeat of Ever Mac Mahon, the Roman Catholic general, the following year, at Skirfolas in Donegal, Coote finally reduced all Ulster under the power of the parliament. After the Restoration, Chas. II., in 1662, granted letters patent to the Irish Society, containing, with very little alteration, all the clauses of the first charter of Jas. I.; this is the charter under which the Society and the corporation of Derry now act. In 1684 the same monarch constituted a guild of the staple, with powers as ample as those enjoyed by any other city or town: in the following year, owing to the decay of trade, the corporation complained to the Society that the government of the town was too expensive for the magistrates to sustain, and solicited an abatement of the rent.

In 1689 this city became the asylum of the Protestants of the north, who, in number about 30,000, fled to it for refuge before the marauding forces of James; and is distinguished in the annals of modern history for the heroic bravery of its inhabitants amidst the extreme privations of a protracted siege. The chief governor having withdrawn the Protestant garrison, and steps being taken to introduce an undisciplined native force influenced by hostile prejudices, the young men of the city closed the gates against its admission, and the bulk of the inhabitants took up arms in their own defence. The magistrates and graver citizens endeavoured to palliate this ebullition of military ardour in their representations to the lord-lieutenant, but in the meantime the armed inhabitants applied to the Irish Society for assistance. Lord Mountjoy, a Protestant commander in the army of James, was, however, admitted, in a great measure from personal regard, but on condition that a free pardon should be granted within 15 days, and that in the interval only two companies should be quartered within the walls; that of the forces afterwards admitted one-half at least should be Protestants; that until pardon was received the citizens should guard the fortifications; and that all who desired it might be permitted to quit the city. By the advice of Mountjoy, who was obeyed as a friend and associate, the arms were repaired, money cheerfully subscribed, ammunition purchased in Scotland, and the agent despatched to England urged to procure supplies. He was succeeded in the command by his first lieutenant, Lundy, whom King William, on sending an officer with some military supplies, commissioned to act in his name; but the dissatisfaction of the citizens was excited by the vacillating character of this commander, who, on the approach of James to besiege the city in person, prepared to surrender it, not withstanding the arrival of two English colonels in the river with reinforcements, which he remanded. The principal officers being about to withdraw, and the town council preparing to offer terms of capitulation, the inhabitants rose tumultuously against the constituted authorities, received with enthusiasm a brave and popular captain who presented himself at the city gates with a reinforcement, and, rushing to the walls, fired upon James and his party advancing to take possession of the place. On deliberation they suffered the timid to depart unmolested; Lundy first concealed himself and afterwards escaped; and two new governors were chosen, one of whom was the celebrated George Walker, rector of Donoughmore. Under their directions the soldiers and able inhabitants were formed into eight regiments, numbering 7020 men, with 341 officers; order and discipline were in some degree established, and, notwithstanding partial jealousies, 18 Protestant clergymen and seven non-conformists shared in the labour and danger of the siege, and by their exhortations stimulated the enthusiastic courage of the defenders with the fervour of devotion. The operations of an army of 20,000 men were thus successfully opposed in a place abandoned as untenable by the regular forces, unaided by engineers or well-mounted guns, and with only a ten days supply of provisions. An irregular war of sallies was adopted with such effect that James, who had hitherto remained at St. Johnstown, six miles distant, returned to Dublin, leaving his army to continue the siege.

The defenders had now to contend against the inroads of disease and famine; and the arrival of Kirke with a fleet in the lough afforded but little prospect of relief, as he deemed it too hazardous an enterprise to sail up to the town in front of the enemy's lines. Although thus apparently left to their own scanty resources, the brave garrison continued the defence with unabated heroism, still making desperate and effective sallies even when too much enfeebled by hunger to pursue their success. To induce a surrender, Marshal Rosen, the besieging general, ordered his soldiers to drive round the walls of the town the helpless Protestant population of the surrounding district, of all ages, who were thus exposed to the horrors of famine for nearly three days before they were suffered to disperse; some of the ablest of the men secretly joined their comrades in the town, and an ineffective body of 500 people were passed from it unperceived by the enemy. When even such miserable resources as the flesh of horses and dogs, hides, tallow, and similar nauseous substances had failed for two days, two of Kirke's ships, laden with provisions and convoyed by the Dartmouth frigate, advanced up the lough in view both of the garrison and the besiegers, in a dangerous attempt to relieve the place, returning with spirit the fire of the enemy. The foremost of the provision ships came in contact with the boom that had been thrown across the channel and broke it, but rebounding with violence ran aground, and for the moment appeared to be at the mercy of the besiegers, who with acclamations of joy instantly prepared to board her; but the vessel, firing her guns, was extricated by the shock, floated, and triumphantly passed the boom followed by her companions. The town was thus relieved and the enemy retired; but of the brave defenders only 4300 survived to witness their deliverance, and of this number more than 1000 were incapable of service; those who were able immediately sallied out in pursuit of the enemy, who had lost 8000 men by the sword and by various disorders during the siege, which had continued 105 days. Culmore fort was reduced to ruin, and was never afterwards rebuilt; and the city sustained so much damage that the Irish Society deemed it necessary to appoint commissioners for its restoration; the twelve chief companies of London advanced £100 each; the Society supplied timber for the public buildings, abatements were made in the rents, the terms of leases were augmented, and other measures necessary for the accomplishment of this object were adopted. In 1692, the corporation failing to negotiate with Bishop King for a renewal of the lease of the quarter-lands, reminded the Society that the bishop's claims to this property were unsubstantial, and agreed to establish their right in consideration of £90.10 per annum, which is still paid. In 1695 the Society procured a resumption of the remainder of the 1500 acres comprised in their letters patent, by an ejectment against the bishop, who, in 1697, appealed to the Irish House of Lords and obtained an order for their restitution, which the sheriffs and other inhabitants of Derry opposing, were taken into custody and conveyed to Dublin. Against this decision the Society applied to the English House of Lords, and in 1703 an act was passed establishing their right not only to the 1500 acres but also to the fisheries, which had previously been an object of dispute, subject to the payment of £250 per annum to the bishop and his successors, which is still continued, with a condition of exonerating him from rent or other demands for his palace and gardens. In 1721 a dispute took place between the corporation and the military governor, who refused to deliver the keys of the city gates to the new mayor, which by the charter he was bound to do; he surrounded the town-hall with troops, and prevented the members of the corporation entering it, but was removed immediately after. A grand centenary commemoration of the shutting of the gates took place in 1788, and was continued with the utmost harmony for three days; and in the month of August following the relief of the city was commemorated.

The city is advantageously situated on the western or Donegal side of the river Foyle, about five statute miles above the point where it spreads into Lough Foyle, chiefly on the summit and sides of a hill projecting into the river, and commanding on all sides richly diversified and picturesque views of a well cultivated tract: this hill, or "Island of Derry," is of an oval form, 119 feet high, and contains about 200 acres. The ancient portion of the city occupies the higher grounds, and is surrounded by massive walls completed in 1617, at the expense of the Society: they form a parallelogram nearly a mile in circumference, and in the centre is a square called the Diamond, from which four principal streets radiate at right angles towards the principal gates. Since the Union the city has considerably increased, particularly on the north along the shore of the river, where several warehouses, stores, and merchants' residences have been erected: on the west is also a considerable suburb, in which, within the last fifteen years, some new streets have been formed; and on the eastern bank of the river is another, called Waterside. The walls, which are well built and in a complete state of repair, are nearly 1800 yards in circuit, 24 feet high, and of sufficient thickness to form an agreeable promenade on the top. The four original gates have been rebuilt on an enlarged and more elegant plan, and two more added; but the only two that are embellished are Bishop's gate and Shipquay gate, the former, built by subscription in 1788, being the centenary in commemoration of the siege. In 1628 the Irish Society was ordered to erect guard and sentinel houses, of which two are yet remaining; and of the several bastions, the north-western was demolished in 1824, to make room for the erection of a butter market; and in 1826 the central western bastion was appropriated to the reception of a public testimonial in honour of the celebrated George Walker. A few guns are preserved in their proper positions, but the greater number are used as posts for fastening cables and protecting the corners of streets. The houses are chiefly built of brick: the entire number in the city and suburbs is 2947. The city is watched, paved, cleansed, and lighted with gas, under the superintendence of commissioners of general police, consisting of the mayor and 12 inhabitants chosen by ballot: the gas-works were erected in 1829, at an expense of £7000, raised in shares of £11. Water is conveyed to the town across the bridge by pipes, from a reservoir on Brae Head, beyond the Waterside, in the parish of Clondermot; the works were constructed by the corporation under an act of the 40th of Geo. III., at a total expense of £15,500, and iron pipes have been laid down within the last few years.

The bridge, a celebrated wooden structure erected by Lemuel Cox, an American, in lieu of a ferry which the corporation held under the Irish Society, was begun in 1789, and completed in the spring of 1791. It is 1068 feet in length, and 40 in breadth: the piles are of oak, and the head of each is tenoned into a cap piece 40 feet long and 17 inches square, supported by three sets of girths and braces; the piers, which are 16½ feet apart, are bound together by thirteen string-pieces equally divided and transversely bolted, on which is laid the flooring: on each side of the platform is a railing 4½ feet high, also a broad pathway provided with gas lamps. Near the end next to the city a turning bridge has been constructed in place of the original drawbridge, to allow of the free navigation of the river. On the 6th of Feb., 1814, a portion of the bridge extending to 350 feet was carried away by large masses of ice floated down the river by the ebb tide and a very high wind. The original expense of its erection was £16,594, and of the repairs after the damage in 1814, £18,208, of which latter sum, £15,000 was advanced as a loan by Government: the average annual amount of tolls from 1831 to 1834, inclusive, was £3693. Plans and estimates for the erection of a new bridge, nearly 200 yards above the present, have been procured; but there is no prospect of the immediate execution of the design. A public library and news room, commenced in 1819 by subscription and established on its present plan in 1824 by a body of proprietors of transferable shares of 20 guineas each, is provided with about 2660 volumes of modern works and with periodical publications and daily and weekly news-papers: it is a plain building faced with hewn Dungiven sandstone, erected by subscription in 1824, at an expense of nearly £2000, and, besides the usual apartments, contains also the committee-room of the Chamber of Commerce. The lower part of the building is used as the news-room, to which all the inhabitants are admitted on payment of five guineas annually. A literary society for debates and lectures was instituted in 1834, and the number of its members is rapidly increasing. Concerts were formerly held at the King's Arms hotel, but have been discontinued. Races are held on a course to the north of the town. Walker's Testimonial, on the central western bastion, was completed in 1828 by subscription, at an expense of £1200: it consists of a column of Portland stone of good proportions, in the Roman Doric style, surmounted by a statue of that distinguished governor by John Smith, Esq., of Dublin: the column is ascended by a spiral staircase within, and, including the pedestal, is 81 feet in height, in addition to which the statue measures nine feet. The city is in the northern military district, and is the headquarters of a regiment of infantry which supplies detachments to various places: the barracks are intended for the accommodation of four officers and 320 men, with an hospital for 32 patients, but from their insufficiency a more commodious edifice is about to be erected, for which ground has been provided in the parish of Clondermot.

The manufactures are not very considerable: the principal is that of meal, for which there are several corn-mills, of which one erected by Mr. Schoales in 1831, and worked by a steam-engine of 18-horse power, and another subsequently by Mr. Leatham, worked by an engine of 20-horse power, are the chief: the recent extension of this branch of trade has made meal an article of export instead of import, as formerly; in 1831, 553 tons were imported, and in 1834 6950 tons were exported. In William-street are a brewery and distillery; there are copper-works which supply the whole of the north-west of Ulster, and afford regular employment to 27 men; two coach-factories; and a corn-mill and distillery at Penny burn, and another at Waterside. A sugar-house was built in 1762, in what is still called Sugar-house-lane, but was abandoned in 1809; the buildings were converted into a glass manufactory in 1820, but this branch of business was carried on for a few years only. This is the place of export for the agricultural produce of a large tract of fertile country, which renders the coasting trade very extensive, especially with Great Britain: the quantity of grain exported to England and Scotland alone, in the year ending Jan. 5th, 1835, was 3680 tons of wheat, 1490 tons of barley, 10,429 tons of oats, 6950 tons of oatmeal, 3050 tons of eggs, 3654 tons of flax, 52,842 firkins of butter, 11,580 barrels of pork, 1900 bales of bacon, 590 hogsheads of hams, 1628 kegs of tongues, and 147 hogsheads of lard. It is still the market for a considerable quantity of linen, of which 9642 boxes and bales were exported in the same year. The number of vessels employed in the coasting trade which entered inwards in 1834 was 649, of an aggregate tonnage of 63,726, and which cleared outwards, 646, of an aggregate tonnage of 62,502, including steam-vessels, which ply regularly between this port and Liverpool and Glasgow. The principal articles of foreign produce imported direct are staves and timber from the Baltic, barilla from Spain, sugar and rum from the West Indies, wine from Spain and Portugal; tobacco from the United States, from which the ships come chiefly to take out emigrants, who resort to this port from the inland districts in great numbers; flax seed, the importation of which has much increased within the last few years, from Riga, America, and Holland; the quantity imported in 1835 was 12,400 hogsheads; but the greater proportion of foreign commodities comes indirectly, or coastwise. The number of vessels employed in the foreign trade which entered inwards in 1834 was 57, of an aggregate burden of 10,406 tons, and that cleared outwards, 16, of an aggregate tonnage of 4869. The salmon fishery of the Foyle affords employment to 120 men, exclusively of the same number of water-keepers: the fish is shipped principally for Liverpool; some is also sent to Glasgow, and some pickled for the London market: the quantity taken annually on an average of three years from 1832 to 1834 inclusive was about 149 tons. The right of fishing in this river up to Lifford is vested by charter of Jas. I. in the Irish Society, who by an act in the reign of Anne, are bound to pay the bishop £250 per annum, as compensation for his claim to some small fishings, and also to a tithe of the whole; but at present the Marquess of Abercorn and the Earl of Erne hold fisheries below the town of Lifford. The fishery off the coast is precarious, and frequently yields only

Londonderry. Drawn by W.H. Bartlett and engraved by S. Bradshaw. From Scenery and antiquities of Ireland, illustrated from drawings by W.H. Bartlett, *vol.1.(London, 1842).*

a scanty supply, from the danger in encountering a rough sea experienced by the boats employed in it, which are only indifferently built; yet at other times the market abounds with turbot taken near Innistrahull and on Hempton's Bank, about 18 Irish miles north of Ennishowen Head; soles and haddock, taken in Lough Swilly and elsewhere; cod, mostly off the entrance to Lough Foyle; and oysters, taken in Lough Swilly from the island of Inch up to Fort Stewart, and in Lough Foyle, from Quigley's Point down to Greencastle. Derry is situated about 19 statute miles above the entrance to Lough Foyle, the approach to which is facilitated by a lighthouse on the island of Innistrahull, and will be rendered still more safe by two others now in course of erection on Shrove Head, Ennishowen, intended to serve as guiding lights past the great Tun Bank lying to the east. A new and very important trade as connected with the port, is the herring fishery; in 1835, upwards of 5800 barrels were cured at the Orkneys, by Derry merchants, and the total quantity imported exceeds 12,000 barrels, one half of which are cured by vessels fitted out from this port; large quantities of oysters have been taken in the river Foyle since 1829.

The limits of the port extend to Culmore, a distance of three miles; the lough has been deepened under the directors of the Ballast Committee, in consequence of which, vessels drawing 14 feet of water, can come close to the quays. At the entrance to the lough is a well-regulated establishment of pilots, under the superintendence of the Ballast Board. The Ballast Office was established by act of parliament in 1790, and remodelled by another act in 1833: the port regulations are under the control of a committee of this establishment, consisting of the mayor and seven other members, of whom the two senior members go out annually by rotation, and who have the power of making by-laws. The corporation alone possessed the right of having quays prior to 1832, when they lost their monopoly, and private quays were constructed: they disposed of their interest in the merchants' or custom-house quays, in Nov. 1831; there are now 21 sufferance or private wharfs or quays, including two at Waterside, in the parish of Clondermot. A patent slip dock was constructed in 1830, at an expense of £4000, in which vessels of 300 tons registered burden can be repaired: prior to that period most vessels were sent for repair to Liverpool or the Clyde, and two large brigs have been built here since that date: naval stores are brought chiefly from Belfast, but sails are manufactured here. The custom-house, a small and inconvenient building, was built as a store in 1805, and since 1809 has been held by Government on a permanent tenure, at an annual rental of £1419.4.6, at first as a king's store, and since 1824 as a custom-house: the premises comprise some extensive tobacco and timber yards, laid out at different periods, and extend in front 450 feet, varying in depth: the duties received here in 1837 amounted to £99,652. The markets are generally well supplied. The shambles, for meat daily, and to which there is a weigh-house attached, are situated off Linen-hall-street, and were built in 1760, by Alderman Alexander and other members of the corporation: the tolls belong to Sir R. A. Ferguson, Bart., who in 1830 purchased the shambles and the fish and vegetable markets of the corporation. The linen market, on Wednesday, is held in a hall occupying an obscure situation in a street to which it gives name, and built in 1770, by the late Fred. Hamilton, Esq., to whose descendant the tolls belong: it consists of a court measuring 147 feet by 15, and enclosed by small dilapidated houses; the cloth is exposed on stands placed in the court and under sheds; on the opposite side of the street is the sealing-room. The butter market, in Waterloo-place, for butter and hides daily, and to which three weigh-houses are attached; the fish market, off Linen-hall-street, daily; the potatoe market, in Society-street, for potatoes and meal by retail daily, with a weigh-house attached; and the vegetable market, off Linen-hall-street, for vegetables, poultry, and butter daily, were all built in 1825 by the corporation, to whom the tolls of the butter and potatoe markets belong. The cow market, for the sale of cows, pigs, sheep, and goats, every Wednesday, is held in a field to the south of Bishop-street, near the river, which was enclosed in 1832 by the corporation, to whom the tolls belong. There are also a flax market in Bishop-street every Thursday, and a market for yarn in Butchers'-street every Wednesday. Six fairs are held annually, but only three are of importance, namely, on June 17th, Sept. 4th, and Oct. 17th; the others are on March 4th, April 30th, and Sept. 20th. Custom was charged on every article of merchandise brought into the city prior to 1826, when it was abolished, except as regards goods conveyed over the bridge; and in lieu thereof, the corporation instituted trespass, cranage, storage, and other dues. The post-office was established in 1784; the amount of postage for 1834 was £4047.17.1½. The revenue police force usually consists of a lieutenant and twelve men; and the constabulary is composed of a chief constable and twelve men.

The municipal government is vested in a mayor, twelve aldermen, and twenty-four burgesses, assisted by a recorder, town-clerk, and chamberlain; and the inferior officers of the corporation are a sword-bearer, mace-bearer, four town-serjeants, two sherffs' bailiffs, &c. The mayor and sheriffs are elected by the common council on the 2nd of Feb., the former from among the aldermen, and the latter from the burgesses, from whom also the aldermen are chosen; the burgesses are appointed from the freemen and inhabitants. The sheriffs exercise jurisdiction both over the entire county and the liberties of the city; and the town-clerk is generally clerk of the peace for the county. The freedom is inherited by the sons of aldermen and burgesses, and is obtained by marriage with their daughters, by apprenticeship to a freeman, and by gift of the corporation. The city returned two representatives to the Irish parliament till the Union, since which it has sent one to the imperial parliament. The right of voting was formerly vested in the burgesses and freemen, in number about 450; but by the late enactments, under which a new electoral boundary has been established, the former non-resident electors, except within a distance of seven miles, have been disfranchised, and the privilege extended to the £10 house holders: the number of registered voters on the 1st of April, 1835, was 724, of whom 504 were £10 house-holders, and the remainder freemen. The mayor, recorder, and all aldermen who have filled the mayoralty, are justices of the peace within the liberties, which comprise the city and a circuit of three Irish miles measured from its centre; and they also exercise jurisdiction by sufferance over the townland of Culmore. The mayor and recorder, or the mayor alone, hold a court of record every Monday, for pleas to any amount; the process is either by attachment against the goods, or arrest of the person. The court of general sessions for the city is held four times a year: there is a court of petty sessions weekly, held before the mayor, or any of the civic magistrates. The mayor also holds weekly a court of conscience, for the recovery of ordinary debts not exceeding £20 late currency or servants' wages to the amount of £6, and from which there is no appeal. The city is in the north-west circuit, and the assizes are held here twice a year: it is also one of the four towns within the county at which the general quarter sessions are held, and where the assistant barrister presides in April and October.

The corporation hall in the centre of the Diamond, and on the site of the original town-house built by the Irish Society in 1622, was erected by the corporation in 1692, and till 1825, when it was rebuilt by the corporation, was called the market-house or exchange: the south front, in which is the principal entrance, is circular. The upper storey contains a common-council room, an assembly-room, and an ante-chamber. On the ground floor, which was formerly open for the sale of meal and potatoes, but was closed in 1825, is a news-room established by the corporation in that year. The court-house, completed in 1817 at an expense of £30,479.15, including the purchase of the site and furniture, is a handsome building of white sandstone, chiefly from the neighbourhood of Dungiven, ornamented with Portland stone, and erected from a design by Mr. John Bowden: it measures 126 feet by 66, and exhibits a facade, judiciously broken by a tetrastyle portico of the enriched Ionic order, modelled from that of the temple of Erectheus at Athens; over the pediment are the royal arms; and the wings are surmounted by statues of Justice and Peace sculptured in Portland stone by the late Edward Smith. The principal apartments are the crown and record courts, the mayor's public and private offices, the offices of the recorder, treasurer, and clerks of the crown and peace, the judges' room, and the grand jury room: in addition to the assizes, sessions, and mayor's count, the county and other meetings are held in it. The gaol, situated in Bishop-street, beyond the gate, was erected between the years 1819 and 1824, by Messrs. Henry, Mullins, and McMahon, at an expense of £33,718, late currency: the front, which is partly coated with cement and partly built of Dungiven stone, extends 242 feet; and the depth of the entire building, including the yards, is 400 feet. It is built on the radiating plan; the governor's house, which includes the chapel and committee-room, is surrounded by a panoptic gallery; and the entire gaol contains 179 single cells, 26 work and day rooms, and 20 airing yards: apart from the main building is an hospital, containing separate wards for both sexes. The regulations are excellent: in 1835 the system of classification was abandoned, and the silent system introduced; the prisoners are constantly employed at various trades, and receive one-third of their earnings.

The DIOCESE of DERRY originated in a monastery founded by St. Columb, about 545, of which some of the abbots at a very early period were styled bishops, but the title of bishop of Derry was not established until 1158, or even a century later, as the bishops, whose see was at Denny, were sometimes called Bishops of Tyrone. The see first existed at Ardsrath, where St. Eugene, the first bishop, died about the end of the sixth century; it was subsequently removed to Maghera, whence it was transferred to Derry. It is called Darnich in the old Roman provincial, and Doire Choluim chille or "Columbkill's Oak Grove," by ancient writers. The town is now called Londonderry, from a colony of settlers from London, in the reign of Jas. I., by whom the present cathedral was built, but the bishoprick retains its ancient name of Derry. The see was constituted at Derry in 1158, by a decree of the Synod of Brigth Thaigh, at which assisted Christian, Bishop of Lismore, the pope's legate, and twenty-five bishops; and Flathbert O'Brolcan, abbot of Denny, was promoted to the episcopal throne. In 1164, with the assistance of Mac Loughlin, King of Ireland, he built the cathedral; the altar of which was robbed in 1196 by McCrenaght, of 314 cups, which were esteemed the best in Ireland, but they were recovered the third day after, and the robber executed. German, or Gervase, O'Cherballen, who succeeded to the bishoprick in 1230, took the church of Ardsrath and many others in Tyrone from the Bishop of Clogher, and forcibly annexed part of the bishoprick of Raphoe to his diocese. In 1310, Edw. II. directed the bishop of Connor to enquire whether the king or any other person would be prejudiced by allowing Richard de Burgo to retain in fee the city of Derry, which the bishop, with the consent of the chapter, had conveyed to him. Prior to 1608, the bishop had one-third of the tithes of each parish; a lay person, called an Erenach, who was the bishop's farmer, had another third; and the remaining third was allowed for the incumbent: but Bishop Montgomery gave the bishop's share to the incumbents of parishes, on the grant by Jas. I. of the termon or Erenach lands, amounting to 6534 acres, to the see in exchange. By an inquisition in 1622, the bishop was found to be entitled to fish for salmon on the Monday after the 4th of June, within the great net fishery belonging to the London Society; also to half the tithe of salmon, &c., caught in the Bann and Lough Foyle. Bishop Hopkins, who died in 1690, was at great expense in beautifying the cathedral, and furnishing it with organs and massive plate, and is said to have expended £1000 in buildings and other improvements in this bishoprick and that of Raphoe. Derry continued to be a separate bishoprick until the death of Dr. Bissett, Bishop of Raphoe, in 1836, when that see, under the provisions of the Church Temporalities act of the 3rd and 4th of Wm. IV., was annexed to the see of Derry, and its temporalities became vested in the Ecclesiastical Commissioners.

This diocese is one of the ten that constitute the province of Armagh: it is partly in the counties of Antrim and Donegal, but chiefly in Tyrone and Londonderry, extending 47 miles in length by 43 in breadth, and comprehending an estimated superficies of 659,000 acres, of which 2500 are in Antrim, 139,300 in Donegal, 233,100 in Tyrone, and 284,100 in Londonderry. The lands belonging to the see comprise 77,102 statute acres, of which 39,621 are profitable land, and 37,481 unprofitable; and the gross yearly revenue derived from these lands and from appropriate tithes, on an average of three years ending Dec. 31st, 1831, amounted to £14,193.3.9½. Under the Church Temporalities act an annual charge of £4160 is, from 1834, payable out of the see estates to the funds of the Ecclesiastical Commissioners: this payment is made to diminish the excess of the revenue of this see above the other bishopricks, and is in lieu of the Ad Valorem tax imposed on all benefices in Ireland. The chapter consists of a dean and archdeacon, and the three prebendanies of Comber, Aghadowy, and Moville. To the dean belong, as the corps of the deanery, the rectories of Templemore, Faughanvale, and Clondermot, the tithes of which, under the composition act, amount to £3235.7.11½ per annum. The deanery lands, which are situated in the parishes of Clondermot and Faughanvale, consist of several townlands, which comprise 2859 statute acres, let on leases at rents amounting to £176.6.4, and renewal fines averaging £269.15.7 annually; and the gross annual revenue of the deanery, as returned by the Commissioners of Ecclesiastical Enquiry, amounts to £3710.13.10 per annum. To the archdeacon belongs the rectory of Dunboe, the tithes of which amount to £480, and the glebe lands comprise 420 statute acres; its gross annual value is £700 per annum. The endowments of the prebends consist of the tithes and glebes of the parishes from which they take their names, and are detailed in the articles on those places. The cathedral has neither minor canons, vicars choral, nor an economy fund. The diocesan school is connected with the free school of Derry, which was founded by the corporation of London in 1617. The consistorial court consists of a vicar-general, surrogate, registrar, deputy-registrar, and 11 proctors. This arrangement extended to the whole of the diocese, so that the bishop, out of 47 parishes, possesses 46 estates, and this is the reason why the clergy of this diocese are generally provided with larger glebes than those of the other dioceses of Ireland. This grant included the patronage of certain churches, since disputed successfully, except those of Dungiven and Coleraine, on the grounds that the powers of the Crown, unsupported by surrender from the bishop, confirmed by an act of parliament, were not competent to make a valid grant. The number of parishes in the diocese is 60, comprised in 57 benefices: that which forms the corps of the deanery is a union of the three parishes of Templemore, Faughanvale, and Clondermot, and is in the patronage of the Crown; 36 are in the patronage of the Bishop; 3 are in the gift of the Provost and Fellows of Trinity College, Dublin; 8 in lay patronage, and the remaining 9, which are perpetual curacies, are in the patronage of the incumbents of the parishes out of which they have been formed. The number of churches is 62, and of school-houses and other places where divine service is performed, 11: the number of glebe-houses is 47.

In the R. C. divisions this diocese is a separate bishoprick, and one of eight suffragan to Armagh. It comprises 36 parochial benefices or unions, containing 70 chapels, which are served by 81 clergymen, 36 of whom, including the bishop, are parish priests, and 45 are coadjutors or curates. The parochial benefice of the bishop is Derry, or Templemore, where he resides.

The cathedral, which also serves as the parish church, was completed in 1633, the former one, erected in 1164, having been destroyed by Sir Henry Docwra. The cost of the building, amounting to £4000, was defrayed by the Corporation of the City of London: it is principally in the later English style, with various decorations since added, which do not harmonize with its prevailing character, and consists of a nave and aisles, separated by stone pillars and arches, with a tower at the west end surmounted by an elegant octagon spire terminating in a cross and spear; on the east gable is a cross springing from the central battlement. The entire structure is 240 feet long, and 66 feet broad; the height of the tower and spire is 228 feet from the churchyard. In 1778, the Earl of Bristol, then Bishop of Derry, completed a new spire of hewn stone, with open ornamented windows, and the old tower was raised 21 feet; but in 1802, owing to the dilapidated state of the tower, the spire was taken down and soon after rebuilt from a fund of £400, half of which was contributed by the Irish Society and half by Bishop Knox and the citizens. The Society also contributed a sum for the embellishment of the cathedral in 1819; and in 1822 the old roof of lead was replaced by a slate roof. A new organ was erected in 1829 by subscription, to which Bishop Knox contributed £100, and Dean Gough and the corporation £50 each. On the north of the communion table is a handsome monument of Italian marble, by Behnes, erected in 1834 to the memory of Bishop Knox, at an expense of £500, raised by subscription: on an elevated plinth is an inscribed tablet, above which is represented a tomb surmounted by a mitre, on the right of which is a full-length figure of Religion, and on the left another of Charity with a babe on her arm and two other children of different ages standing at her knees. There are various other tablets, one of which, to the memory of the father of the Rev. Wm. Hamilton, D.D., is inscribed with the epitaph of that distinguished naturalist. The bishop's palace, built about the year 1761, during the prelacy of Bishop Barnard, is a substantial and commodious building, occupying the site of the Augustinian convent: it was almost rebuilt by the Earl of Bristol, when bishop, and after the damage which it sustained by being occupied as a barrack in 1802, was repaired by Bishop Knox. The gardens in the rear comprise nearly two acres, and extend to the city wall; having at the above period been appropriated as a parade, that designation is still applied to the adjacent part of the wall. The deanery, a large unadorned edifice of brick, was built in 1833 by the Rev. T. B. Gough, the present dean, at an expense of £3421.16.8$^{1}/_{2}$, to be reimbursed by his successor.

Adjacent to the city wall on the west is a chapel of ease, a rectangular building, erected by Bishop Barnard, whose descendant, Sir Andrew Barnard, became the patron: the chaplain's original stipend of £50 is now paid out of the property of Wm. J. Campbell, a minor, who claims the advowson. A free church was built on the north of the city by Bishop Knox, in 1830, at an expense of £760; and a gallery was erected in 1832, at a further expense, including the cost of a vestry-room and the introduction of gas, of £145, raised by subscription. The R. C. chapel occupies the site of the monastery of St. Columb, and is situated in a street called the Long Tower, from the lofty round tower which formed the belfry of the Dubh-Regles, the original church built by St. Columb. This chapel was completed in 1786, at an expense, including the cost of some additions in 1811, of £2700, of which £210 was contributed by the Earl of Bristol, and £50 by the corporation. The Presbyterian meeting-house, in Meeting-house-row, has a chaste and handsome front, of which the pediment and corners are of Dungiven freestone: it is supposed to have been built about the year 1750, at an expense of nearly £4000, and was repaired in 1828 at an additional cost of £700. The Primitive Wesleyan Methodist chapel, in the same street, was originally a store, which was used by Wesley on his visit to this city in 1763: his congregation built the Wesleyan Methodist chapel in 1783, but on the separation taking place the Primitive Methodists returned to their former place of worship; part of the building is still let for a store, and the chapel is used as a Sunday school between the intervals of divine service, for which the dean pays a rent of £20. The old Wesleyan Methodist chapel was vacated on the completion of a new chapel built in 1835, at an estimated expense of £1100, raised by subscription, towards which the Irish Society contributed £100; the ground floor is used as a vestry-room and a school-room for 300 children. There are also places of worship for Presbyterians in connection with the Seceding Synod, a plain building erected in 1783, at an expense of £450; for Covenanters, built in 1810 at a like expense; and for Independents, built in 1824 at an expense of £500.

The Diocesan school, or Foyle College, was originally founded within the walls as a free grammar school in the reign of Jas. I., and was rebuilt on its present site to the north of the city in 1814, chiefly through the exertions of Bishop Knox, who gave £1000 towards the expense, which amounted to £13,714.13.6, and was further defrayed by donations from the Irish Society and London Companies, sale of stock, and grand jury presentments. It is a simple hut handsome edifice of stone, consisting of a centre and two wings, and pleasantly situated on the bank of the river: it is sufficiently capacious to accommodate 80 boarders; there are at present about 30 boarders and as many day-scholars, exclusive of 20 who are free; the day pupils not free pay £4.4 per annum for mercantile, and £7.7 per annum for classical instruction. The school has no endowment, but the Irish Society, the bishop, and the clergy of the diocese subscribe annually to the amount of about £200; this, with the emoluments arising from the boarders and the day scholars who are not free, constitutes the income of the master: the bishop and the dean and chapter are trustees. The school has deservedly been held in great estimation owing to the high literary acquirements of the masters. Attached to the institution is an excellent library of works on divinity, collected by Bishop Hopkins, and purchased and presented to it by his successor, Bishop King, which has also been augmented by a donation of £100 from James Alexander, Esq., of London; it is open to the clergy of the diocese at all times. The parish school originated in an act of the 28th of Hen. VIII., confirmed by one of the 7th of Wm. III.: the present building, situated without the walls, was erected in 1812 through the liberal contributions of Bishop Knox and the trustees of Erasmus Smith's charity, the latter of whom allow annually £30 for the boys' and £15 for the girls' school; and, in addition, the girls' school is aided by annual grants of £40 and £10 late currency from the Irish Society and the Bishop of Derry respectively: there are about 108 boys and 97 girls, who, except 20 of the boys who are free scholars, pay one penny each weekly. In connection with the Presbyterian meeting-house is a school established in 1820, in lieu of a blue-coat school which had existed upwards of a century, in which there are at present about 100 boys and 96 girls, who pay one penny each weekly; the boys' school is further supported by a subscription of £10 per annum from the congregation, and an annual grant of £20 by the Irish Society; and the girls' school by subscriptions among the ladies, aided by £10 per ann, late currency from the Irish Society: the school-rooms were built and enlarged by subscription at an expense of £450. St. Columb's school, founded in 1813 under the auspices of the Roman Catholic bishop and clergy, but for some time suspended from a difference which arose between the prelate and one of his curates, was finally established in 1825: the building, including the erection of a lofty enclosure, cost nearly £1000. It is in connection with the National Board of Education, who grant £30 per annum for its support, which is further aided by £10 per annum from the Irish Society, and an annual collection in the Roman Catholic chapel amounting to £30; 143 boys and 166 girls are instructed. The London Ladies' Society school, in Fountain-street, was established in 1822; attached to it is a small library for the use of the poor. Gwyn's Charitable Institution was founded by Mr. John Gwyn, a merchant of the city, who died in 1829, and endowed by him with a bequest of £41,757, producing at present £1882 per ann., for boarding, clothing, and educating as many poor boys as the funds may admit of. This excellent school, which is under the management of 21 trustees, was opened on the 1st of April, 1833, in a hired house formerly the city hotel: the trustees have purchased 10 statute acres of ground at the rear of the infirmary, where it is in contemplation to erect premises capable of accommodating 200 pupils, at an estimated expense of £6000: there are at present 81 boys in the school. A Sunday School Union was formed in 1832, by which the liberties have been divided into six districts, each under the superintendence of one or two members; the number of schools in the parish at present in connection with the union is 16, attended by 162 teachers, and the number of pupils on the books is 1726.

The lunatic asylum for the counties of Londonderry, Donegal, and Tyrone, situated on rising ground to the north of the city, was commenced in June 1827, and opened in 1829; the entire expense, including the purchase of the site and furniture, amounted to £25,678.2.4, advanced by Government, and to be repaid by the three counties by instalments. The facade fronting the river consists of a centre with pavilions, from which extend wings with airing-sheds, terminating in angular pavilions, all of Dungiven sandstone; above the centre rises a turret, of which the upper part forms an octagonal cupola; in the rear are several commodious airing-yards, separated by ranges of brick building, including the domestic offices and workshops: the entire length of the front is 364 feet; the depth of the building, with the airing-yards, 190 feet; and the height to the eave, 25 feet. The grounds comprise eight acres, including a plot in front ornamentally planted, and a good garden The asylum was originally intended for 104 patients, but has been enlarged so as to admit 150: it is still too small, from the cells being partially occupied by incurables, persons afflicted with epilepsy, and idiots. The average annual expenditure for the last three years ending 1835 was £2554.3.6: the average number of patients discharged recovered in each year was 42; discharged relieved, 6; and incurable, 4; and the average number of deaths was 17 in each year: the number of patients at the commencement of

1836 was 155; about 100 of the patients are constantly employed. The infirmary and fever hospital, for the city and county, on the north of the city, was built in 1814, in place of an old poor-house which previously occupied the site of the present fish and vegetable markets, and is supported by parliamentary grants, Grand Jury presentments, governors' subscriptions, and contingencies: it contains 120 beds. The average annual income for five years ending Jan. 5th, 1833, was £1475.15.10$^1/_2$, and the expenditure, £1456.10; the entire number of patients deriving relief from this institution on the 5th of Jan., 1835, was 463, A dispensary for the city and north-west liberties was established in 1819 by the late Bishop Knox and the inhabitants, and is supported by voluntary contributions, an annual grant of £30 by the Irish Society, and presentments by the Grand Jury; the number of patients relieved in that year was 920, and the expenditure, £235.8.2. The clergymen's widows' fund originated in voluntary subscriptions, to which Bishop Knox, a munificent benefactor to most of the charitable institutions of Derry, gave £1000, and most of the Protestant clergy of the diocese contributed: the widows now receive each £35 per annum, and the six senior widows have houses rent-free, called the Widows'-row, adjacent to the cathedral. The charitable loan fund was instituted by Bishop Knox, and the corporation contributed to it £31.10 per ann. until the year 1829, from which period it was unsupported till 1833, when the Irish Society granted £10 annually towards the expense of management: the capital, which is decreasing, amounted on July 31st, 1835, to £423. The ladies' penny society has an average annual income of about £200, including a bequest of £30 per ann., and an annual grant of £30 by the Irish Society, which is applied in distributing clothing and a few articles of food among the poor: it has also a branch called the flax fund, to which the Society contribute £20 per annum, for the distribution of certain portions of flax among poor applicants, who are paid for spinning it into yarn. The poor-shop, instituted in 1821, under the management of a committee of ladies, for providing the poor with clothes and bedding at first cost, on condition of their giving security for payment by weekly instalments at the rate of one penny in the shilling, is supported by subscriptions. A mendicity association was instituted in 1825, chiefly through the exertions of Bishop Knox; and a penitentiary for reclaiming abandoned females, to which there is a school attached, was established in 1829. A religious tract depository, in connection with which is a religious, moral, and historical society, was established in 1822: the library formed by the society comprises about 500 publications, and at least one half of the funds must be expended on works purely religious. The above and many other charitable institutions are in a great degree attributable to the indefatigable exertions of the late Lady

Walker's monument, Londonderry. Drawn by T.M. Baynes and engraved by H. Ogg. From G. N. Wright, Ireland illustrated *(London, 1831).*

Hill. Alderman Peter Stanley, in 1751, bequeathed £42 per annum late currency for 31 inhabitants of the city and liberties on the western side of the river; and in 1831, Margaret Evory gave £20 per annum for the poor of the entire parish.

MACOSQUIN, or CAMUS-juxta-BANN, a parish, in the barony of COLERAINE, county of LONDONDERRY, and province of ULSTER, 2 miles (S. S. W.) from Coleraine, on the road to Dublin; containing 6639 inhabitants. The place derived its latter name, which is the more ancient, from the foundation of a monastery at Cambos or Camus, on the river Bann, by St. Comgal, in 580; and the former, by which it is more generally known, from the Cistercian abbey of St. Mary de Fontana or Macosquin, founded in 1172 by the family of O'Cahan. Both these establishments, of which the former became very celebrated as the resort of numerous pilgrims, continued to flourish till the dissolution, and were granted in 1609 by Jas. I. to the Irish Society, by whom the church of the latter was made parochial. The parish, which is chiefly the property of the Richardson family by purchase from the Merchant Tailors' company, is situated on the river Bana, by which it is bounded on the east, and comprises, according to the Ordnance survey, 17,804$^1/_4$ statute acres, of which 65$^3/_4$ are in the river Bann, and 12,923 are applotted under the tithe act, and valued at £6851.5 per annum. The land is generally of good quality, in a profitable state of cultivation, and well fenced and drained; there are extensive tracts of bog and mountain, which might be brought into cultivation at a moderate expense. Basaltic stone of excellent quality for building is scattered over the parish, and is quarried for that purpose and for mending the roads; granite, porphyry, and clay-slate are found in the channels of several of the numerous rivulets by which it is intersected; and iron ore is also very abundant, especially in the townland of Drumcroon, but the mines have never been worked in consequence of the high price of coal. There are several gentlemen's seats in the neighbourhood, most of them surrounded with extensive and thriving plantations, which form a conspicuous and interesting feature in a district generally destitute of timber. Of these, the principal are Somerset, the residence of the Rev. T. Richardson; Greenfield, of S. Bennett, Esq.; Ardverness, of R. Bennett, Esq.; Drumcroon, of J. Wilson, Esq.; Dromore, of J. Gamble, Esq.; Ballyness, of Miss Heyland; Castleroe, of Capt. Hannay; Castleroe, the property of Rowley Heyland, of Dublin, Esq., at present untenanted; and Camus House, of Curtis McFarland, Esq. The linen manufacture was formerly carried on to a very great extent, especially in the finer fabrics, and there are four large bleach-greens, capable of finishing 60,000 pieces annually, all of which were in full operation; but the trade has so much declined, that one only is now kept at work by the proprietor, for the humane purpose of affording employment to the numerous families which had settled around them. The salmon fishery, first granted to Sir Arthur Chichester in 1605, and afterwards to the Irish Society, is situated at a place called "the Cutts," to which the tide flows up; but the river Bann, though navigable here, is unavailable to the benefit of the parish, as no vessel can pass under the bridge of Coleraine; the navigation is also prevented by fords, and by the "Cutts," where the great salmon fishery of the Bann is carried on, about a mile from the bridge. The courts leet and baron attached to the manor have not been held for some time; the jurisdiction of the court of Coleraine extends over this parish, and all pleas are now referred to it.

The living is a rectory, in the diocese of Derry, and in the patronage of the Bishop, but the advowson is claimed by the Richardson family; the tithes amount to £600. The glebe-house was built about 70 years since at an expense of £738.9.2$^3/_4$; the glebe comprises 200 Cunningham acres, valued at £200 per annum. The church, a very spacious structure (formerly the abbey church of Macosquin), was new-roofed and repaired in 1826, at an expense of £500, of which one-half was paid by assessment and the other by the incumbent. In the R. C. divisions the parish forms part of the union or district of Killowen or Coleraine. There are places of worship for Presbyterians in connection with the Synod of Ulster, of the third class, at Englishtown, and with the Associate Synod, of the second class, at Crossgare; also one for Covenanters at Ringrash. About 500 children are taught in the public schools of the parish, of which the parochial school, near the church, is partly supported by the rector; one for girls by the lady of the rector, who gave the school-house; one at Ballywilliam by the Ironmongers' company; one at Castleroe, established by the late F. Bennett, Esq., who, in 1820, endowed it with £10 per annum, charged on the Castleroe estate, built a large and handsome school-house, and directed £5 per annum to be paid to a minister for officiating in it occasionally; it is further aided by a donation from T. Bennett, Esq., who also contributes £3 per annum and a house to a school at Camus; and there is a school built by Mr. Richardson and afterwards endowed by Dr. Adam Clarke with a sum of money left by an English lady to found schools in Ireland, after which it was connected with the Methodists for some time, but has now reverted to the patronage of its original founder. There are also four private schools, in which are about 200 children, and eight Sunday schools. The small remains of the monastery founded by St. Comgal were taken down to build a wall round the burial-ground; among them was a very ancient stone cross having four compartments, in each of which were three of the apostles sculptured in high relief, and profusely ornamented with scrolls and wreaths; it was removed from its socket and now forms a gate pillar in the wall: There was also an ancient font, to which, previously to the removal of the cross, the people resorted in great numbers. Several stone and bronze celts have been found, chiefly in the bogs; also fossilized tubs of butter, one of which, weighing 22 lb., is in the possession of J. Wilson, Esq., of Drumcroon. There are five ancient forts and several

Salmon Leap. Drawn by T.M. Baynes and engraved by S. Lacey. From G.N. Wright, Ireland illustrated *(London, 1831).*

artificial caves, one of which, at Ballywilliam, contains five apartments. There are also several strong chalybeate springs in the parish, of which those at Drumcroon and Greenfield contain iron, sulphur, and magnesia in solution, with a considerable portion of carbonic acid gas.

MAGHERA, a market and post-town, and a parish, in the barony of LOUGHINSHOLIN, county of LONDONDERRY, and province of ULSTER, 16 miles (S.) from Coleraine, and 102 (N.) from Dublin, on the mail coach road to Coleraine; containing 14,091 inhabitants, of which number, 1154 are in the town. This place is evidently of great antiquity, and though there is no precise account of the original foundation of an abbey for Canons Regular, said to have been established here at a very early period, yet it is certain that the ancient see of Ardstra or Ardsrath was removed, in 597, to this town, which continued to be the seat of the diocese till 1158, when it was united to the see of Derry, and the cathedral church established in that city. The town appears to have declined rapidly in importance after that period, and few events of historical interest occur, except occasional depredations during the insurrections of the O'Nials, to whom the surrounding territory belonged, and in the war of 1641, during which it was burned by the insurgents under Macdonnell. In 1688, the town, which had scarcely recovered from its former devastation, was assaulted by the Irish adherents of Jas. II., and the inhabitants were compelled to abandon their houses and seek refuge in the city of Derry. During the disturbances of 1798 it enjoyed comparative tranquillity, and has since been gradually increasing in extent and importance. It consists of one long and spacious street, from which several smaller streets branch off, and contains 210 houses, most of which are modern buildings of stone roofed with slate and of handsome appearance; it is a great thoroughfare, and is amply supplied with excellent water. The inhabitants are principally employed in agriculture and in the linen manufacture, which is extensively carried on in the parish; and at Upperlands is a bleach-green, in which about 8000 pieces are annually finished for the English and American markets; there are also numerous corn and flax-mills on the different streams, of which the Moyola forms part of the southern boundary of the parish. The market, on Tuesday, is amply supplied with all kinds of provisions; a market is also held on Friday, chiefly for grain; and there are fairs on the last Tues day in every month for cattle, sheep, pigs, and pedlery. The market-house, the property of A. Clarke, Esq., of Upperland, is a large neat building, erected in 1833 on a rising ground in the centre of the town; and over it is a spacious room in which the petty sessions are held on alternate Saturdays, and a manorial court monthly, in which debts under 40s. are recoverable. Here is also a chief constabulary police station.

The parish comprises, according to the Ordnance survey, 24,791 $^{1}/_{4}$ statute acres, of which 22,056 are applotted under the tithe act, and valued at £10,650 per annum. The greater portion is good arable and pasture land; there is also some

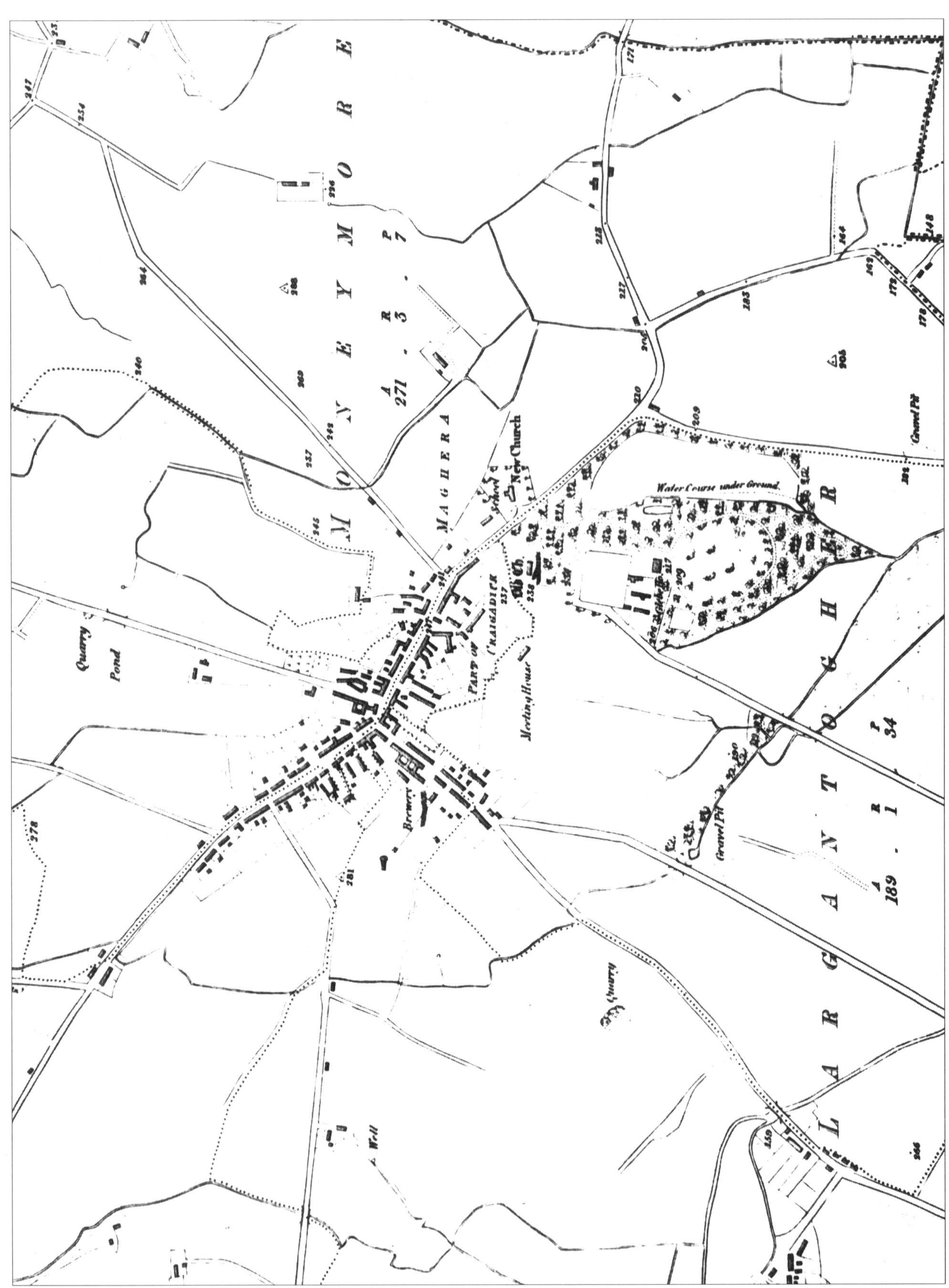

Maghera. Part of O.S. map of Co.Londonderry, sheet 36, published 1833 (reproduced at 140%).

of inferior quality and a very large tract of waste land and bog. The mountain district of the parish is very extensive and abounds with grouse and every other kind of game. The system of agriculture is improved, and the highlands afford excellent pasturage for cattle. The vale of the Moyola and the vicinity of the town are extremely productive; and in the bogs are several fertile spots, called by the country people "islands," which are in a good state of cultivation. Limestone, found on the estate of the Mercers' Company, is extensively quarried, and is productive of great benefit to the neighbourhood. On the plantation of Ulster, the lands of the ancient see of Maghera were confirmed to the Bishop of Derry, and other parts of the parish were also assigned by Jas. I. to the Mercers', Vintners', Salters', and Drapers' Companies of London, who still retain possession of their manors. The principal seats are Maghera House, the residence of A. Clarke, Esq.; Fairview, of J. Henry, Esq.; Rowens Gift, of Capt. Crofton; Upperland, of A. Clarke, Esq.; Clover Hill, of R. Forrester, Esq.; and the glebe-house, of the Rev. J. Spencer Knox. The living is a rectory, in the diocese of Derry, and in the patronage of the Bishop; the tithes amount to £1015.7.7$^1/_2$. The glebe-house was built in 1825, at an expense of £3077.6, of which £1278.2.2 was a grant from the late Board of First Fruits, and the remainder was defrayed by the incumbent. The glebe comprises 907$^3/_4$ acres, valued at £651.10 per ann. The church, a neat edifice of stone with a square embattled tower crowned with pinnacles, towards which the same Board granted a loan of £1363.6.2$^1/_2$, was erected in 1819; the east window is embellished with stained glass, presented by the lady of the late Bishop Knox. In the R. C. divisions the parish is the head of a union or district, comprising also the parish of Killelagh and part of that of Termoneeny; the chapel at Lamny is a plain modern edifice, and there is also a chapel at Fallagloon, a handsome building with a campanile turret and bell. There are places of worship for Presbyterians in connection with the Synod of Ulster, of the first and second classes, and for those in connection with the Seceding Synod, of the second class. About 1000 children are taught in 16 public schools, of which the parochial schools, held in a large building near the church, erected in 1821 at an expense of £400, of which £100 was a parliamentary grant and £125 was given by the Mercers' Company, are supported by the rector; a national school at Curran is aided by Lord Strafford; two at Swattragh by the Mercers' Company; and one at Craigadick by the rector and Mr. Clarke. There are also 15 private schools, in which are about 550 children, and three Sunday schools. A voluntary poor fund and a dispensary have been established. The ruins of the old church are highly interesting, and some portions bear marks of very remote antiquity; over the west entrance is a representation of the Crucifixion, rudely sculptured in high relief, with ten of the apostles; and in the churchyard are the tomb and pillar of Leuri, the patron saint, whose grave was opened some years since, when a silver crucifix was found in it, which was carefully replaced. About three miles from the town is Doon Glady, a very large and perfect rath, which gives name to one of the townlands; it is encompassed with treble walls and a trench. There are also several other raths and forts in the parish. Numerous celts, swords, spear heads, and ornaments of bronze and brass, have been found in the parish and vicinity, and are in the possession of the Rev. Spencer Knox, the rector. There are some remains of ancient iron-works, established at Drumconready in the reign of Chas. I., and destroyed in 1641; they consist of the foundations of the buildings and heaps of half-smelted ore and charcoal.

MAGHERAFELT, a market and post-town, and a parish, in the barony of LOUGHINSHOLIN, county of LONDONDERRY, and province of ULSTER, 30 Miles (N. W. by W.) from Londonderry, and 96 (N. N. W.) from Dublin, on the road from Armagh to Coleraine; containing, with part of the post-town of Castle-Dawson (which is separately described), 7275 inhabitants, of which number, 1436 are in the town of Magherafelt. This place suffered materially in the war of 1641; the town was plundered by the insurgents, who destroyed the church, put many of the inhabitants to death, and carried off several of the more wealthy, with a view to obtain money for their ransom. In 1688 the town was again plundered, but on the approach of the assailants, the inhabitants took refuge in the Carntogher mountains, and subsequently found an asylum in Derry; on this occasion the church, having been appropriated by the enemy as a barrack, was preserved. The town, which is large and well built, consists of a spacious square, from which four principal streets diverge at the angles, and from these branch off several smaller streets in various directions; the total number of houses is 276, most of which are of stone and roofed with slate. The linen manufacture is carried on very extensively by the Messrs. Walker, who employ more than 1000 persons in weaving at their own houses; and nearly 100 on the premises in preparing the yarn and warps; the manufacture is rapidly increasing. There is also a very large ale and beer brewery near the town. The principal market is on Thursday, and is abundantly supplied with all kinds of provisions; great quantities of pork, butter, and flax are exposed for sale. There are also very extensive markets on alternate Thursdays for linen and yarn, which are sold to the amount of £33,000 annually; and a market on Monday for barley and oats, and on Wednesday for wheat. Fairs, which are among the largest in the county, are held on the last Thursday in every month, for cattle, sheep, and pigs. The market-house is a handsome building of hewn basalt, situated in the centre of the square; in the upper part are rooms for transacting public business. The quarter sessions for the county are held here in June and December, and petty sessions on alternate Wednesdays; a manorial court is also held monthly by the seneschal of the Salters' Company, for the recovery of debts under £2; and there is a constabulary police station. The court-house is a

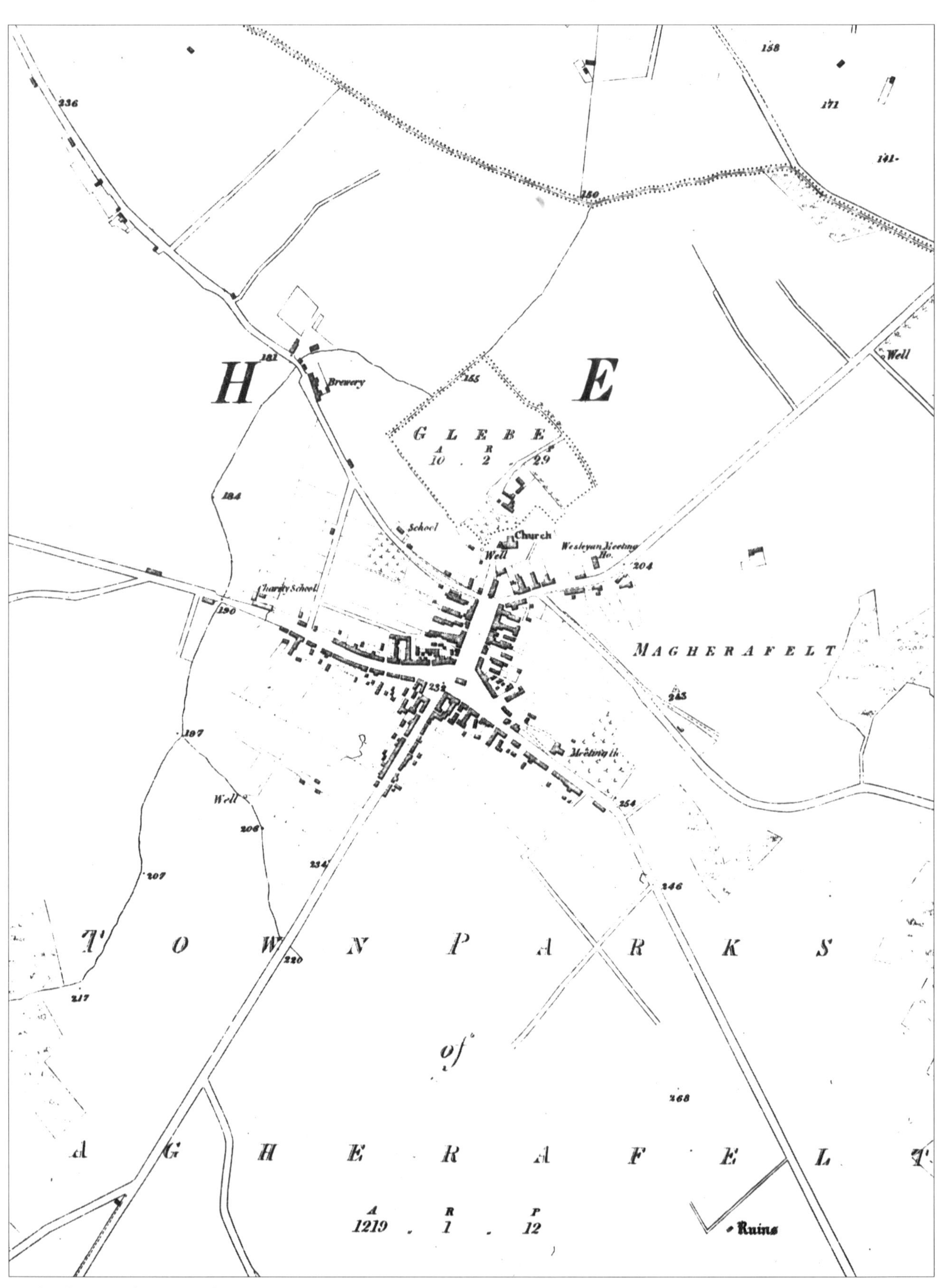

Magherafelt. Part of O.S. map of Co. Londonderry, sheet 42, published 1833 (reproduced at 140%).

commodious edifice, and there is a small bridewell for the confinement of prisoners charged with minor offences.

The parish, which is situated on the river Moyola, comprises, according to the Ordnance survey, 8290¼ statute acres, of which the greater portion is very good land, and the system of agriculture is improved. The principal substratum is basalt, which, in the townland of Polepatrick, has a columnar tendency; limestone of good quality is abundant, and coal is found in some parts. The principal seats are Millbrook, the residence of A. Spotswood, Esq.; Farm Hill, of Capt. Blathwayt; Glenbrook, of S. J. Cassidy, Esq.; Prospect, of the Rev. T. Wilson; and the glebe-house, of the Rev. T. A. Vesey. Considerable improvements are contemplated, tending greatly to promote the prosperity of the surrounding district. The lands immediately around it belong to the Salters' Company, and are at present leased for a limited term of years to the Marquess of Londonderry and Sir R. Bateson, Bart.; other lands, in the manor of Maghera, belong to the see of Derry; some, in the manor of Moneymore, to the Drapers' Company; some, in the manor of Bellaghy, to the Vintners' Company; and the manor of Castle-Dawson to the Rt. Hon. G. R. Dawson. The living is a rectory, in the diocese of Armagh, and in the patronage of the Lord-Primate: the tithes amount to £450. The glebe-house was built in 1787, at an expense of £574.18, of which £92.6.1¾ was a gift, and the remainder a loan, from the late Board of First Fruits; the glebe comprises 403a.2r.17p. statute measure, valued at £270 per annum. The church, situated in the town, is a handsome edifice built in 1664, enlarged by the addition of a north aisle in 1718, and ornamented with a tower and spire in 1790; it has been recently repaired by a grant of £121.0.9 from the Ecclesiastical Commissioners. In the R. C. divisions the parish is the head of a union or district, comprising also parts of the parishes of Woods-chapel, Desertlyn, and Ballyscullion; the chapel is at Aghagaskin, about a mile from the town. There are places of worship for Presbyterians, in connection with the Synod of Ulster, and Wesleyan Methodists. A free school was founded here by Hugh Rainey, Esq., who, in 1710, erected a school-house, and bequeathed money to purchase an estate for its endowment; the estate was afterwards sold under an act of parliament, subject to an annual payment of £175 Irish currency, with which the school is endowed; it is under the patronage and direction of the Lord Primate and John Ash Reiny, Esq., who resides at the school; 14 boys are clothed, boarded, and educated for three years, and afterwards placed out as apprentices with a premium. About 400 children are also taught in four other public schools, of which the parochial schools are supported by the rector, the Marquess of Londonderry, and Sir Robert Bateson, Bart.; and a female work school by the Marchioness of Londonderry and Lady Bateson, by whom the school-house was built: there are also four private schools, in which are about 130 children. A dispensary and a Ladies' Clothing Society have been established in the town. There are several forts in the parish, but none entitled to particular notice.

MONEYMORE, a market and post-town, partly in the parish of DESERTLYN, but chiefly in that of ARDTREA, barony of LOUGHINSHOLIN, county of LONDONDERRY, and province of ULSTER, 24 miles (S.) from Coleraine, and 92 (N.) from Dublin, on the road to Coleraine; containing 1025 inhabitants. This place, which is one of the oldest post-towns in the country, is noticed by Pynnar, in his survey of Ireland, as consisting of an ancient castle, which he describes as a fine old building, and of six good houses of stone and lime, supplied with water conveyed by pipes to the castle and to each of the houses from a well near the lime stone quarry at Spring Hill. Cormick O'Hagan, a follower of Sir Phelim O'Nial, took the castle by stratagem in 1641, and it remained for a long time in the possession of the insurgents, by whom it was subsequently destroyed. Sir Phelim, some time after, rendezvoused his troops at this place, whence he marched to plunder the house of Lissan, then the property and residence of Sir Thomas Staples. The castle which was one of the most perfect in Ireland, was taken down about the year 1760, to afford room for a small public-house, and only some portions of the walls are at present remaining. In lowering the high street and the hills some years since, some of the old water pipes were discovered, the wood of which crumbled into dust, but the iron hoops were in a tolerably perfect state and are now in the possession of Mr. Miller; some more of the pipes were also found in trenching a field adjoining the spring, proving the accuracy of Pynnar's statement. The town consists of two principal and five smaller streets, and contains 184 houses, which are very neatly built, and several others are now in progress of erection. About a quarter of a mile above it is Spring Hill, the seat of W. L. Conyngham, Esq., a line mansion more than 200 years old, pleasantly situated in grounds tastefully arranged and commanding some finely varied scenery; the demesne is enriched with some remarkably fine beech, oak, ash, and fir trees, and close to the house is a remarkably fine cedar. A very elegant house has been recently built by Rowley Miller, Esq., agent of the Drapers' company, and another by J. R. Miller, Esq.; the glebe-house, built in 1831 by the Hen, and Rev. J. P. Hewitt, is a very handsome residence; and Desertlyn Cottage, the residence of J. Smyth, Esq., is pleasantly situated and the grounds tastefully laid out. There are also, in the immediate vicinity of the town, handsome houses belonging to Z. Maxwell and E. L. Batchelor, Esqrs., the Rev. J. Barnett, the Rev. G. Thompson, Mrs. Hamilton and others.

The surrounding district has been greatly improved by the Drapers' company, who are the proprietors, since the year 1817, when, on the expiration of a lease granted to Sir W. Rowley, the estates returned into their possession, and have since been managed under their superintendence. The annual rent roll is £10,300, the whole of which is expended by the company in the improvement of the country

Moneymore, from a window of the Drapers' Arms Inn. Drawn by W.J. Booth, 1827, and engraved by T.M. Baynes. From Reports of... the Drapers' Company *(London, 1829).*

generally, and more especially of their own property. They have planted more than 800 statute acres, and have completed more than 50 Irish miles of good road at their own expense, for the convenience and benefit of their tenantry; they have expended more than £1000 in the erection of bridges, and are about to plant 800 acres of mountainous land, in addition to the former plantations. They have thus not only added to the improvement and embellishment of the surrounding district, but have contributed greatly to the benefit of the poor by affording employment to the industrious, and have given directions to their agents to afford employment to all that may stand in need of it, The system of agriculture has been greatly improved under the auspices of the North-West Farming Society; there is little or no waste land, and scarcely sufficient bog to supply the inhabitants with fuel. There are many limestone quarries, from which lime is procured chiefly for manure; sandstone and freestone of good quality abound, and from the quarries of the latter was raised the stone for the erection of the new church; coal has also been found near the surface, and about two years since an attempt was made to explore the vein, but without success. The linen manufacture is carried on extensively throughout the district; and there is a considerable traffic by means of Lough Neagh, which is within four miles of the town, and across which merchandise brought by the canal from Belfast and Newry is conveyed to Port Ballyronan, where corn, butter and other agricultural produce of this neighbourhood are shipped to those places for exportation to Liverpool and other English ports. The market is on Monday, and fairs are held on the 21st of each month, at which, in addition to horses, cows, swine, sheep, and agricultural produce, large quantities of linen are also sold. These are the largest linen fairs in the North of Ireland; the sales, on an average, amount to £40,000 per annum. An additional linen market, established in 1835, is held on the first Monday in every month; it is well attended, and promises to equal the other linen fairs in the extent of its sales. The market and court-house, and the linenhall, erected in 1818, are neat and well-arranged buildings; and near them is a spacious and handsome hotel, erected about the same time. A new marketplace and a spacious cornstore are now being erected, a little off the main street, which will diminish the' pressure of the people on market and fair days; and here corn, potatoes, butchers' meat and other articles will be exposed for sale. A constabulary police force is stationed in the town; petty sessions are held on alternate Tuesdays, and a court for the manor once every month, in which debts to the amount of 40s. late currency are recoverable. The manor is co-extensive with the whole estates belonging to the Drapers' company, which include portions of the several parishes of Arboe, Ardtrea, Ballynascreen, Derryloran, Desertlyn, Desertmartin, Kilcronaghan, Lissan; Maghera, and Tamlaght. This estate comprises 64 townlands, nine of which are native freeholds, each paying a chief rent to the company, and of which seven are in the parish of Kilcronaghan.

The parish church of Desertlyn, situated in the town, is a very handsome structure, in the Norman style, and was erected in 1832, at an expense of £6000, wholly defrayed by the Drapers' company. There are also a handsome R. C. chapel, towards the rebuilding of which the same company contributed £230; a place of worship for Presbyterians in connection with the Synod of Ulster, built by the company at an expense of £4000; and one for those in connection with the Seceding Synod, built on ground presented by the company, who also contributed £250 towards its erection; these last pay an annual rent of 5s., and the ground around them has been tastefully laid out and planted by the company. Two large and handsome school-houses, with residences for a master and mistress, were built in the town in 1820, and are supported by the Drapers' company, who also have built and support four others in the rural parts of their estate; in these schools about 1400 children are gratuitously instructed, and ten of the boys annually apprenticed to handicraft trades; the masters have each a salary of £50 and the mistresses of £35 per ann., with a house rentfree and a supply of fuel. Two dispensaries, with houses for resident surgeons, were built and are supported by the company, one here and one at Draperstown, for the benefit of their tenantry; and two county dispensaries at the same places were also erected and are solely supported by the same company, for the benefit of such inhabitants of the surrounding district as do not reside on their estates. The company allow £1000 per ann., for the maintenance of the schools and dispensaries, which are regulated by a Board of Governors, consisting of the clergy of all denominations, the resident gentry of the neighbourhood, and the respectable farmers on the estate. There are several Danish forts in the parish, two of which, on the townland of Tulnagee, are in a perfect state; and adjoining the linen-hall are some slight vestiges of the ancient castle.

MUFF, a village, in the parish of FAUGHANVALE, barony of TIRKEERAN, county of LONDONDERRY, and province of ULSTER, 6 miles (N. E. by E.) from Londonderry, on the old road to Coleraine; containing 192 inhabitants. This place owes its origin to the Grocers' Company of London, to whom, on the settlement of Ulster, Jas. I. granted the adjacent lands, on which the company erected a large bawn and a strong castle, defended by a garrison of their own tenantry. The castle was besieged in 1641 by the insurgents under Col. McDonnell, and gallantly defended by the garrison during the winter of that year, till relieved in the following summer by the troops from Derry, but it afterwards fell in the hands of the parliamentarians, by whom it was dismantled. The company, in 1626, erected a church here, which has ever since been the parish church of Faughanvale; and on the expiration of the leases, which they had granted for long terms, resumed the management of their estate in 1819, since which period very considerable improvements have been made. The company's manor comprehends 38 townlands, extending into the parishes of Lower Cumber and Clondermot, and comprising 16,500 statute acres. The village has been entirely rebuilt; the houses are large and of handsome appearance, the streets spacious and regularly laid out, and the roads leading to it well constructed and kept in good repair. In conjunction with the resident gentry of the neighbourhood, the company established an agricultural school at Templemoyle, with which a classical school at Fallowlee is connected, and for its use allotted 130 acres for experiments in practical farming, in consideration of which they send three free pupils into the school. Fairs are held on the first Thursday in Feb., May, Aug., and Nov., for cattle, sheep, pigs, and various articles of merchandise. A penny post has been established to Londonderry, a constabulary police force is stationed here, and petty sessions are held on the first Tuesday in every month. A manorial court is held monthly before the seneschal, for the recovery of debts under 40s,; the court and market-house is a spacious and handsome building in the centre of the village. The old church built by the company having fallen into decay, a new church in the early English style was erected in 1821, towards which a loan of £1000 was granted by the late Board of First Fruits; the glebe-house (erected by the Company), a dispensary, and an almshouse for 20 poor widows, are also in the village. There are some remains of the old parish church; but not a vestige of the bawn or castle, except the vaults of the latter, can be traced.

NEWTOWN-LIMAVADY, a corporate, market and post-town (formerly a parliamentary borough), in the parish of DRUMACHOSE, barony of KENAUGHT, county of LONDONDERRY, and province of ULSTER, 12$^{3}/_{4}$ miles (E. N. E.) from the city of Londonderry, and 131 (N. by W.) from Dublin, on the road from Londonderry to Coleraine; containing 2428 inhabitants. The district in which the town stands was anciently the territory of the O'Cahans or O'Canes, the head of a powerful and warlike sept, whose castle on the brow of a romantic glen was called Lima-vaddy, or "the Dog's Leap." The estimation in which these chieftains were formerly held appears from the fact that Dermod O Cahan was summoned by Edw. II. to attend him with his forces on his disastrous expedition against Scotland. He went, but instead of joining the army of the invader, was found in the ranks of the Scottish king at the battle of Bannockburn. After the general forfeiture of Ulster, in 1608, arising out of the attainder of the Earls of Tyrone and Tyrconnel, Sir Thomas Philips, surveyor of the forfeited

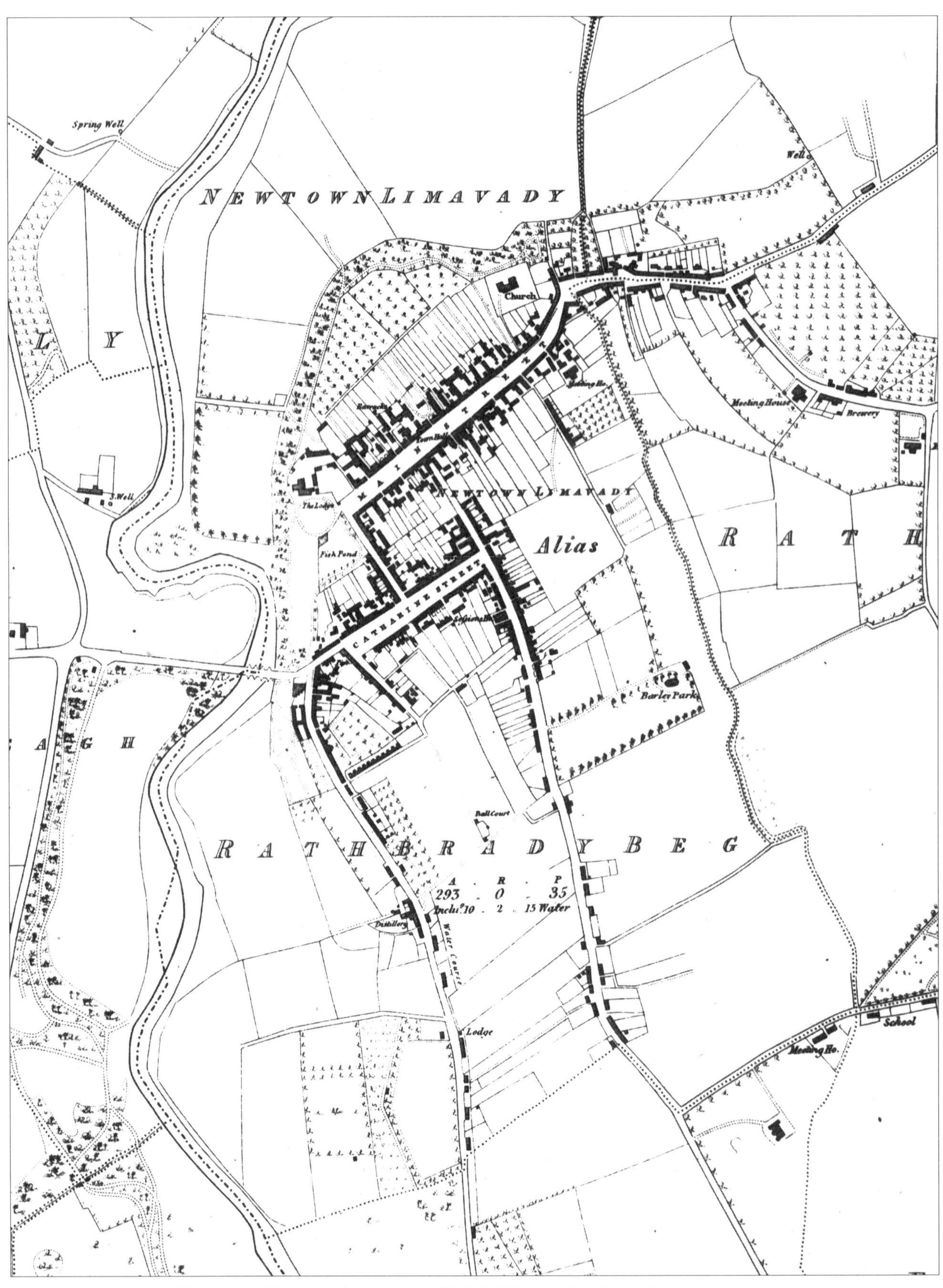

Newtown-Limavady. Part of O.S. map of Co. Londonderry, sheet 9, published 1833 (reproduced at 140%).

estates, obtained a grant of 1000 acres in this district, on which he erected a castle and a bawn on the eastern bank of the Roe, on a spot near the site on which a town, named Ballyclose, now a suburb of Newtown-Limavady, previously existed. The town took its name from the circumstance of its modern erection; and to distinguish it from several others, it acquired the adjunct of Limavady from its contiguity to O'Cahan's castle. It increased rapidly under the fostering care of its founder, who, in 1610, brought hither 25 English families. In 1613 the town obtained a charter, which is stated to have been granted on the petition of the inhabitants and for the better plantation of Ulster. By this charter the inhabitants were incorporated under the name of "the provost, 12 burgesses and commonalty," and a court of record was created, of which the provost was to be judge, and also to be clerk of the market and collector of the tolls and customs, which he retained for his own use: it also conferred a licence for holding a market on Monday, and a fair on July 1st (to which three others were added a few years afterwards), granted 300 acres of land for a common, and 375 for the maintenance of a free school, to be erected at Limavady, and the right of sending two members to parliament; a discretionary power of electing freemen was given to the provost and burgesses by the same charter. In the war of 1641, the castle was besieged by the Irish army under Col. O'Nial, but the garrison under Capt. Philips, the governor, supported by many of the townspeople, among whom were some women, held out during the entire winter, until relieved by the approach of the parliamentary forces under Col. Mervyn, who routed the besieging army with much slaughter: the castle, however, was subsequently taken by the Irish and burnt, together with the church and the entire town. A new town sprang up from the ruins, which suffered a similar fate in the war of 1688, being burned by the army of Jas. II. on its retreat from Derry, It was again rebuilt after the Revolution, and some of the houses then erected are still standing. The borough was disfranchised at the Union, from which period the corporation has declined; the only official proof of its existence being the collection of the tolls and customs, which was relinquished in consequence of the resistance given to the payment of them: on the death of the provost some years since, no successor was appointed, and the corporation may now be considered extinct. The land granted for commonage seems to have merged in the general estate on its sale by the Philips' family, in the reign of Chas, II. The school was never founded, nor can any particulars be procured relative to the lands set apart for its endowment. The borough and manor courts are discontinued, and the place is now, like all the rest of the county, governed by the magistrates and the police.

In point of size the town is the third in the county and the first in the barony. It comprises four principal and several smaller streets; three of the streets are large and well built. There is a handsome sessions-house, where the general sessions for the county are held in June and December, and petty sessions on alternate Tuesdays; adjoining it is a small bridewell. It is a constabulary police station, which is provided with a good barrack in one of the main streets. The market-house is a large, old, inconvenient building, over an arch which connects two of the principal streets. Large and commodious grain stores and shambles were erected in 1820, by Edw. Boyle, Esq., who also established grain markets on Tuesday and Friday, which are well attended and productive of much advantage to the town and neighbourhood: connected with these buildings is a news-room, well supplied with journals and periodicals. The Monday market is the mart for cattle, butter, and flax: the potato market is held in an adjoining street. The fairs are held on the second Monday in February, March 28th, June 13th, July 12th, and Oct. 29th: they are all well attended and largely supplied with cattle of every description: that of February is a great horse fair. Distillation is carried on extensively in the neighbourhood. A dispensary in the town is maintained in the usual manner. The church, which is the parochial church of Drumachose, is a large and handsome edifice, built in 1750 on the site of a former one, and enlarged in 1825 by the addition of an aisle, by a loan of £200 from the late Board of First Fruits: it now consists of a nave and a north aisle, in the Grecian style. In the suburb of Ballyclose are meeting-houses for Presbyterians in connection with the Synod of Ulster, and with the Remonstrant and Associate Synods: near the church is a meeting-house of the Wesleyan Methodists. Of the castle built by Sir Thos. Philips nothing now remains: the site is pointed out as being in the grounds and gardens of the Lodge, at the north-western extremity of the main street. The environs of the town are extremely beautiful: to the north-west is the rich vale of Myroe, extending to the shores of Lough Foyle; to the east and north-east the lofty range of Benyevenagh, and to the south the summits of Donald's Hill and Benbradagh, beneath which is spread out the vale of the Roe, with its numerous plantations, villas, mills, and bleach-greens, the rich foliage of the oak woods and the plantations of Roe Park, the beautiful residence of Edm. Chas. McNaghten, Esq., and the other seats interspersed throughout the district, which are noticed in the article on the parish, as are also the schools.

PORTSTEWART, a sea-port and town, in the parish of BALLYACHRAN, liberties of COLERAINE, county of LONDONDERRY, and province of ULSTER, $3^1/_2$ miles (N.) from Coleraine, to which it has a penny post; containing 475 inhabitants. It is situated at the foot of a branch of the great basaltic range of promontories, and commands an extensive view of the estuary of the Bann, the entrance into Lough Foyle, and the promontory of Downhill, with the peninsula of Ennishowen in the distance. The exertions of the proprietors, John Cromie and Henry O'Hara, Esqrs., have raised this place, in the space of a few years, from a group of fishermen's huts to a delightful and well frequented summer residence. Its principal street, which commands the view already described, consists of well-built hotels and shops, having the mansion of Mr. Cromie near its centre; at a little distance to the south is another street of smaller houses, and westward are a number of detached villas, lodges, and ornamented cottages, chiefly built for bathing-lodges by the gentry of the surrounding counties. In this portion is a castle, built in 1834 by Mr. O'Hara, on a projecting cliff over the sea, the road to which is cut in traverses through the rock on which it stands, thus giving it the character of a chieftain's fortress of the feudal ages. A mail coach passes through the town every day; numerous vehicles ply to Coleraine; and steamers frequently arrive from Liverpool, the Clyde, Londonderry, and occasionally from Belfast. A mile from the town is the parish church of Agherton; divine service is also performed in a school-house in the place. There are a meeting-house for Presbyterians in connection with the Synod of Ulster, and a chapel for Wesleyan Methodists. The town is plentifully supplied with wild fowl, round and flat fish and herrings, of which last one of the most productive fisheries is off this port and on the coast of Ennishowen. The air here is serene and pure, the scenery grand and picturesque, the country well cultivated, planted, and embellished with elegant mansions, the principal of which, besides those already noticed, are Cromore, the seat of John Cromie, Esq.; Flowerfield, of S. Orr, Esq.; Low Rock, of Miss McManus; and Blackrock, of T. Bennet, Esq. The vicinity presents a variety of objects of geological interest, especially at the castle and near the creek of Port-na-happel, where there is a rock of the colour and appearance of Castile soap, which, on being burnt,, emits a sulphureous smell, and leaves a purple cinder: here also are large layers of zeolite, stentite and ochre among the rocks of basalt. Not far from the town is the old channel of the Bann, from which the new channel has shifted nearly a mile westward: between both are large drifts of sand blown in from the sea, and covering many acres of excellent land.

SWATTERAGH, a village, in the parish of MAGHERA, barony of LOUGHINSHOLIN, county of LONDONDERRY, and province of ULSTER, $3^1/_2$ miles (N.) from Maghera, on the road to Coleraine, and on the river Clady; containing 204 inhabitants and comprising 50 houses, which, with the exception of one, are small and indifferently built. Here is a small corn-mill, the water from which, after passing under the bridge, divides, and making a curious circuit, forms an extensive island. The country around is barren and badly cultivated, being esteemed the worst part of the Mercers' Company's estate; but a change may be expected, as the leases haye lately fallen into their own hands, In the village is a meeting-house for Presbyterians in connection with the Synod of Ulster, of the third class; also a large and handsome school-house, chiefly supported by the rector and his lady.

TAMLAGHT, a parish, partly in the barony of LOUGHINSHOLIN, county of LONDONDERRY, but chiefly in that of DUNGANNON, county of TYRONE, and province of ULSTER, $3^1/_4$ miles (S. by E.) from Moneymore, on the roads from Toome to Moneymore and from Cookstown to Magherafelt and on the river Ballinderry; containing 2854 inhabitants. The river here forms the southern boundary of the county of Londonderry, and on its south bank, close to its junction with Lough Neagh, stands the village of Coagh, which is described under its own head. According to the Ordnance survey, the parish comprises $4954^3/_4$ statute acres, $2447^3/_4$ acres being in the barony of Dungannon, and 2507 in that of Loughinsholin, all fertile land, except about 300 acres of waste and bog: about two-thirds of the surface are arable and the rest meadow and pasture; there is no mountain land. The inhabitants combine with agriculture the weaving of linen cloth, here carried on to a great extent. There are several quarries of good limestone, much of which is burned for manure. A little westward of the church are seen strata of white limestone, which enter from Seagoe and Marahin, in the county of Down, pass under Lough Neagh, nearly due east and west, and here emerging from their subterranean bed, continue to the neighbourhood of Moneymore, and so on to the Magilligan strand. Here were formerly two extensive bleach-greens in full operation, neither of which is now worked. Tamlaght was created a parish in 1783, by Primate Robinson, by separating 6 townlands from the parish of Ballyclog, in the barony of Dungannon, and $5^1/_2$ from that of Ballinderry, in the barony of Loughinsholin: the Primate also built the church and purchased the glebe, with which he endowed it, together with the tithes of the $11^1/_2$ townlands. The living is a rectory, in the diocese of Armagh, and in the patronage of the Lord-Primate; the tithes amount to £200. The glebe-house was built in 1781, at an expense of £496, of which £92 was a gift from the late Board of First Fruits, the residue having been supplied by the then incumbent. The church is a small plain edifice in the Londonderry portion of the parish. In Coagh is a meeting-house for Presbyterians in connection with the Synod of Ulster, of the second class; within the parish is a meeting-house for those in connection with the Associate Synod; and there are places of worship for Baptists and Wesleyan Methodists, the latter in the market-place of Coagh. The parochial schools at Tamlaght are supported by the rector, who also contributes to the support of a school at Aghery; and there is a school at Coagh, supported by W. L. Cunningham, Esq.; in these schools are about 280 children. There are also three private schools in which about 90 children are educated; and four Sunday schools. On the glebe stands a cromlech called Cloughtogel, composed of a stupendous table stone of granite, weighing 22 tons, raised 13 feet above the ground on six uprights of basalt, and under it there is a chamber or vault of considerable extent: there were formerly several other cromlechs connected with this, extending in a line due east and west, the whole surrounded by a circle of upright stones; but, in the process of fencing and other alterations, all have been removed except the first-named. In a field called the "Honey Mug," not far distant, is a large upright pillar of marble of a singular kind, beneath which is an artificial cave: and there are other remarkable stones in the neighbourhood.

TAMLAGHTARD, or MAGILLIGAN, a parish, in the barony of KENAUGHT, county of LONDONDERRY, and province of ULSTER, $4^1/_2$ miles (N. E.) from Newtown-Limavady; containing 3607 inhabitants. The former of these names, which signifies "the cemetery on the height," is derived from the situation of the ancient burial-ground, which is still used for that purpose; and the latter from a family of that name who were proprietors of a native freehold in it, until it was forfeited to the Crown after the war of 1641. In the year 584, St. Columbkill founded a monastery here, which afterwards acquired great wealth and celebrity, and became so pre-eminent among the other monastic foundations of this saint, that it obtained the title of the "Throne or shrine of St. Columba"; kings, princes, prelates, and other men of eminence, repaired thither to close their days in its recesses, and the remains of many others were brought hither for interment: the most remarkable of the latter were those of St. Aidan, Bishop of Lindisfarne, which were raised by Colman, one of his successors, and buried here in a tomb of hewn stone that still exists near the eastern window of the old parish church; near which is also a fine well, called Tubberaspug-Aidan, "the Well of Bishop Aidan." The monastery was plundered, in 1203, by Diarmit Hua Lochluin, at the head of a party of foreigners, who were afterwards met by the chiefs of the country, and routed in a battle in which their leader was slain. On the dissolution of monasteries, the buildings and lands of this were granted to the see of Derry.

The parish, which contains, according to the Ordnance survey, 13,137 statute acres, of which 28 are under water, is situated at the northern extremity of the county, having Lough Foyle on the west and the Northern ocean on the north; the river Roe forms part of its southern boundary. The soil of the upland portion consists of clay and bog, and in the lowlands a mixture of sand and bog: three-fourths of the surface consist of mountain and barren land. Its border to the sea is a fine strand, extending in its entire length from west to east upwards of 10 miles in an unbroken line, and backed in many parts by a range of basaltic cliffs, or by the sandy tract forming the great rabbit-warren of Magilligan. In the south the land rises into the lofty mountain of Benyevenagh, whose summit, 1260 feet above the level of the sea, and on the southern boundary of the parish, commands a most extended range of prospect, embracing the celebrated island of Iona and others of the western isles of Scotland: on the side towards Lough Foyle it rises with a bold and almost precipitous elevation. The vicinity of the ocean gives the air a mild and genial temperature, which is increased by the shelter afforded by this mountain against the eastern blasts. The vegetable productions of the parish are of great variety. Innes, in his natural history of it, published by the Royal Society of London in 1725, states that "the herb-doctors, who then were in high repute in Ireland, esteemed the breast of Benyevenagh mountain a kind of physic garden, which supplied them with medicines to be found in no other place;" adding that "the abundance and great variety of flowers rendered Magilligan honey so delicious, that the produce of the townland of Tirereevan commanded a higher price than any other brought to the Dublin market." There are few trees except in the demesnes, where they are protected from cattle; although the side of the mountain of Benyevenagh affords excellent sites for their cultivation, which have been taken advantage of only in one tract that is finely planted. Alders and osiers succeed well in the lowlands, and the growth of trees in general, when properly protected and attended to, is very rapid. The insect tribe is very prolific and often extremely troublesome: the grub worm abounds in boggy lands to the great injury of the corn crops; early sowing is the only protection against the ravages of this insect. Fleas often multiply in a wonderful manner on the low lands; no house in which sand is admitted can be kept free from them. Earwigs, which are great enemies to the few stocks of bees now reared here, are very numerous and troublesome in summer: the minnow-worm, used for bait in flounder-fishing, is to be had in abundance on the strand. The fishes most frequently taken are flounders and cockles in the shallows and sands; farther out, herrings and oysters; and in the deep sea, cod, haddock, and turbot. Salmon are some. times taken off the north shore and in the river Roe, where also trout and mullet are caught: eels are scarce. Some eagles breed in the heights of Benyevenagh; kites and hawks abound there, The barnacle frequents the lough strand in countless numbers, forming an article of considerable profit to the residents in the neighbourhood, who send them in quantities to Londonderry and the inland towns. The widgeon, heron, curlew, and seagull also frequent these shores; pigeons are so abundant as to cause much annoyance to the farmers.

This parish is remarkable for one of the largest rabbit-warrens, and, until lately, the most profitable in Ireland. In 1786, it was worth £1500 per annum: the number of skins then sold there annually amounted to three or four thousand dozen; they were purchased by the hatters. The price has now fallen from 15s. to 3s. per dozen; the discovery of cheaper materials for the manufacture has occasioned this depression, and a diminution in quantity has also been caused partly by the havoc committed on the rabbits by rats of the Norway breed, which have increased here to a most pernicious degree, not only as regards the warren, but in the corn fields and about the haggards, and partly by the increased culture of rye on the sandy lands, which by the judicious exertions of the proprietor, Conolly Gage, Esq., are gradually being converted from their previously unproductive state into arable land. The process adopted to produce this beneficial effect is by covering the surface with soil, mud, and shells brought up in boats from the banks of Lough Foyle, near the mouth of the Roe. About 50 years since, foxes were so abundant that the parish vestry gave a reward of 2s. for every skin brought in; they are now extirpated. The last wolf known to exist in Ulster was started about 90 years since upon Benyevenagh, and hunted into the woods near Dungiven, where it was killed. The population is chiefly engaged in agricultural pursuits; most of the low lands produce abundant crops of wheat, oats, flax, and potatoes: the first-named of these, introduced by Mr. Gage in 1830, now forms part of the rotation of most of the more wealthy farmers; but the old and less profitable systems of agriculture are still adhered to by many with much pertinacity: the burning of soil in the lowlands has been in some parts carried to such excess as to threaten the total extinction of the productive qualities of the soil: the quantities of white limestone raised in the mountain districts have tended much to aid the exertions of the landholders in the improvement of their farms. The high lands also afford excellent pasturage for sheep and young cattle, and many tracts heretofore unproductive have been brought into a state of profitable cultivation. In the year 1831, no less than 1131 persons were engaged here in trades, manufactures, and handicraft arts, with whom agriculture was only an occasional occupation. Little flax has been at any time raised, the soil not being well adapted to it, and still less latterly, in consequence of the low prices of yarn: wool is manufactured into a substantial and well-looking cloth worn by the farmers. A kind of matting is manufactured from the bent grass, or basque, planted on the sandy tracts to prevent the drifting of the sands: a ready sale is found for it in the inland parts of the country. The trade of the parish is mostly confined to the disposal of this article and to the sale of wild fowl, rabbits, poultry, and eggs in Londonderry. The principal seats are Belarena, the residence of Conolly Gage, Esq., whose highly embellished demesne, on the banks of the Roe and the side of Benyevenagh, contributes much to the beauty of the scenery of this secluded district; Castlelecky, the romantic seat of the late Averell Lecky, Esq., and still occupied by some of his family; Ballycarton, of B. Lane, Esq.; Ballymaclary, of T. Church, Esq.; Doaghs, of Mr. Jas.Reynolds; and Magilligan Glebe, of the Rev, John Graham, rector of the parish.

The living is a rectory, in the diocese of Derry, and in the patronage of the Bishop: the tithes amount to £425: the glebe-house stands on a glebe of 23 acres, valued together at £36.15.4 per annum: the gross value of the benefice, tithe and glebe included, is £450 per annum. The church, situated near the ancient monastery of Duncrun, is a large and handsome edifice, in the early English style of architecture, built in 1778; it has a steeple, which has been lately furnished with a bell: the Ecclesiastical Commissioners have recently granted £229 towards its repair. The old church, being in a decayed state and in an inconvenient situation, was relinquished as a Protestant place of worship, and was given to the R. C. congregation, with the consent of the late Earl of Bristol, then Bishop of Derry; but being after some time found unsuited to its purpose, a large and commodious chapel was built in the neighbourhood, towards the erection of which Dr. Knox, the late Bishop of Derry, and other Protestant gentlemen, contributed. The churchyard, being the burial-place of most of the old families of every religious persuasion, has been enclosed with a wall and iron-gate by parish assessment. In the R. C. divisions the parish is the head of a union or district, comprising also parts of those of Dunboe and Aghanloo. There is at Margymonaghan a meeting-house for Presbyterians in connection with the Synod of Ulster, of the third class. There are four schools in the parish; three are in connection with the Kildare-place Society, and one under the Board of National Education: the rector pays the teacher's salary in one of these, and Sir Hervey Bruce, Bart, and Conolly Gage, Esq., patronise two of the others. In these schools are about 200 boys and 90 girls: there are also a private school of 13 girls and a Sunday school. Hodgson Gage, Esq., bequeathed £200 and the Rev. John Leathes, rector of the parish, in 1703, £100 to the poor; the interest is paid annually through the Rev. Mr. Graham by Sir Hervey Bruce and Conolly Gage, Esq., two of the seven proprietors of the soil. The remains of an ancient encampment and the foundations of a castle were lately discovered in a strong position about half-way up the mountain; it is supposed to have been one of the fastnesses in which the Irish secured themselves and their property during the wars of Elizabeth and Chas. I. and II. The foundations of the ancient abbey of Duncrun, and near them those of the old church, are the only traces of their former existence: the surrounding scenery is peculiarly grand and romantic. The ruins of Screen abbey, noticed by Colgan in his Trias Thaumaturga, may still be traced on the townland of Craig. The Rev. John Graham is author of the Siege of Derry, Derriana, Annals of Ireland, and various historical, statistical, and poetical publications. Dennis Hampson, the celebrated Irish harper, resided in this parish.

TAMLAGHTFINLAGAN, a parish, in the barony of KENAUGHT, county of LONDONDERRY, and province of ULSTER, $2^1/_4$ miles (W. by S.) from Newtown-Limavady, on the mail coach road to Londonderry; containing 7356 inhabitants. The parish, which comprises, according to the Ordnance Survey, 17,402 statute acres, of which $81^1/_2$ are under water, and one-sixth consists of mountain, derived its name from an abbey founded by St. Columbkill, in 585, in the townland of Tamlaght, over which he placed Fion Lugain, as its first abbot: at what time it ceased to be a monastic institution is now unknown, but it is classed as a parochial church in Pope Nicholas's Taxation in 1291. The lands belong to three proprietors, in the proportions of three-fifths to the freehold estate of Newtown, as granted to Sir Thos. Phillips; two-fifths to the Fishmongers' Company, and one-fifth to the see of Derry; and are in three distinct manors, but no courts are held in any of them. Lough Foyle forms about one-half of the western boundary. In the vale of Myroe, which exhibits some of the most beautiful and romantic scenery in the North of Ireland, and throughout all the northern districts, is some of the very finest and most productive land, bearing heavy crops of all kinds of grain: in the southern portion the land rises into considerable ranges of mountain and bog, by much the greater part of which is capable of cultivation, and from which spring the sources of the numerous streams and rivulets that irrigate and fertilise the lower grounds. In the same portion, near the sources of the Rush and Ballykelly waters, are large deposits of excellent blue limestone, and in several places throughout the parish are indications of calcareous sandstone; but the prevailing rock is of schistose formation. The vicinity of the shores of Lough Foyle affords great facilities for water-carriage, of which full advantage has not yet been taken, though a large sum has been expended, somewhat injudiciously, towards the construction of a landing-place at the mouth of the Ballykelly water. The inhabitants unite to their agricultural employment, which is the chief source of their incomes, the weaving of linen cloth: at the Dog-leap are extensive and very complete mills for bleaching linen, which are at present unemployed: there are several tanyards, in which a considerable quantity of leather is manufactured; three flour-mills, three corn-mills, and a plating-mill or forge for the manufacture of spades, shovels, and other agricultural implements. By much the greater number of the farms in the northern or lowland portion of the parish are well fenced, drained, and cultivated: green crops have latterly been attended to. The old oak woods at Walworth, Roe Park, and the Dog-leap, and the modern plantations in various parts, add much to the richness of aspect that characterises the greater portion of the parish. The same effect is still farther heightened by the numerous seats with which it is studded. The principal are Roe Park, the residence of Edm. C. McNaghten, Esq.; Walworth, of the Rev. G. V. Sampson; Drummond, of A. Sampson, Esq.; Walworth Lodge, of Major Stirling; Finlagan, of the Rev.O. McCausland; Farloe, of John Given, Esq.; Bessbrook, of F. McCausland, Esq.; Rush Hall, of Hugh Boyle, Esq.; Oatlands, of John Church, Esq.; Culmore, of J. Martin, Esq.; and Ardnargle, of Jas, Ogilby, Esq.

The living is a rectory, in the diocese of Derry, and in the patronage of the Bishop: the tithes amount to £1000, The glebe-house is situated half a mile east of the church, upon a glebe of 188 Cunningham acres, which is valued at £235 per annum. The church was built in 1795, near the village of Ballykelly, at the joint expense of the Earl of Bristol, then Bishop of Derry, and of John Beresford, Esq.: it is a small but very handsome edifice, in the early English style, with a large square tower and lofty octagonal spire: the windows are embellished with the armorial bearings of the Irish Society, the Fishmongers' Company, and the Beresford family, in stained glass. In it is a very neat monument to the memory of the Rev. G. V. Sampson, author of the Memoir and Map of Londonderry and of the Statistical Survey of the same county: another belonging to the ancient family of the Hamiltons, and a third, of modern and elegant execution, to a junior branch of the Beresford family. A grant of £124 for its repair has been lately made by the Ecclesiastical Commissioners. In the R. C. divisions the parish forms part of the union or district of Newtown-Limavady: the chapel is situated at Oghill, near Ballykelly; in which village there is a large meeting-house for Presbyterians in connection with the Synod of Ulster, of the first class, built by the Fishmongers' company in 1827, in the Grecian style: at Largy and Myroe there are also meeting-houses of Presbyterians in connection with the Synod of Ulster. Handsome male and female schools, with residences for the teachers, have been erected by the same company, and are conducted under its patronage on the most im proved system: the parochial male and female schools, at Tamlaght, were built by the rector in 1832, and are supported by him: two others in the parish were built and are supported by the Fishmongers' company; one, at Glasvey, is in connection with the London Hibernian Society; and there are schools at Ballinarig, Dromore, Largy, Crindale, Carraghmenagh, and Lomond, in connection with the Kildare-place Society. These schools afford instruction to about 500 children: there are also 10 private schools, in which are about 300 boys and 230 girls; and a large and handsome dispensary at Ballykelly. The remains of Walworth castle, erected by the Fishmongers' company, in 1619, shew it to have been a large and spacious edifice, defended by a bawn and flankers, three of which are still in a tolerable state of preservation. Closely adjoining are the remains of a church, built by the Hamilton family in 1629. The ruins of the old parish church, which was destroyed in the war of 1641, occupy the site of the ancient abbey. There are numerous raths, of which that called Daisy Hill, in Roe park, and another near it, called Rough Fort, are the most remarkable.

TAMLAGHTOCRILLY, a parish, partly in the barony of COLERAINE, but chiefly in that of LOUGHINSHOLIN, county of LONDONDERRY, and province of ULSTER, 3 miles (N. W.) from Portglenone, on the river Bann; containing 10,070 inhabitants, The parish comprises, according to the Ordnance survey, 16,839 statute acres, the general quality of which is light and cold, with a good deal of moss or bog, being chiefly composed of decomposed basalt, in some places there are escars of sand and rubble, and in others the bare rocks of basalt rise above the land; in some districts large detached masses of basalt are scattered in great confusion, so that not more than three-fourths of the land can be said to be available for tillage, the system of which is rapidly improving; good crops of corn, flax, and potatoes are produced, and are likely to be still further augmented by reason of the increasing application of lime as manure. There are considerable tracts of turbary in various parts of the parish, in which large trunks of oak and fir are imbedded. Five townlands of the parish belong to the Mercers' Company, and are in the manor of Kilrea; seven belong to the see of Derry, and are in the manor of Maghera, as are also the several glebes. There are three inconsiderable villages, situated on the western side of the river Bann, namely, Tamlaght, Glenone, and Innisrush. The gentlemen's seats are Innisrush, the residence of Hercules Ellis, Esq.; Glenburn, of J. Courtenay, Esq.; Termoneeny glebe-house, of the Rev. C. S. Foster; Herveyhill, of the Rev. W. Napper, the incumbent; and Glenone, of the Rev. M. Bloxham, curate of the chapel of ease.

The living is a rectory and perpetual cure, in the diocese of Derry, the former in the patronage of the Bishop, and the latter in that of the incumbent: the tithes amount to £435.19, payable to the rector; the glebe comprises 564 acres, valued at £522.2 per annum. The income of the perpetual curate arises from £92.6.2, payable by the rector, and £4.7.6, the rent of two houses; he has also a glebe.house, and a glebe of 15 acres, valued at £18.15 per annum. The peculiarity of the glebes is worthy of notice: Lisgorgan belongs to the rector of Desertmartin, 6 miles distant; Ballymacpeake belongs to the rector of Maghera and Termoneeny, upon which stands the glebe-house of the latter; Killymuck belongs to the rector of Kilrea; and Moneystaghan to the rector of Ballyscullion, besides the glebe of the rector of Tamlaght and the curate of Tyanee chapelry. The church is in the village of Tamlaght: it was rebuilt in 1815 by aid of a loan of £1000 from the late Board of First Fruits. The chapel at Tyanee is a small neat edifice, in the early English style, built at the private expense of the late Earl of Bristol, Bishop of Derry, and to the repairs of which the Ecclesiastical Commissioners have recently granted £150. In the R. C. divisions the parish is part of the union or district of Desertoghill; it contains two chapels, a small one at Greenlough, and a larger one at Drumagarner, both plain buildings. At Boveedy is a meeting-house for Presbyterians in connection with the Seceding Synod, of the second class; one lately erected in the village of Tamlaght in connection with the Synod of Ulster; and one at Drumbolg for Covenanters. About 1200 children are educated in seventeen public schools, of which the parochial school on the glebe is supported by the rector; those at Lismoyle and Lisnagrott are partly supported by the Mercers' Company; one at Gortmacrane is aided by R. Heyland, Esq; those at Tyanee and Greenlough are under the National Board, and twelve are in connection with the London Hibernian Society. There are also two private schools, in which are about 70 children; and seven Sunday schools. The Rev. Ralph Mansfield, about 80 years since, bequeathed £100 to the poor of the parish, of which only £50 remains, the interest of which is distributed twice a year. There are some remains of ancient fortifications; and at Tivaconway is a Druidical circle. On a rising ground above the village is the sepulchral cave, or Tamlachta, from which the parish derives its name.

TEMPLEMORE, a parish, in the North-west liberties of the city of LONDONDERRY, county of LONDONDERRY, and province of ULSTER; containing, with the city of Londonderry, 19,620 inhabitants, of which number, 10,130 are in the city. This parish, also called Templederry, and more anciently Derry, or Derry Columbkille, derives its name Templemore, "the Great Church," from the cathedral of Derry, to which that name had been applied, in a popular acceptation, to distinguish it from the smaller churches in its immediate vicinity, and, after the cathedral had been used as the parish church, the name was extended to the parish. The most ancient name of the district in which it was situated was Moy-Iha, "the Plain of Ith," uncle of Milesius, whose sons led into Ireland the celebrated colony that bore his name. This district, which comprehended the tract between Loughs Foyle and Swilly, and extended as far south as the river Fin, was afterwards divided between Owen and Enda, the two sons of Nial of the Nine Hostages, under the names of Inis-Owen, "Owen's Island," and Tir-Enda, "Enda's Territory." Previously to the 12th century, Moy-Iha was occupied by a branch of the Kinel-Owen, called Clan-Conor, of which the most distinguished families were those of O'Cathan, O'Cairellan, O'Murry, O'Kennedy, O'Corran, O'Quin, and O'Dugan, most of whom having crossed the Foyle into Derry, their places here were occupied by the Kinel-Moen, another branch of the Kinel-Owen, of whom the O'Gormlys and O'Loonys were chiefs: these in turn were driven across the Foyle by the Kinel-Connell in the 15th century. From inquisitions taken in the reign of Jas. I. it appears that about half the parish was then considered to belong to Inishowen, or O'Dogherty's country; that Sir John O'Dogherty had several townlands now in Templemore, which were included in a regrant of Inishowen made to him on a surrender in the 30th of Elizabeth: he forfeited this property in 1599 by rebellion, but it was regranted to his son, Sir Cahir O'Dogherty, with the exception of some townlands reserved for the fort of Culmore. In 1608, Sir Cahir also rebelled, in consequence of which all his estates were granted to Arthur, Lord Chichester, of Belfast, who leased them to Sir Faithful Fortescue, Arthur Ussher, Tristram Beresford, and Chas. Pointz. Of the 24 townlands into which the parish is now divided, one, on which is the fort of Culmore, belongs to the King; one to Capt. Hart; one and a part to the Bishop of Derry in right of his see; two to Lord Templemore, a branch of the Chichester family; three to the Marquess of Donegal, the head of the same family; and fifteen and a part to the Irish Society. Until the year 1809 the parish extended into the county of Donegal. and included the three parishes of Burt, Inch, and Muff, which were then severed from it and erected into perpetual euracies.

The parish, as at present constituted, contains 12,611 statute acres, according to the Ordnance survey, valued at £8363, without the buildings on it, and with these, at £26,716, per ann.: it is bounded by the river and Lough Foyle on the east, and by the county of Donegal on every other side, extending about eight miles in length from north-east to south-west, and less than three in its greatest breadth in the contrary direction. The surface is beautifully undulating, presenting a succession of hills, mostly cultivated or under pasture. A wide valley, extending from the Foyle at Pennyburn, separates the hills into two groups. Of these the southern is the most prominent, rising at its southern extremity into Holywell hill, 860 feet above the sea; the highest point of the northern group, in Elaghmore, is not more than 354 feet. The lake of Ballyarnet, occupying portions of the three townlands of Ballyarnet, Ballynashallog, and Ballynagard, contains only 3a. 3r. 27p.;

its height above the sea is about 100 feet. Except the Foyle, which is navigable for small craft to Castlefin, there is no other body of water entitled to the name of river; the numerous small streams which irrigate the parish, flow eastward into the main river or lough, with the exception of one, which, passing by Coshquin, terminates in Lough Swilly. Springs are numerous; not fewer than eight occur within a tract of about 20 acres, in Springhill and Creggan; several of them are slightly chalybeate. The coast of Lough Foyle, where it borders the parish, is low, and destitute of any striking characteristic features. It is the general opinion of the intelligent farmers here that a marked amelioration has taken place in the climate; the seasons both of seed time and harvest have advanced considerably: the extended cultivation of wheat, and the increasing number of quails are further proofs of it. The soil in the higher grounds is occasionally, though rarely, stony, sandy, and meagre; but in by far the greater portion of the parish it is a light productive clay or loam, which in the very low grounds becomes stiffer, though never to an injurious extent. The subsoil is more generally a coating of gravel resting on the rock than the rock itself; and is often in a very indurated state, owing to the abundance of iron proceeding from the decomposition of the schistose rocks: it is then called "till," and more generally "red till," from its prevailing colour, and is considered to be injurious to vegetation.

The geological structure of the parish is simple; the great mass of the primary schistose rocks which occupies much of the western portion of the county, spreads over its whole surface, with the exception of a considerable patch of detritus at Culmore in the north-east, which probably conceals a part of the new red sandstone, that rock being visible at the northern extremity of the parish, and also with the exception of several very limited deposits of mud and clay which skirt the Foyle on the south-east, Mica slate, passing into quartz slate, is the prevailing rock, occupying at least two-thirds of its substance. Limestone is found only in small quantities at its southern extremity, where the quarries have been abandoned; and greenstone, of a dense, close-grained and homogeneous character, at Conn's Hill, where the opening of the quarry is, strictly speaking, without the bounds. The schistose rocks are in the harder varieties too coarse, and in the softer not sufficiently cohesive, for being used as roofing slates; but they are much employed in building: plenty of clay for bricks is to be had; but the manufacture has been relinquished on account of the scarcity of fuel. The bogs are of great local importance, though they are now only the relics of a more extensive tract, which has been nearly exhausted by continued use: portions are occasionally reclaimed, and when the peat has been entirely cut away, the subsoil is easily brought into cultivation: large trunks and roots of trees have been raised from them. The natural meadows are extensive, particularly on the sides of some of the bogs: the mountain pasture is generally poor. Wheat, which formerly was considered unsuitable to the climate and soil, is now in much estimation: green crops are occasionally adopted. Forced or sown meadows are by no means general; when prepared for cutting the first year, they are sown with perennial rye-grass and red clover; when for grazing, white grass and white clover are sown. There are several nurseries. Most of the timber in the parish appears to have been planted more for ornament than profit: the most common trees along the Foyle are beech, elm, sycamore, and ash: a small patch of natural wood is to be seen at Ballynagalliagh. Manures are easily attainable, being partly stable dung, partly lime, drawn from the city; and partly a compost of bog earth, dung, lime, and shells; the shells are procured at a bank called Shell Island, in Lough Foyle: kelp is occasionally used.

The manufactures carried on in the rural parts of the parish are chiefly those arising directly from agricultural produce. The mill at Pennyburn ground 1,513,200 lbs. of wheat, and 1,164,800 of oats, in the year 1834; three others ground an aggregate of 543,000 lbs. of oatmeal: seven flax-mills worked up 4250 cwt. of flax and 1059 cwt. of tow: a brewery made 5200 barrels of beer, and two distilleries 208,800 gallons of spirits: two tanneries converted 5300 hides into leather: there were two limekilns, 1 brick-kiln, 2 rope-walks, 80 linen looms, 28 cotton looms, and 1 woollen loom at work: all these totals are the results of returns collected in that year, and are exclusive of the manufactures of the city, to which the commerce of the district is wholly confined: the salmon fishery gives employment to 232 persons. The jurisdiction of the corporation of Londonderry extends over the whole parish, but in Culmore only by sufferance, that townland being the exclusive property of the Crown, and under the control of the governor of the fort. The condition of the peasantry in the low lands is comfortable, the dwellings neat, and orchards and kitchen gardens are frequently to be seen, attached to well-fenced farms of considerable extent and in good condition. In the mountain lands, which are much frequented on account of free turbary being granted with their cabins, the cottiers are very poor, and several of the farm-houses are nearly as wretched as the huts of the labourers. Three main roads from Londonderry to Greencastle, Lifford, and Letterkenny, intersect the parish: they are not kept in good order, and would admit of much improvement as to the line of direction: the cross roads and bye-roads are sufficiently numerous: there is a ferry across the mouth of the Foyle at Culmore, below the fort. It has long been contemplated to connect Loughs Foyle and Swilly by a canal; but though the distance be short, and the district through which the line would pass well adapted for it, a difficulty presents itself in the Swilly at the Burnfoot, which is separated from the Foyle by a neck of land only three miles broad, rising and falling at spring tides 18 feet, which is twice as much as at Londonderry, and therefore the surfaces of the loughs at high water stand at different levels, The principal seats are The Farm, the property of Sir R. A. Ferguson, Bart.; Boom Hall, the property of the Earl of Caledon, and the residence of the Bishop of Derry; Brook Hall, remarkable for the beauty of its grounds, the property and residence of the Rt. Hon. Sir G. F. Hill, Bart.; Thorn Hill, of Capt. Simeon; Ballinagard, of Capt. Hart; Belmont, lately the residence of W. Miller, Esq., deceased; Troy or Troyvale Cottage, of Chas. O'Doherty, Esq.; Foyle Hill, of W. Holland, Esq.; Milton Lodge, of Capt. H. Lecky; Ballougry, of Capt. McNeil; Green Raw House, of W. K. McClintock, Esq.; Mullennan, of R. Harvey, Esq.; Culmore Point, of A. McCausland, Esq.; Bellevue, of Hans Riddall, Esq.; Pennyburn, of A. Bond, Esq.; and Troy House, of J. Murray, Esq. The bishop's demesne, though it is not his residence, may be included under this head. Casina, erected by the late Earl of Bristol, is situated in the suburbs of the city, close to the bishop's garden, commanding a fine view of the river and the scenery on its opposite bank; although irregularly built, it presents a handsome front, and the principal apartment is decorated with paintings in chiaro-oscuro.

The living is a rectory, united by patent of Jas. I. to the rectories of Faughanvale and Clondermott, forming together the corps of the deanery of Derry, in the patronage of the Crown: the tithes amount to £1607.0.1. The deanery-house was rebuilt in 1834, at an expense of £3330, provided out of the funds of the present incumbent, the whole of which will be chargeable on his successor: the glebe, containing 3 acres, is valued at £9 per ann.; the gross value of the benefice, tithe and glebe inclusive, amounts to £3224.7.11$^1/_2$. The cathedral of Londonderry is used as the parish church, and there are two other churches in the parish, the particulars of all which are given in the account of that city, which see. The old church was situated in the northern part of the parish, near Culmore fort. The R. C. parish is co-extensive with that of the Established Church; it is also the head of the diocese and the mensal of the Bishop. Besides the schools described in the article on the city, there is one at Ballougry, to which the Irish Society gives an annual grant of £30; also four private schools, in all of which, including the city schools, there are about 500 boys and 450 girls; there are also 9 Sunday schools. In Ballinagard demesne, on the western bank of the Foyle, is a rath measuring 73 yards by 60; it is surrounded by a fosse and parapet, and is now covered with trees. In Ballymagrorty there is a small cromlech, the table stone of which is 4 feet by 3; and on the summit of Holywell Hill are the remains of a cairn, about 40 feet in diameter, in the centre of which is a small pit, 3 feet square and 5 deep; the rock of the mountain forms its bottom, and it is called the Holy well, from a small pool of rain water being found in it, which is supposed to possess healing virtues. There are also two cairns of modern construction; one is called "Jenny's Cairn," from having been the spot where a young woman was murdered under very atrocious circumstances; the other, in the bed of a rivulet, is called the "Priest's Burn," from a tradition that a priest was killed on the spot. The old church of Killea, in the townland of the same name, was one of the five chapels of ease to the mother church; its foundations still remain in a cemetery surrounded by an old stone wall. The church of Culmore, though a ruin, is of no great antiquity, having been built a short time before the war of 1688 and burnt by James's army, since which it has never been repaired: it was cruciform and consisted of a nave and transept; the walls are still entire, except at the western end. The castle of Aileagh or Elagh, the property of W. McCorkell, Esq., now a small ruin, stands on a commanding eminence on the verge of the parish, about two miles from the more ancient fortress of the same name in the county of Donegal, formerly a royal castle. The forts of Culmore and Donnalong were erected by the English in the reign of Elizabeth or Jas. I., to secure their newly acquired possession of Derry: the former, situated on a projecting point on the western bank of the Foyle, where it opens into the lough, was a small triangular fort with a bastion at each corner, and a square tower at the point next the river: though not occupied as a military station for upwards of a hundred years, a governor is still appointed to it. General Hart, the late governor, substantially repaired the tower, but the outworks are now nearly obliterated. Donnalong, or Donolonge, which was a place of more importance, was built on the eastern bank of the Foyle, in the parish of Donagheady; there are no remains. Templemore gives the title of an English baron to a branch of the Chichester family.

TERMONEENY, a parish, in the barony of LOUGHINSHOLIN, county of LONDONDERRY, and province of ULSTER, near the post-town of Mayhera; containing 2551 inhabitants. This parish, which is bounded on the north by the river Moyola, comprises, according to the Ordnance survey, 4773 statute acres, of which about 40 acres are in plantations, and 1000 bog; the remainder is principally arable, with a moderate proportion of pasture. The land varies greatly in quality; around the old church of Mullach it is extremely fertile, producing abundant crops; but in the neighbourhood of Knockleighrim, high, rocky, and unproductive. The substratum is principally basalt, and many of the rocks of that formation rise abruptly above the surface, especially Knockleighrim, a bold and almost detached rock of basalt, which rises to a considerable height and is difficult of access, except on the east, to which its whole surface inclines; it has some indications of the columnar formation, and is a conspicuous object from every part of the barony. The principal seats are Clover Hill, the residence of R. Forrester, Esq.; and Brough, of D. Cunningham, Esq.; there are also many good houses in the parish. The inhabitants are partly engaged in weaving linen, and also calico for the Belfast manufacturers; there is a large bleach-green at Brough, where about 8000 pieces of linen are bleached and finished annually. Four townlands of the parish belong to the see of Derry, and are in the manor of Maghera; the remaining five belong to the Vintners' Company, of London, and are in the manor of Bellaghy. The living is a rectory, in the diocese of Derry, and in the patronage of the Bishop: the tithes amount to £220. The glebe-house was built in 1822, at an expense of £433.6.11, defrayed by the then incumbent; the glebe comprises 290 acres, valued at £158 per annum. The church was erected in 1801, on which occasion the late Board of First Fruits contributed a gift of £554 British. In the R. C. divisions the parish is partly in the union of Maghera, and partly a district of itself: there is a chapel at Lammy, without its limits. A place of worship is alternately occupied on Sundays by Covenanters and Seceders. About 200 children are taught in two public schools, of which the parochial school is partly supported by the rector; and there is a private school, in which are about 90 children.

TUBBERMORE, or TOBARMORE, a post-town, in the parish of KILCRONAGHAN, barony of LOUGHINSHOLIN, county of LONDONDERRY, and province of ULSTER, 18 miles (S.) from Coleraine, on the road to Armagh, and 98 (N. by W.) from Dublin; containing 679 inhabitants. It is situated on the river Moyola, and comprises 132 small thatched houses, in one wide irregular street. Fairs are held on Jan. 17th, Feb. 13th, March 28th, May 31st, July 5th, Aug. 12th, and Oct. 19th. Here are chapels for the Independents and Pres-byterians. The ancient fountain, or Tober-mor, which gave name to the town, and is now dry, was once sufficiently powerful to supply a mill close by, now in ruins.

WOODS-CHAPEL, or CHAPEL-IN-THE-WOODS, a district parish, in the barony of LOUGHINSHOLIN, county of LONDONDERRY, and province of ULSTER, $2^1/_2$ miles (E.) from Magherafelt, on the road from Belfast to Londonderry, by Toome bridge; containing 7471 inhabitants. Prior to the Reformation this district was a parish, called in ecclesiastical records the parish of Ross-Aglish, with a church, glebe, and glebe-house, as appears by the return made to Hen. VIII. in 1540. It was granted by Queen Elizabeth, together with Ardtrea and Kiltinny, now called Upper Aglish, to the Provost and Fellows of Trinity College, Dublin, when the three were united into a single parish under the name of Ardtrea, and so continued until 1823, when this district was severed from it, and constituted a perpetual curacy, according to the ecclesiastical, and a distinct parish according to the civil, arrangements. The district, which consists of 15 townlands taken from the parish of Ardtrea, extends from near Moneymore, along the shore of Lough Neagh, by Ballyronan, Castledawson, and Toome, to the neighbourhood of Bellaghy, on the shore of Lough Beg; comprising an extent of $10,440^1/_2$ statute acres. The soil in general is light, with an occasional intermixture of rich land; that in the neighbourhood of Ballyronan is very fertile and highly cultivated, well fenced and planted. The crops most usually raised are wheat, oats, barley, potatoes, turnips, and flax; mangel-wurzel, clover, and vetches sometimes form part of the rotation. In the neighbourhood of Toome, between the lakes and towards Bellaghy, it consists altogether of low marshy meadow, mostly covered with water during winter, but in summer yielding excellent and abundant pasturage. The Lough Neagh Improvement Company proposes to draw off the surplus waters of that lake through this tract, and thus not only to effect the thorough drainage of this extensive tract of rich land, but, by reducing the waters of Lough Neagh to their summer level, to reclaim many thousand acres now under water, and consequently unprofitable during a great portion of the year. The soil rests mostly on a substratum of basalt, which shews itself frequently above the surface in knolls of rock, much broken and decomposed; some veins of the coal formation from Castledawson appear near Warwick Lodge, and a few scattered fragments of the limestone formation from Springhill: but in neither case does the appearance of the seams hold out encouragement for an expenditure of capital to work them. The proposed line of railway from Armagh to Coleraine is intended to pass through the parish, but no progress has yet been made towards its accomplishment beyond the marking out of the line. Close to the shore of Lough Neagh is the village of Ballyronan, which see. The houses of the farmers, though generally small, are well built, comfortably furnished, and for the most part surrounded with small orchards and gardens. The plantations about Lakeview, the seat of D. Gaussen, Esq., being arranged partly in hedgerows and partly in clumps or groves, give the neighbourhood a lively and prosperous appearance. Warwick Lodge is the residence of W. Bell, Esq.; Lisnamorrow, of T. Dawson, Esq.; and Ballyneil House, of the Rev. L. Dowdall, a lineal descendant of the celebrated Geo. Dowdall, Archbishop of Armagh, whose opposition to the orders of Hen. VIII. respecting the changes to the liturgy gave rise to the long-continued controversy between the Archbishops of Armagh and Dublin, as to the right of each to the primacy of the Church of Ireland.

The living is a perpetual curacy, in the diocese of Armagh, and in the patronage of the Rector of Ardtrea: the income of the perpetual curate amounts to £89.4.$7^1/_2$, of which £69.4.$7^1/_2$ is payable by the rector of Ardtrea, and £20 from the augmentation fund of the Ecclesiastical Commissioners: the glebes appear to have been comprised in the grant by Jas. I. to the London Society, or they have since merged into the estate of the Salters' Company, which has an extensive and valuable property there. The church, at Lisnamorrow, ten miles distant from the mother church, and between two and three east of Magherafelt, was built in 1730, and enlarged in 1825, at an expense of £415 British, by a loan from the late Board of First Fruits: the Ecclesiastical Commissioners have lately granted £183 for its repair. The ruins of the old church still remain; and its yard is used as a burial-ground. In the R. C. divisions the parish forms part of the union or district of Moneymore, and has a chapel, a small plain edifice, at Derrygarve. At Ballymaguigan, or Gracefeld, there is a small Moravian settlement, with a chapel, burial-ground, and school attached to it. The male and female parochial schools, at Lisnamorrow, close to the churchyard, are chiefly supported by the rector; one at Ballyronan is supported by the Marquess of Londonderry, Sir R. Bateson, Bart., and D. Gaussen, Esq.; and there are others at Aughrim, Anahorish, Ballymuldey, Ballymuldeymore, Creagh Moyola, and Derrygarve, in connection with different societies: these schools afford instruction to 320 boys and 250 girls, and there are also five Sunday schools.

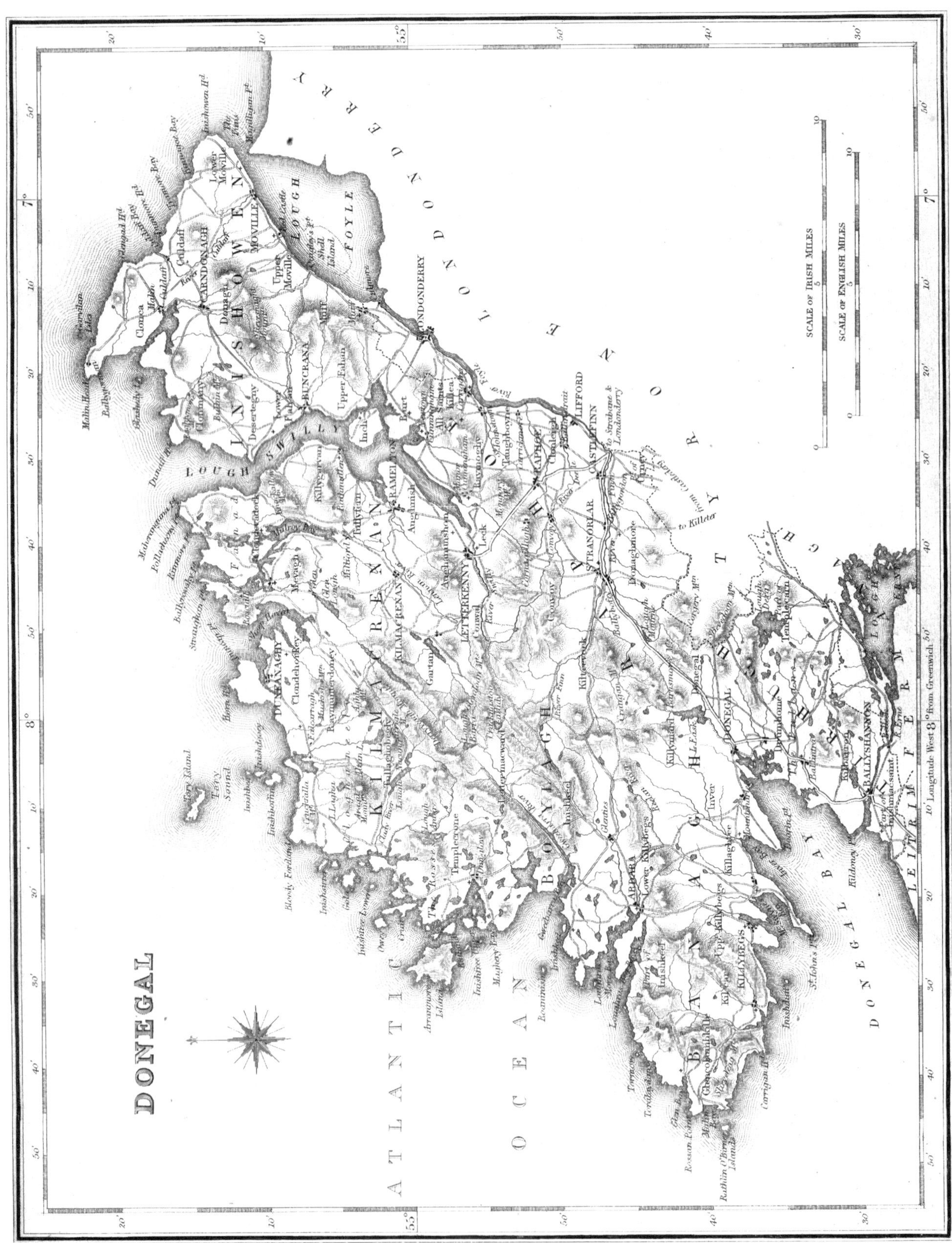

Donegal. Drawn by R.Creighton and engraved by I.Dower. From Lewis's Atlas *(London, 1837.*

COUNTY DONEGAL

A

TOPOGRAPHICAL DICTIONARY

DONEGAL (County of), a maritime county of the province of ULSTER, bounded on the east and south-east by the counties of Londonderry, Tyrone, and Fermanagh, from the first-named of which it is separated by Lough Foyle; on the south, by the northern extremity of the county of Leitrim and by Donegal bay, and on the west and north by the Atlantic. It extends from 54° 28′ to 55° 20′ (N. Lat.), and from 6° 48′ to 8° 40′ (W. Lon.); comprising, according to the Ordnance survey, a surface of 1,165,107 statute acres, of which 520,736 are cultivated land, and 644,371 unimproved mountain and bog. The population, in 1821, was 248,270, and in 1831, 291,104.

In the time of Ptolemy it was inhabited by the Vennicnii and the Rhobogdii, the latter of whom also occupied part of the county of Londonderry, The Promontorium Vennicnium of this geographer appears to have been Ram's Head or Horn Head, near Dunfanaghy; and the Promontorium Rhobogdium, Malin Head, the most northern point of the +peninsula of Innisoen or Ennishowen. The county afterwards formed the northern part of the district of Eircael or Eargal, which extended into the county of Fermanagh, and was known for several centuries as the country of the ancient and powerful sept of the O'Donells, descended, according to the Irish writers, from Conall Golban, son of Neil of the Nine Hostages, monarch of Ireland, who granted to his son the region now forming the county of Donegal. Hence it acquired the name of Tyr-Conall, modernised into Tyrconnel or Tirconnel, "the land of Conall," which it retained till the reign of Jas. I. The family was afterwards called Kinel Conall, or the descendants or tribe of Conall. Fergus Ceanfadda, the son of the founder, had a numerous progeny, among whom were Sedna, ancestor of the O'Donells, and Felin, father of St. Cohunt. Cinfaeladh, fourth in descent from Ceanfadda, had three sons, one of whom was Muldoon, the more immediate ancestor of the O'Donells; and another, Fiamhan, from whom the O'Dohertys, lords of Innisoen, derive their descent. A second Cinfaeladh, eighth in descent from Fergus Ceanfadda, was father of Dalagh, from whom the O'Donells are sometimes styled by the Irish annalists Siol na Dallagh, the sept of Daly, or the O'Dalys. Enoghaine, his eldest son, was father of Donell, from whom the ruling family took the surname it has borne ever since. His great grandson, Cathban, chief' of the sept in the reign of Brian Boroimhe, first assumed the name of O'Donell as chief, which was adopted by all his subjects and followers. Besides the O'Dohertys, the septs of O'Boyle, Mac Sweeney, and several others were subordinate to the O'Donells of Tyrconnel.

The chieftaincy of Nial Garbh, who succeeded his father Turlogh an Fhiona in 1422, was the commencement of a sanguinary era of internal discord aggravated by external warfare. This chieftain, after having endured much opposition from his brother Neachtan, and maintained continual hostilities with the English, by whom he was at length taken prisoner, died in captivity. The first effort of importance made by the English to subjugate this territory commenced by their seizure of the convent of Donegal and a castle of the O'Boyles, giving them a temporary command over the adjacent territory, from all which they were quickly expelled by the celebrated Hugh Roe, or Red Hugh, O'Donell, who succeeded to the chieftaincy in 1592. This powerful toparch, at an early period of his government, marched into Tir Owen against Tirlogh Luineagh O'Neil, chief of the sept of the same name and a partizan of the English, whom O'Donell, although he had recently entered into terms of amity with the Lord-Justice of Ireland, expelled from his principality in 1593, forced him to resign the title of O'Neil in favour of Hugh, Earl of Tyrone, and afterwards compelled the whole province of Ulster to acknowledge his superiority and pay him tribute. He then sent an embassy to the king of Spain to aid him in the total expulsion of the English, and having obtained a reinforcement of mercenaries from Scotland, carried on a successful war far beyond the limits of his own territory.

The English government, after various disasters, particularly the defeat of Sir Conyers Clifford in the Curlew mountains, resolved to transfer the seat of war into O'Donell's country, for which purpose a large fleet, having on board a force of six thousand well-appointed troops, was sent from Dublin under the command of Sir Henry Docwra. Having landed in Ennishowen in the summer of 1600, they possessed themselves of the forts of Culmore, Dunnalong, and Derry. Each of these fortresses was immediately invested by O'Donell, who, while his troops maintained the blockade, made two expeditions into Connaught and Munster. During his absence, his brother-in-law, Nial O'Donell, and his brothers were prevailed upon to join the English, and to give them possession of Lifford, which they fortified. Here also they were hemmed in by the Irish, as likewise at the monastery of Donegal, which they had afterwards gained. The landing of the Spaniards in the south caused a total suspension of arms in Ulster, and the subsequent defeat of the invaders at Kinsale compelled O'Donell to proceed to Spain in quest of further suecours, where he died in September, 1602, being the last chief of the sept universally acknowledged as the O'Donell.

On the attainder in 1612 of Rory O'Donell. to whom Jas. I. had given the title of Earl of Tyrconnell and the greater part of the family possessions, the district, which had been erected into a county called Donegal, by Sir John Perrot, in 1584, was included by that king in his plan for the plantation of Ulster. By the survey then taken, the whole county was found to contain 110,700 acres of cultivable, or, as it was styled, profitable land. Of these, the termon lands, containing 9160 acres, were assigned to the bishoprick of Raphoe, to which they had previously belonged; 3680 acres were allotted for the bishop's mensal lands; 6600 acres for glebe to the incumbents of the 87 parishes into which the county was to be divided; 9224 acres of monastery lands to the college of Dublin; 300 acres to Culmore fort; 1000 acres to Ballyshannon, and 1024 acres, named the Inch, to Sir Ralph Bingley. The remainder, amounting to 79,074 acres, were to be divided among the settlers or undertakers, as they were called, in 62 portions, 40 of 1000 acres, 13 of 1500, and 9 of 2000 each, with a certain portion of wood, bog, and mountain, to constitute a parish. Of these portions, 38 were to be granted to English and Scotch undertakers, 9 to servitors, and 15 to natives. The 2204 acres still undisposed of were to be given to corporate towns to be erected and entitled to send burgesses to parliament, 800 to Derry, and 200 each to Killybegs, Donegal, and Rath: Lifford had 500 acres previously assigned to it. The residue of 604 acres was to be equally allotted to free schools at Derry and Donegal. All fisheries were reserved to the Crown. The distributive portions thus assigned do not corres pond with the general total above stated, and the proposed provisions both as to distribution and regulation were far from being rigidly observed in practice.

The county is chiefly in the diocese of Raphoe, but parts of it extend into those of Derry and Clogher. For purposes of civil jurisdiction it is divided into the baronies of Raphoe, Kilmacrenan, Ennishowen, Tyrhugh, Bannagh and Boylagh. It contains the disfranchised borough, sea-port and market-towns of Ballyshannon, Donegal, and Killybegs; the disfranchised borough and market-town of Lifford; the disfranchised borough of St. Johnstown; the market and post-towns of Letterkenny, Ramelton, Raphoe, Carn, Stranorlar, Buncran a, and Moville Upper; the post-towns of Castlefin, Dunfanaghy, Ardara, Dungloe, and Narin, and several other small towns and villages, of which Bundoran, Mount-Charles, and Rathmullen have each a penny post. Prior to the union the county sent 12 members to parliament; two for the county at large, and two for each of the above-named boroughs, but, subsequently, it has been represented by the two county members only, who are elected at Lifford. The number of voters registered in January, 1836, was 1745; of whom 181 were free-holders of £50, 169 of £20, and 1159 of £10 per ann.; 33 clergymen of £50, and 1 of £20, being the free-holds of their respective benefices; I rent-charger of £50, and 10 of £20; and 48 leaseholders of £20, and 143 of £10. It is included in the north-western circuit. Lifford, where the county gaol and court-house are situated, is the assize town; quarter sessions are held four times in the year at Donegal, twice at Letterkenny, and once at Lifford and Buncrana. There are bridewells at Letterkenny and Donegal, and session-houses at each of those places and at Buncrana. The local government is vested in a lieutenant, 19 deputy-lieutenants, and 66 other magistrates, with the usual county officers. The number of persons charged with criminal offences and committed, in 1835, was 472, and of civil bill commitments, 49. There are 29 constabulary police stations, having a force of one stipendiary magistrate 7 chief and 30 subordinate constables and 116 men, with nine horses, the expense of whose maintenance is defrayed by equal Grand Jury presentments and by Government. The district lunatic asylum is in Londonderry and the county infirmary at Lifford. There are dispensaries at Lifford, Ballintra, Raphoe, Taughboyne, Killybegs, Moville, Clonmany, Killygarvan, Kilmacrenan, Kilcar, Letterkenny, Donegal, Muff, Culdaff, Stranorlar, Rutland, Donagh, Killygorden, Dunkaneely, Ramelton, Buncrana, Careygart, Ballyshannon, Dunfanaghy, and Mount-Charles, maintained by voluntary subscriptions and Grand Jury presentments in equal proportions. The amount of Grand Jury presentments for 1835 was £27,609. 1. 4., of which £163.10, was for the public roads of the county at large; £14,799.2.4 for the public roads, being the baronial charge; £5301.18.11½ for public buildings and charities, officers' salaries, &c.; £3480.10.3 for police; and £3863.19.9½ in repayment of a loan advanced by Government. In the military arrangements the county is in the northern district. There are infantry barracks at Lifford and Ballyshannon, and artillery forts at Greencastle, Inch island, Rutland island, and at several places along the shores of Lough Swilly, each of which, except Greencastle, is garrisoned by a single gunner.

Donegal is the most western of the three northern counties of Ireland. The surface, which is much varied, may be arranged into two great divisions of mountain and champaign. The latter, which is subdivided into two portions by the Barnesmore mountains, comprises the barony of Raphoe and the maritime parts of that of Tyrhugh, round Ballyshannon and Donegal. The mountain region, comprehending all the remainder of' the county, is interspersed with fertile valleys and tracts of good land, especially in the baronies of Kilmacrenan and Ennishowen, The most elevated mountains are Errigal, which, according to the Ordnance survey, rises 2463 feet above the level of the sea; Blue Stack, 2213 feet; Dooish West, 2143; Slieve Snaght, 2019; Silver Hill, 1967; Slieve League, 1964; and Aghla, 1958. There are also five others which have an elevation of more than 1500 feet, and twelve more exceeding 1000 feet in height. The most improved and populous district is that on the borders of the rivers Fin and Swilly, and the eastern confines near Lifford. In the western champaign district, between Ballintra and Ballyshannon, the surface is in many places moory, heathy and rocky, particularly near the south-east, where at a distance of three or four miles from the sea it rises into a tract of mountains ten or twelve miles broad, which sweeps round by Pettigo, Lough Derg, and the confines of Fermanagh; from these a range extends westward by Killybegs to Tellen Head, whence a vast expanse stretches by Rutland, the Rosses, and the shores of the Atlantic across Loughs Swilly and Foyle, into the counties of Londonderry and Antrim. From Barnesmore to Donegal and Ballintra, the country is composed of bleak hills, many of which, though high, are covered with a sweet and profitable vegetation, while several points in the ascent from Killybegs into the mountains of the north present fine views of the bay and harbour of that port. Even amidst the wilds of Boylagh and Bannagh are cultivated and well-peopled valleys, but the district of the Rosses presents mostly a desolate waste. On its western side is a region of scattered rocks and hills, some on the mainland, others insulated: the larger of these rocks are thinly covered with peat and moss; a few admit of some degree of cultivation, while almost all the innumerable smaller rocks are entirely bare. Collectively, this group is known by the name of the islands of the Rosses. Arranmore, the largest, containing about 600 acres, is about two miles from the mainland; on Innis Mac Durn is the little town of Rutland; the largest of the rest are Irvan, Inniskeera, Inisfree, Owey and Gruit. Northward of the Rosses lies the district of Cloghanealy, in Kilmacrenan, entirely composed of disjointed rocks and dark heath, except where, at a lesser elevation near the sea, a stunted sward appears.

On the northern coast, about five miles from the shore, is the island of Tory. The peninsula of Rossguill, formed by the bays of Sheephaven and Mulroy, and that of Fannet by Mulroy and Lough Swilly, are of similar character, except that in the latter the mountains attain a greater altitude, are separated by larger and more fertile valleys, and command prospects of such extent and variety as to attract visiters from distant parts. Lough Swilly, an arm of the sea penetrating far into the land, and receiving at its southern extremity the river from which it derives its name, has on its western shores a tract of rich arable soil losing itself gradually in the mountains, while its eastern side presents a tract of similar character extending towards Derry, under the general denominations of Blanket-nook and Laggan. To the north of the city of Londonderry lies the barony of Ennishowen, a large peninsula bounded on the east and west by the gulfs of Lough Foyle and Lough Swilly. It consists of a central group of mountains with a border of cultivation verging to the water's edge: in the mountains of Glentogher is an expanse of 4000 acres of peat and heath. Besides the great inlets on the northern coast already noticed, the shores are indented with numerous smaller recesses. The islands, except some of those of the Rosses, are very small, the principal being Rockiburn island, off Tellen Head; Inisbarnog, off Lochrusmore bay; Roanmish, off Iniskeel; Gold island, Inismanan, Inis-Irhir, Inisbeg, Inisduh, and Inisbofin, off Kilmacrenan barony; and Seal island, Ennistrahull and the Garvilands, off Ennishowen. The lakes are numerous but small. The principal are Lough Derg near the southern boundary of the county, celebrated for St. Patrick's Purgatory, a place of annual resort for numerous pilgrims, the particulars of which will be found in the account of Templecarne parish; and Lough Esk, near Donegal, a fine expanse of water environed with wild and romantic scenery. The others are Loughs Fin and Mourne (the head waters of rivers of the same name), Salt, Glen, Muck, Barra, Bee, Killeen, Broden, Veagh, Cartan, Dale, Kest, Fern, Golagh, and Nuire, with several others round the base of Slieve Snaght mountain; one near Dobeg, in Fannet; others in the Rosses, and others near Nairn, Ardara, Glenona, Glenleaghan, Lettermacaward, Brown Hall, Ballyshannon and elsewhere.

The climate was formerly cold and unhealthy, with an incessant humidity of atmosphere; but the drainage of some of the lakes and marshes, and the lowering of the levels and deepening of the beds of several rivers, during late years, have produced a very beneficial change, both as to the health of the inhabitants and the increase of arable land: the soils are very various: the richest are those of the champaign district in the south-east. Near Leitrim county it is deep, coarse, and sometimes incumbered with rushes, but in the vicinity of Ballyshannon it assumes a richer character. The change arises from the subsoil, here limestone, the bed of which extends to the neighbourhood of Donegal, supporting a light, gravelly, brown soil; thence to the mountains of Boylagh and Bannagh the soil gradually deteriorates, having a brown clay and rubbly substratum. From Dunkanealy to Killybegs and to Tellen Head the soil of the cultivable glens is a light gravelly till, resting on variously coloured earths and rocks; while that of the mountain region, with the exception of a few green spots, consists of a thin surface of peat on a substratum of coarse quartz gravel, under which are found variously coloured clays, based for the most part upon granite. The soil of the little dales in Fannet is a brown gravelly mould, or a kind of till based on gravel, soft freestone or clay-slate of various colours: but both here and at Horn head, to the west of Sheep Haven, the drifting sands, impelled by the gales from the Atlantic, have covered much good land. The soil of the arable lands of Ennishowen is mostly similar to that of those last described.

The chief tillage district is the barony of Raphoe, in which, besides potatoes, wheat, oats, and barley, flax is grown and manufactured largely. From Ballyshannon to Donegal and Killybegs tillage is general; and in Boylagh and Bannagh much land is now under cultivation, though formerly scarcely sufficient was tilled to supply the inhabitants with potatoes and grain. Oats and potatoes, the former chiefly for distillation, are the principal crops throughout the mountainous districts; but latterly the growth of barley and flax has been encouraged. Agriculture, as a system, however, is not much practised except among the resident gentry, by whom great improvements are annually made. They have formed and strenuously support farming societies, have awarded premiums, and recommended improved implements and a better rotation of crops. The effects of their exertions shew themselves in a very striking manner in the baronies of Raphoe and Tyrhugh, in each of which there is a farming society, which has been attended with very beneficial effects; wheat has been raised in both these baronies with the greatest success. Ballyshannon formerly imported flour to the amount of several thousand pounds annually; during the last two years, considerable quantities of wheat were exported. Turnips, vetches, mangel-wurzel and other green crops are common. In the two last-named baronies the fences, also, have been much improved: they are now generally formed of quickset hedges, while in most other parts, except the north of Ennishowen, they are sod ditches or dry stone walls. The iron plough is in general use among the gentry and larger farmers, but the old cumbrous wooden plough is still used in many parts. The angular harrow is becoming very general, and all other kinds of agricultural implements are gradually improving. A light one-horse cart, with iron-bound spoke wheels, has nearly superseded the old wooden wheel car, and the slide car is seldom seen out of the mountain districts, in which the implements are still rude in construction and few in number, consisting, on many farms,

Lough Foyle, looking from Co. Londonderry to Co. Donegal. Drawn by H.Gastineau and engraved by H. Hinchliffe. From S.C.Hall, Ireland: its scenery, character &c. *vol.iii (London, 1846).*

merely of the loy (a spade with a rest for the foot on one side only), the steveen (a pointed stake for setting potatoes), and the sickle.

Good grasses of every species grow in the champaign tracts; but in the mountains they are coarse and bad. Cattle, which have been fed for twelve months on the latter, where the vegetation consists of aquatic grasses, rushes, and heath, are seized with a disorder called the cruppan, a sort of ague that is cured only by removal to better herbage; yet the change of pasture, if long continued, gives rise to another disease, called the galar, no less fatal, unless by a timely removal to the former soil. Even the pastures of the champaign parts are unfit for fattening and are therefore used only for grazing sheep, young cattle, and milch cows. A peculiar herbage, called sweet-grass, formed of joints from two to three yards in length, grows on the shores of Innisfree, several feet under the high water mark of spring tides, to which the cattle run instinctively at the time of ebb. In Raphoe, irrigation is general. Besides the composts usually collected for manure, lime is in universal demand. In the maritime district from Ballyshannon to Killybegs, sea-weed and shelly sand are the chief manures; throughout the mountains, sea-corac alone, except on the grounds of a few gentlemen where lime is used. The character of the cattle has been much improved by the introduction of the English and Scotch breeds, particularly the Durham, Leicester, and Ayrshire. A cross between the Durham and old Irish produces an animal very superior in appearance, but not found to thrive. The favourite at present is a cross between the old Leicester and the Limerick, which, being again crossed by the North Devon, or Hereford, grows to a large size and fattens rapidly. The breed of pigs has also been greatly improved; when fattened, they are by some sent to market alive, by others slaughtered at home and the carcases carried to Strabane or Londonderry for the provision merchants there. Fowl and eggs in large quantities are transmitted to the sea-ports for exportation. The county is very bare of wood, though there is some good ornamental timber in many of the demesnes, and young plantations, formed in several places, are very thriving. Well stocked orchards and gardens are to be met with round many of the farm-houses in Raphoe.

Granite forms the summit of all the mountains, and with the new red sandstone, rests on a substratum of limestone mostly of the primitive formation and containing no organic remains, although secondary limestone abounds in several parts. The limestone is found through all the level districts near the sea and elsewhere, and in the mountains forming the manors of Burleigh and Orwell. On the eastern shore of Lough Swilly, and in some other parts of Ennishowen, is found a species of calcareous argillite, having the appearance of grey limestone, but containing too much silex to burn freely. Round Carndonagh, in the same barony, is a dark blue limestone of superior quality. Many species of valuable marble have been discovered. One of these, of a pure white, free from flaws or discolouration, and capable of being raised in blocks of any dimension at a trifling expense, has been found in the Rosses; but the want of roads, though the quarries are at a short distance from the sea, prevents its exportation. Grey and black marble of very fine quality have also been found. Little advantage has hitherto been derived from any of the other mineral productions. Lead ore has been discovered in several places in the barony of Boylagh; in the river flowing from the mountain of Killybegs; on the surface near the western shore of Loughnabroden; at the foot of the Derryveagh mountains; in the Barra river; in Arranmore and other parts of the Rosses; and at Kieldrum, in the barony of Kilmacrenan, where there is a considerable deposit of ore collected for a lead-work which was carried on a few years since, but discontinued as being unprofitable from the want of experienced miners. Copper ore and iron pyrites may be traced in Errigal and Muckish mountains, and detached masses are found in several of the mountain streams and near Ballyshannon. Both these ores are abundant; and in several other parts the numerous vitriolic springs indicate larger deposits. Iron ore abounds in several parts. As long as fuel could be procured from the forests of Donegal, Derryveagh, Slievedoon and Kilmacrenan, the mines were wrought and the ore smelted. The remains of bloomeries are often met with in the mountains and the foundations of forges near some of the rivers. Manganese is also abundant. Coal appears in a thin seam at Dromore, on the shore of Lough Swilly, and indications of it are frequent in Innishowen, but no attempts have yet been made to raise it. The same remark applies to steatite or soap-stone, here called "camstone," though found in abundance in all the mountains of Kilmacrenan and Bannagh: it is mostly of a bright sea-green colour. At Drumarda, on the shores of Lough Swilly, on Tory island, and in the Rosses, are extensive beds of potter's clay, which is used in a small degree in manufacturing coarse pottery. Pipe clay and other kinds of useful clays are found frequently, but little used. Silicious sand of a very superior kind is abundant at Lough Salt, and in the Ards, whence considerable quantities are exported for the manufacture of glass. Excellent slates are raised near Letterkenny, Buncrana, and in some other places.

The manufacture of linen cloth of every kind of texture, chiefly from home-raised flax, is carried on to a considerable extent. Several bleach-greens are in full operation, and an extensive factory has been recently established at Buncrana. Cotton cords, velveteens, fustians, and checks are woven to a considerable extent for exportation, as are friezes for home consumption. Woollen stockings of excellent quality, manufactured in the barony of Boylagh, are in great demand. Whiskey is made very largely both in licensed and unlicensed distilleries: the latter are chiefly in the Rosses, Boylagh, and Ennishowen, which last place has long been celebrated for the quality of the spirit produced there. The north-western coast fisheries are chiefly confined to

Donegal. They had declined greatly for many years in consequence of the herring, the chief object of capture, having deserted the coast. In 1830 it was ascertained that the shoals had returned, and the fishery consequently revived, insomuch that the value of the take in 1834 exceeded £50,000, and in the two succeeding seasons has been still greater. The coast every where affords the means of an abundant summer fishing; but the want of proper boats and tackle deters the fishermen from venturing to struggle against the stormy seas that break upon the shores during the winter. The white fishing for cod, ling, haddock, and glassen, and that of turbot and other fiat fish, all of which are in inexhaustible abundance, is little attended to beyond the supply of the neighbourhood. The sun fish resorts hither and is sometimes taken. Seals are caught in large numbers in Strabreagy bay and near Malin. There are several salmon fisheries: the principal is that on the Erne at Ballyshannon; there are others in Loughs Foyle and Swilly and in some of the smaller bays. Eel and trout abound in all the lakes and rivers.

The bays and harbours are numerous, capacious, and safe, The principal are Lough Foyle, forming the entrance to the port of Londonderry and navigable for vessels of the largest draught to that city, and by lighters of 20 tons' burden to Lifford, and thence by the Finwater to Castlefin; the small but secure bay of Strabreagy, well sheltered by Malin Head; Lough Swilly, the entrance to which is safe and easy; Mulroy; Sheephaven; the numerous inlets in the Rosses; Guibarra and Loughros bays, and the capacious bay of Donegal, containing within its scope the smaller harbour of Ballyshannon, on the improvement of which several thousand pounds have been expended by Col. Conolly.

The principal rivers are the Foyle, the Swilly, and the Erne. The first-named, and by far the most important in a commercial point of view, rises in Lough Fin, in the mountains of Branagh, and under the name of the Fin-water proceeds to Lifford, where, on its confluence with the Mourne from the east, the united stream takes the name of the Foyle, and flowing past the city of Londonderry, of which it forms the capacious port and harbour, opens out into Lough Foyle. The Swilly rises in the mountains of Glendore, and passing by Letterkenny forms a large estuary between Ramelton and Newtown-Conyngham, which at flood tide appears like a large arm of the sea, but at low water exhibits a dreary and muddy strand. Further on, and opposite to Rathmullen, is Inch island, beyond which the waters expand into a deep and spacious gulph, which was considered of such importance during the late war with France, as to be protected by numerous batteries and martello towers, The Erne, anciently called the Samaer, flows from Lough Erne, enters the county at Belleek, and after a rapid course of four miles forms the harbour of Ballyshannon, which, should a rail-road be formed between it and the Lough, would acquire a large accession of trade, and by the union of Loughs Erne and Neagh, so as to form a more speedy communication between the north and west of Ireland, become an important harbour. The Burndale river rises in Lough Dale in the mountains of Cork, and flowing eastward, joins the Foyle: it is navigable to Ballindrait for vessels of 12 tons. The other rivers are the Esk, Inver, Awen-Ea, Onea, Barra, Golanesk, Guidore, Clady, Hork, Awencharry, Lenan, Binnian, Awencranagh, Awenchillew, Sooley, and many smaller streams.

The roads, although, in consequence of the late Grand Jury act, considerably improved, and several new lines opened, require much to be done. They are, in general, badly constructed and not properly repaired, although the best materials are in abundance. Near the junction of the county with that of Fermanagh is a relic called "the Giant's Grave;" it is a cave, the side walls of which are formed of large blocks of unhewn stone, and the ceiling of flags of limestone. Another singular relic of antiquity connected with the O'Donell family is called "the Caah." It consists of a small box containing the Psalter of Columbkill, said to be written by the saint himself. Another, consisting of a flagstone raised 18 inches from the ground on other stones, perfectly circular and regularly indented with holes half an inch deep and one inch in diameter, is in the deer-park of Castleforward. The ruins of seven religious houses still visible out of 41 are those of Astrath near Ballyshannon, Bally MacSwiney, Donegal, Kilmacrenan, Lough Derg, Tory island, and Rathmullen, The principal castles yet remaining, wholly or in part, are Kilbarron, Killybegs, Donegal, Castle MacSwiney, Dungloe, Ballyshannon, Fort Stewart, Burt, Doe and Green castle at the mouth of Lough Foyle. The modern seats, which are neither numerous nor peculiarly ornamental, are noticed in the accounts of their respective parishes. The farm-houses are comfortable, but defective in cleanliness. The cabins of the peasantry, especially near the coast, are wretched and extremely filthy, the cattle and swine generally associating with the family, a custom also observable at times in the champaign country. The fuel is turf: the food, potatoes, oaten bread, and fish with some milk and butter; the clothing mostly frieze, though articles of cotton are common, especially for the women's wear. The English language, pronounced with a Scotch accent, is general in the flat country, but in the mountain region it is little spoken. The most extraordinary natural curiosity is a perpendicular orifice in one of the cliffs projecting over the sea near Dunfanaghy, which in certain states of the tide throws up a large jet of water with a tremendous noise: it is called MacSwiney's Gun. Not far from Bundoran is a similar orifice, called the Fairy Gun, from which a perpetual mist issues in stormy weather, accompanied by a chaunt ing sound observable at a great distance. Near Brown hall is a subterraneous river with numerous caves, the water of which possesses a petrifying quality: reeds and pieces of boughs are very soon encrusted with the calcareous matter, and large deposits of sulphur are found on the banks. Natural caves are found on the shores near Bundoran, and numerous others in various parts. In Drumkellin bog, in Inver parish, a wooden house was found perfectly framed and fitted together, having a flat roof: its top was 16 feet below the present surface of the bog.

ALL SAINTS, a parish, in the barony of RAPHOE, county of DONEGAL, and province of ULSTER, 6 miles (W.) from Londonderry, on Lough Swilly, and on the road from Londonderry to Letterkenny; containing 4066 inhabitants. It consists of several townlands formerly in the parish of Taughboyne, from which they were separated and formed into a distinct parish, containing, according to the Ordnance survey, 9673$^3/_4$ statute acres, of which 102 are covered with water. The land is generally good and in a profitable state of cultivation; the system of agriculture is improving; the bog affords a valuable supply of fuel, and there are some good quarries of stone for building. Castle Forward, the property of the Earl of Wicklow, is at present in the occupation of W. Marshall, Esq. A distillery and a brewery are carried on to some extent; and petty sessions are held on the first Friday in every month. The living is a perpetual curacy, in the diocese of Raphoe, and in the patronage of the Incumbent of Taughboyne. The church, a neat small edifice, was formerly a chapel of ease to the church of Taughboyne. In the R. C. divisions this parish is the head of a union or district, called the union of Lagan, and comprising also the parishes of Taughboyne, Killea, and Raymochy; there are three chapels, situated respectively at Newtown-Conyngham (in All Saints), Raymochy, and Taughboyne. There are two places of worship for Presbyterians, one in connection with the Synod of Ulster, of the third class; and the other with the Seceding Synod. The parochial school is aided from Robinson's fund; a school of 28 girls is supported by Lady Wicklow, and a school is supported by subscription; there are also three pay schools, in which are about 90 boys and 20 girls, and a Sunday school. The interest of £200, bequeathed by a respectable farmer, is annually divided among the poor.

ARDARA, a post-town and district parish, in the barony of BANNAGH, county of DONEGAL, and province of ULSTER, 7$^1/_2$ miles (N.) from Killybegs, and 134$^1/_2$ miles (N. W.) from Dublin; containing 456 inhabitants. This place is situated on the river Awinea, at the bottom of Lockrusrnore bay on the northern coast, and on the road from Narin to Killybegs. The village consists of 85 houses: it is a constabulary police station, and has a fair on the 1st of November; petty sessions are held at irregular intervals. The parochial district was formed by act of council in 1829, by disuniting 38 townlands from the parish of Killybegs, and 49 from that of Inniskeel. The living is a perpetual curacy, in the diocese of Raphoe, and in the alternate patronage of the Rectors of Killybegs and Inniskeel. The income of the curate is £90 per annum, of which £35 is paid by each of the rectors of the above-named parishes, and £20 is given from Primate Boulter's augmentation fund. The church is situated in the village. The R. C. parochial district is co-extensive with that of the Established Church, and contains a chapel. The Wesleyan Methodists assemble in a school-house once every alternate Sunday. A parochial school is aided by an annual grant from Col. Robertson's fund; and there is a school under the Wesleyan Missionary Society. In these schools are about 160 boys and 80 girls; and there are also two pay schools, in which are about 70 boys and 20 girls, and a Sunday school. On an island in the lake of Kiltorus, off Boylagh, near Mr. Hamilton's, of Eden, are the ruins of an old fortified building, near which were formerly some rusty cannon.

ARRANMORE, an island, in the parish of TEMPLECROAN, barony of BOYLAGH, county of DONEGAL, and province of ULSTER, 3 miles (W. N. W.) from Rutland; containing, in 1834, 1141 inhabitants. This is the largest of a group of islands called the Rosses, lying off the north-west coast, about two miles from the shore, in lat. 54° 51′ 45″ (N.), and lon. 8° 31′ 45″ (W.): it is three miles in length and three in breadth, and is about nine miles distant from the mainland; comprising, according to the Ordnance survey, 4355 statute acres, of which about 650 only are under cultivation and in pasture, and the remainder is rugged mountain. In 1784 a large herring fishery was carried on successfully on this part of the coast, in which 400 sail of vessels and about 1000 small boats were employed; but within the last thirty or forty years it has been entirely discontinued. On the north point of the island, which is a large rock of granite, was formerly a lighthouse, fitted up with an improved apparatus in 1817 by the corporation for the improvements of the port of Dublin, which has since been removed to Tory Island; the house remains, but is not lighted. There is good anchorage on the east side of the island in an open roadstead. In the R. C. divisions this place forms part of the parish of Templenane or Templecroder, in which is the chapel, where divine service is performed every third Sunday.

AUGHANUNCHON, or AGHANINSHON, a parish, in the barony of KILMACRENAN, county of DONEGAL, and province of ULSTER, 1$^1/_2$ mile (N. E.) from Letterkenny; containing 1848 inhabitants. This parish, which is situated on Lough Swilly, and on the road from Letterkenny to Ramelton, comprises, according to the Ordnance survey, 4011$^1/_2$ statute acres, including 184$^1/_4$ acres of tideway. The living is a rectory and vicarage, in the diocese of Raphoe, and in the patronage of the Bishop: the tithes amount to £147. The church is in a very dilapidated state. The glebe-house, a comfortable residence, was built in 1782, by aid of a gift of £100 from the late Board of First Fruits; the glebe comprises 300 acres. In the R. C. divisions it forms part of the union or district of Aughnish. The parochial school is supported by an endowment from Col. Robertson's fund, aided by the rector; and there are two other schools.

AUGHNISH, a parish, in the barony of KILMACRENAN, county of DONEGAL, and province of ULSTER, containing, with part of the post-town of Ramelton, 4937 inhabitants.

This parish is situated on Lough Swilly, and on the road from Letterkenny to Rathmullen: it comprises, according to the Ordnance survey, 9194$^1/_2$ statute acres, of which 8146 are applotted under the tithe act, and valued at £3954 per annum. The land is principally arable and pasture, with a small quantity of bog; agriculture is improving, and the waste lands are being reclaimed. There are extensive bleach-greens and flour-mills belonging to Mr. Watts; and the parish is benefited by its vicinity to the river Lannon, which is navigable for vessels of 150 tons burden to Ramelton. Fairs are held on the Tuesday after May 20th and Dec. 11th, and on the 17th of July; and petty sessions are held every alternate Thursday at Ramelton. The gentlemen's seats are Fort Stewart, the residence of Sir J. Stewart, Bart., and Shellfield, of N. Stewart, Esq. The living is a rectory, in the diocese of Raphoe, united subsequently to the 15th of Jas. I. to the rectory of Tully or Tullaferne, together forming the union of Aughnish or Tullyaughnish, which is in the patronage of the Provost and Fellows of Trinity College, Dublin. The tithes amount to £509.7.4, and the entire tithes of the benefice to £1100. The church, which is at Ramelton, is a plain structure, rebuilt by aid of a gift of £200 and a loan of £800, in 1826, from the late Board of First Fruits, and a donation of £800 from the late Dr. Usher. The glebe-house, in the centre of the parish, one mile from the church, was built in 1828, at an expense of £6000, of which £1384.12 was a loan from the same Board, and the remainder was either charged on the revenues of the living or contributed by the incumbent. The glebe lands in Aughnish consist of 389a. 3r., and in Tullaferne, of 512a. 0r. 15p., each portion valued at 10s. per acre. The R. C. parish is co-extensive with that of the Established Church, and is one of those held by the Bishop of Raphoe; the chapel is a spacious building. There is a place of worship for Presbyterians of the Synod of Ulster, of the first class, also for Seceders and Wesleyan Methodists. The parochial school is aided by Col. Robertson's fund; and there are four other public schools: about 200 boys and 250 girls are taught in these schools, besides which there are about 150 boys and 60 girls educated in private schools, and there is a Sunday school at Glenlary. A school-house is in course of erection by the Synod of Ulster. There are also a dispensary, a loan fund, a fund for supplying flax, and a Ladies' Society. – See RAMELTON.

BALLIBOPHAY, a village, in the parish of STRANORLAR, barony of RAPHOE, county of DONEGAL, and province of ULSTER, 10$^1/_2$ miles (W. by S.) from Lifford, and 118 miles (N. W. by N.) from Dublin; containing 168 houses and 874 inhabitants. It is situated on the river Finn, and on the road from Donegal to Strabane, and consists principally of one street. A market for grain and provisions is held in a market-house every Thursday; and cattle fairs are held on May 21st and Dec. 20th. Here is a chief station of the constabulary police. – See STRANORLAR.

BALLINTRA, a village, in the parish of DRUMHOLM, barony of TYRHUGH, county of DONEGAL, and province of ULSTER, 4$^1/_2$ miles (N. N. E.) from Ballyshannon; containing 439 inhabitants. This village, which is situated on the road from Ballyshannon to Donegal, and at an equal distance from both those towns, consists of one street containing about 90 houses, and has a daily penny post to Donegal and Ballyshannon. Within a mile is Brown Hall, the seat of the Rev. Edward Hamilton, a handsome mansion in a beautifully picturesque demesne, through the groves of which winds a river that in some parts rushes down thickly wooded precipices, and within view of the house is a small lake. This scenery, which is called the Pullins, is strongly contrasted with the dreary tracts of country that surround it, especially on the south and east. Fairs are held on the 1st of February, March 25th, May 20th, June 24th, Aug. 1st, Oct. 3rd, and Nov. 30th, for general farming stock. This is a station of the constabulary police; petty sessions are held on alternate Mondays: and in the village are situated the parish church, a place of worship for Wesleyan Methodists, and a dispensary. – See DRUMHOLM.

BALLYGORMAN, a village, in the parish of CLONCHA, barony of ENNISHOWEN, county of DONEGAL, and province of ULSTER, 4 miles (N. W. by N.) from Malin containing 227 inhabitants. It is situated at the extremity of the promontory of Malin Head, and is the most northern village in Ireland. A signal tower has been erected by order of the Board of Admiralty; and, not far distant, a small pier and harbour are in course of formation, by excavating the solid rock. There are two coast-guard stations, one at the Head and another at Glengad. On a ledge of rock near the Head a small basin has been scooped out, where, at every tide, is deposited a small quantity of water, which the country people consider efficacious for sores. – See CLONCHA.

BALLYSHANNON, a sea-port, market, and post-town (formerly a parliamentary borough), partly in the parish of INNISMACSAINT, but chiefly in that of KILBARRON, barony of TYRHUGH, county of DONEGAL, and province of ULSTER, 35 miles (S. W.) from Lifford, and 102 miles (N. W.) from Dublin; containing 3775 inhabitants, of which number, 1390 are in the Purt. In remote ages this town was called Athseanaigh, and the chieftains of Tyrconnell had a castle here in which Hugh O'Donnell, prince of Tyrconnell, received his son, Hugh Roe, after his escape from the castle of Dublin, in 1592. In 1597 the neighbourhood was the scene of the most important military operations of that period. An English force, consisting of 22 regiments of infantry and 10 of cavalry, under the command of Sir Conyers Clifford, crossed the Erne by a ford, although vigorously opposed by O'Donnell's troops, and succeeded in establishing their headquarters at the monastery of Asharouagh. Here they received heavy ordnance from Galway by sea, and laid close siege to the castle of Ballyshannon, but met with an unexpectedly strong resistance, and many of their best officers and men were killed or wounded. After continuing the siege for five days, the English were compelled to make a precipitate retreat,

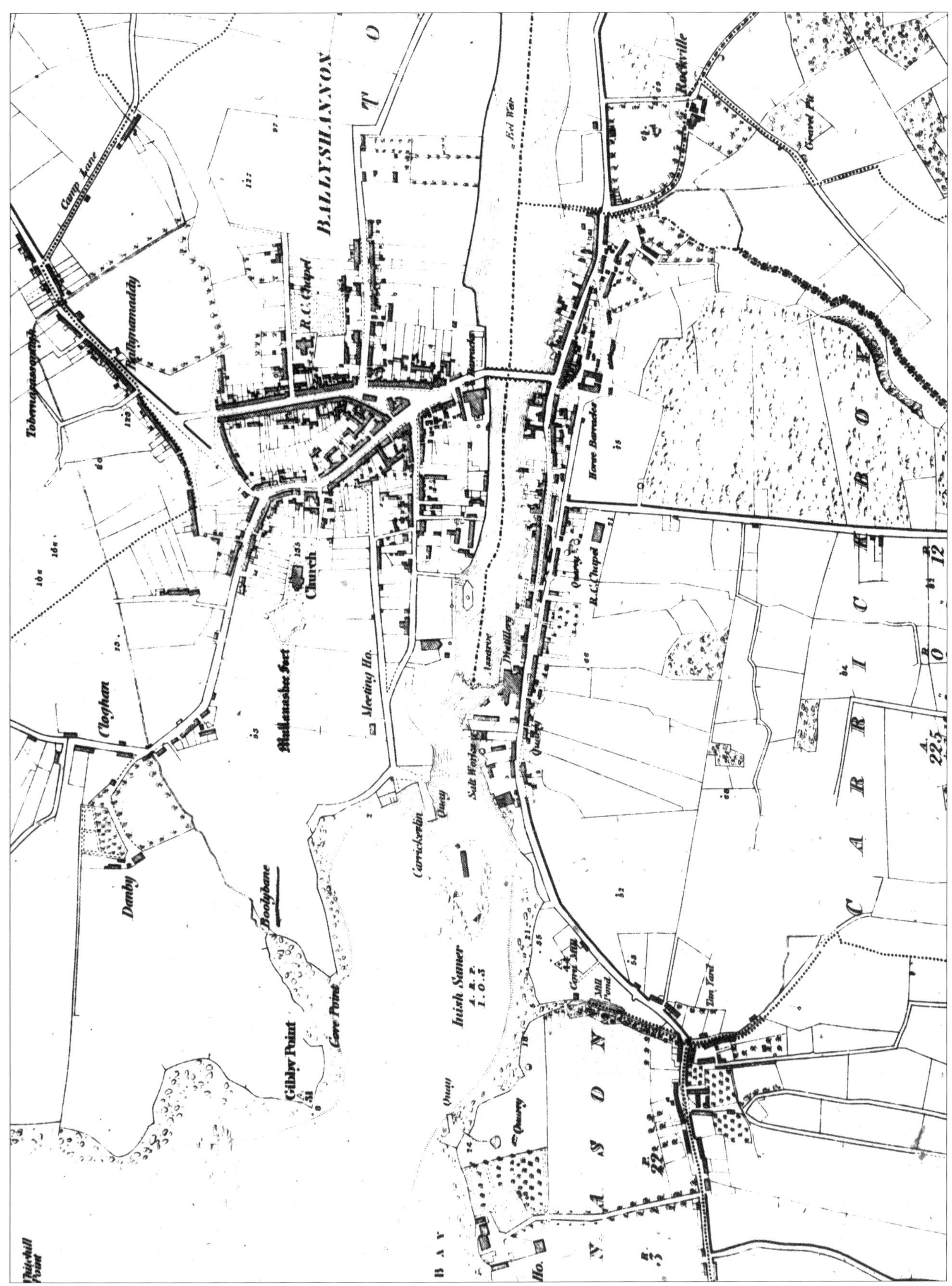

Ballyshannon. Part of O.S. map of Co.Donegal, sheet 107, published 1836 (reproduced at 140%).

closely pursued by O'Donnell and his allies, and being unable to cross the Erne at the ford by which they advanced, they tried another that was seldom attempted, where many were killed or drowned, and thus one of the first expeditions into this long independent territory terminated very disastrously. On the grant by Jas. I. of the earldom and territory of Tyrconnell to Rory O'Donnell, in 1603, he reserved the castle of Ballyshannon and 1000 circumjacent acres. The castle was taken in 1652 by the Earl of Clanricarde.

This town is situated at the head of the harbour of the same name, at the mouth of the river Erne, which is here crossed by a bridge of fourteen arches, and divides the town into two parts; that on the south side, in the parish of Innismacsaint, being called the Purt of Ballyshannon. It comprises three streets and the suburb of the Purt, and in 1831 contained 689 houses, of which 287 were in the parish of Innismacsaint. Here is an artillery barrack for about 40 men, with stabling for 40 horses. A distillery is carried on, manufacturing above 100,000 gallons of whiskey annually, and which increased its trade one-third in 1835; and there is a large brewery. The imports are timber, coal, slate, rock salt, bark, iron, earthenware, and grocery; and the exports are grain, and fresh, salted and pickled salmon. There is a fine salmon fishery in the river Erne, which produces from 60 to 80 tons annually. Here is a small custom-house. The town is favourably situated for commerce and manufacturers, having a large population, and a fertile country around it: it is within four miles of Lough Erne, which embraces an inland navigation of more than fifty miles through the richest part of Ireland, and for purposes of manufacture the river Erne, in a course of four miles, affords numerous sites for mills, having a succession of falls amounting to 140 feet. The surrounding country contains much mineral wealth; a rich mine of zinc has been lately discovered at the Abbey, a lead mine near Bandoran, and rich specimens of copper in the vicinity. The harbour, the entrance to which was formerly obstructed by a bar, has been rendered accessible to vessels of 250 tons' burden. This great improvement, which will probably render the place a respectable port, was made at the sole expense of Col. Conolly, who has formally resigned any claim on the loan of £5000 sanctioned by the Commissioners of Public Works in furtherance of the undertaking, and in an exemplary manner has promoted to a great extent the making of roads and other improvements throughout the entire district. The navigation of the river is stopped abruptly by a grand cascade called the Fall, where the whole body of water descending from Lough Erne, in a

Ballyshannon. Drawn by W.H. Bartlett and engraved by J.T. Willmore. From The scenery and antiquities of Ireland, illustrated from drawings by W.H. Bartlett *(London, 1842).*

stream about 150 yards wide, falls about 16 feet with a tremendous roar down a steep cliff into a basin forming the head of the harbour. This cascade is seen to most advantage in winter, when the river is swollen by rains, and at the recess of the tide the noise of the descending water may be heard many miles off. Plans have been suggested for opening a communication with Lough Erne; among others it has been lately proposed to avoid the falls, not by cutting a canal, but by forming a rail-road to Belleek, which, however, has not been yet carried into effect. The market is held in the market-house on Tuesday and Saturday, for potatoes, pigs, oats, oatmeal, &c.; and fairs are held on the 2nd of every month, except September, when it is held on the 18th. A branch of the Provincial Bank of Ireland has been established, and a chief constabulary police force stationed here.

The town was incorporated by a charter of Jas. I., dated March 23rd, 1613; and the corporation was entitled "the Portreeve, Free Burgesses, and Commonalty of the Town of Ballyshannon." From the time of its incorporation till the Union, when it was disfranchised, it returned two members to the Irish parliament, and the £15,000 compensation was paid to the Earl of Belmore. A court of record was created under the charter, but has fallen into disuse. A seneschal's court is held once in three weeks under the lord of the manor, having jurisdiction to the amount of 40s.; it was established by charter of Jas. I., dated April 9th, 1622, granting large possessions to Henry Folliott, Baron of Ballyshannon. Petty sessions also are held generally once a fortnight. The gentlemen's seats in the vicinity are enumerated in the articles on Kilbarron and Innismacsaint, which see. On an eminence called Mullinashee, adjoining the town, stands the parish church of Kilbarron; and there are two R. C. chapels, two places of worship for Methodists and one for Presbyterians. There are also three public schools, and a dispensary. A small portion of the ruins of the once celebrated castle of the O'Donnells, Earls of Tyrconnell, is in the town; and near to it, on the road to Belleek, are a few vestiges of the ancient church of Sminver.

BUNCRANA, a market and post-town, in the parish of LOWER FAHAN, barony of ENNISHOWEN, county of DONEGAL, and province of ULSTER, 11 miles (N. N. W.) from Londonderry, and 129$^1/_2$ miles (N. W. by N.) from Dublin; containing 1059 inhabitants. Though of some importance in the reign of Elizabeth, this place subsequently fell into great decay, but was restored and laid out in its present form by Sir John Vaughan, in 1717. The town is beautifully situated on the eastern shore of Lough Swilly, at the foot of the mountains of Ennishowen, and, from the romantic and picturesque beauty and salubrity of its position, has of late years become a bathing-place of considerable resort. It consists of three principal and several smaller streets, remarkably clean, and contains 248 houses, of which the greater number are large and well built of stone; the environs are adorned with several handsome houses, villas, and bathing-lodges. Buncrana Castle, close to the town, was the residence of the O'Donnells and O'Doghertys; but after the flight of O'Nial, O'Donnell, and other northern chieftains, in 1607, the territory escheated to the Crown. In the following year, Sir Cahir O'Dogherty, having rebelled against the English authority and carried on a sanguinary war for nearly six months, was defeated and taken prisoner by Sir Arthur Chichester, and was closely confined in this castle, which was shortly after granted to Sir Arthur: one of the towers, with the staircase of stone and the dungeon beneath, remains tolerably entire. A new castle, now the property and residence of Mrs. Todd, was built by Sir John Vaughan in 1717; it is approached by a very handsome bridge over the river, and in front are extensive gardens and terraces, all in excellent preservation. Lough Swilly here expands into an arm of the sea, bounded by mountains and rocks of majestic character, and forming a capacious haven of easy access, suitable for vessels of any burden. On the south side of the entrance are the Swilly Rocks, about half a mile from the shore; on the west side, at Fannet Point, there is a lighthouse, with a fixed light of nine lamps, showing a deep red colour seaward and a bright light towards the lough. Two rivers empty themselves into the laugh, one on each side of the town, after falling over several ledges of rock in their channels: in the northern, or, as it is commonly called, the Castle river, is an extensive and valuable salmon fishery; on the southern river are flax, oatmeal, and flour-mills. From its central situation the town has been chosen as the head-quarters of the artillery forces attached to the batteries on the Foyle and Swilly. At Naiads' Point is a battery, which is one of six erected on the threatened invasion of the French, 'with accommodation for one officer and 27 men, now under the care of a master-gunner and five men; and at Ballynary there is a coast-guard station.

Considerable portions of the adjacent mountain district are being brought into cultivation: copper and lead ores are found, and slate of excellent quality abounds in these mountains, but has never been worked. In 1745 the linen manufacture was introduced by Cal. Vaughan, and flourished for some time, and, in 1784, various branches of the cotton trade, particularly the weaving of velvets, fustians, corduroys, and plain cloth, to which the printing of cotton was added, but, although carriedon with much spirit, it declined after his death. A manufactory for sail-cloth and ducking was afterwards established, and continued to flourish till the year 1830, when the premises were destroyed by fire. There are now in course of erection extensive mills and factories for weaving fine and coarse linens for the Manchester market, also a large flour-mill and fulling-mill nearby adjoining. Several vessels are engaged in fishing for soles, plaice, and turbot, which are taken off these shores in large quantities and of a superior kind, carried over land to Derry, and sent from that port by steam to Liverpool. Oysters of large size and good flavour are also

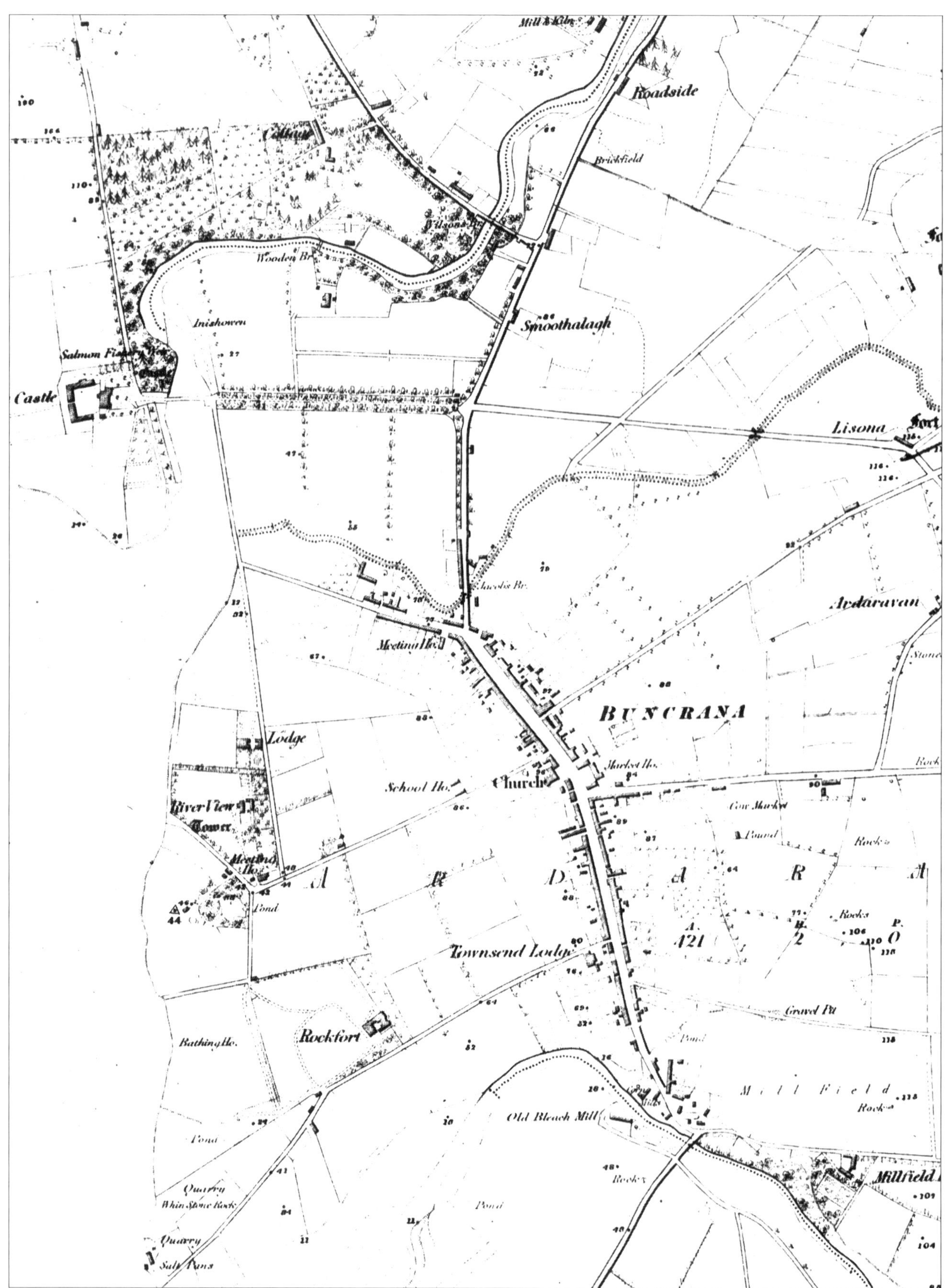

Buncrana. Part of the O.S. map of Co.Donegal, sheet 29, published 1836 (reproduced at 140%).

taken in the lough. The markets are on Tuesday and Saturday, and in the winter season there is a large market on the last Friday in every month. Fairs are held on May 9th, July 27th, Sept. 8th, and Nov. 15th. General quarter sessions are held once, and road sessions six times, in the year; and petty sessions are held every alternate week. The court-house, a large and handsome building in the centre of the town, was erected at an expense of £1300 by the late Wm. Todd, Esq., and presented to the county on this being made a town for holding quarter sessions. A court for the manor of Buncrana is held on the first Monday in every month, for the recovery of debts under 40s. Here is a station of the constabulary police. The parochial church, situated in the town, is a neat edifice. It was built in 1804, considerably enlarged and improved in 1816, and, being still too small, is again about to be enlarged, for which the Ecclesiastical Commissioners have recently granted £370.6.8. There are places of worship for Presbyterians in connection with the Synod of Ulster, and for Primitive and Wesleyan Methodists. A large and handsome building for a school was erected by the trustees of Erasmus Smith's charity, by whom and the incumbent the school is supported; and at Cock Hill there is a national school. A dispensary is maintained in the customary manner. – See FAHAN (LOWER).

BUNDORAN, a village, in the parish of INNISMACSAINT, barony of TYRHUGH, county of DONEGAL, and province of ULSTER, 4 miles (S. W.) from Ballyshannon: the population is returned with the parish. This village, which consists of one street on the road from Ballyshannon to Sligo, is situated on Ballyshannon harbour, on the western coast, and on the confines of the county of Sligo: the coast is bold and rocky. It is a favourite place of resort for sea-bathing during the summer; several small but respectable houses have been built for the accommodation of visiters; and extensive hot and cold sea-water baths have been fitted up. There is a daily penny post to Ballyshannon and Sligo.

BURT, a parish, in the barony of ENNISHOWEN, county of DONEGAL, and province of ULSTER, 6 miles (N. W.) from Londonderry; containing 3765 inhabitants. This parish, which anciently formed part of the parish of Templemore, is situated on tough Swilly, and comprises, according to the Ordnance survey, 10,672½ statute acres. The living is a perpetual curacy, in the diocese of Deny, and in the patronage of the Dean, to whom the tithes are payable: the curate's stipend is £100 per annum late currency, of which £75 is paid by the dean, and the remainder is advanced from the augmentation funds of the Ecclesiastical Commissioners. The church, a neat small edifice, was built about a century since. There is no glebe-house. In the R. C. divisions the parish forms part of the union or district of Iskahan, Burt and Inch, and contains a chapel. There is also a place of worship for Presbyterians in connection with the Synod of Ulster, of the first class. A parochial school, in which are about 40 boys and 4 girls, is supported by the Dean of Derry; and there are three pay schools, in which are about 80 boys and 30 girls, and three Sunday schools. On the shore of lough Swilly are the ruins of the castle of Burt or Birt, erected by Sir Cahir O'Dogherty in the 15th century, consisting of a single tower, situated on a commanding eminence.

CARN, or CARNDONAGH, a market and post-town, in the parish of DONAGH, barony of ENNISHOWEN, county of DONEGAL, and province of ULSTER, 17 miles (N.) from Londonderry, and 135½ (N. N. W.) from Dublin; containing 618 inhabitants. This place, which is pleasantly situated on an eminence near the head of the bay of Straghbregagh, or Strabeagy, and on the road from Londonderry to Malin, consists of a small square and four good streets, and contains 198 houses, many of which are large and well built; a river runs through it, and another has its course a little to the north. The market is on Monday; and fairs are held on the 21st of Feb., May, Aug., and Nov. Here is a chief constabulary station, with barracks for the police; and it is the head of a coast-guard district, comprising also the stations of Dunree Fort, Dunaff Head, Malin Head, Port Redford, and Green Castle. In the vicinity are many excellent houses, the principal of which are, Tunalague, the residence of R. Cary, Esq., proprietor of the town; the glebe-house, of the Rev. G. Marshall; Fairview, of J. Magill, Esq.; and Bridge House, of M. Rankin, Esq. The parish church, near which is an ancient and curious stone cross, and the R. C. parochial chapel, a large and handsome edifice, erected in 1826, are situated in the town. There are also a meeting-house for Presbyterians in connection with the Synod of Ulster, male and female parochial schools, a large and handsome national school, and a dispensary. – See DONAGH.

CARRICK-McQUIGLEY, a village, in the parish of UPPER MOVILLE, barony of ENNISHOWEN, county of DONEGAL, and province of ULSTER, 2½ miles (S.) from Moville: the population is returned with the parish. It is situated near Lough Foyle, on the road from Derry to Moville. A grant ot a market and four fairs was made to the inhabitants in the reign of Chits. I.; the market has long been discontinued, and the fairs are very indifferently attended. Near the village are several handsome gentlemen's seats, which are noticed more particularly in the article on Upper Moville.

CASTLEFINN, a post-town, in the parish of DONAGHMORE, barony of RAPHOE, county of DONEGAL, and province of ULSTER, 4½ miles (W. by S.) from Lifford, and 111¾ (N. W. by N.) from Dublin: the population is returned with the parish. This place, which was anciently called Castle-Fynyn, belonged about the close of Elizabeth's reign to Sir Neill Garbh O'Donnell It is situated on the river Finn, which is navigable to the Foyle for vessels of 14 tons' burden, and is on the road from Strabane to Stranorlar; it consists of a single street. Here is a R. C. chapel. – See DONAGHMORE.

CLONCHA, or CLONCA, a parish, in the barony of ENNISHOWEN, county of DONEGAL, and province of ULSTER, 5 miles (N.) from Carn; containing 6654 inhabitants. This parish is bounded on the north by the

Atlantic ocean, and the west by Strabregagh Bay, and comprises, according to the Ordnance survey, 19,643 acres. The land is much diversified, but generally cold, wet, and barren: the higher grounds form the mountains of Knockamany and Knockbrack, whose summits and sides are covered with heath, coarse herbage, and bog. These mountains are principally composed of schist, or clay-slate, but in the lower districts there are considerable masses. Coral, jasper, chalcedony, opal, agate, and cornehian, are sometimes deposits of coarse blue limestone, and granite and porphyry are sometimes found in detached found in small masses on the shores, and are called in the neighbourhood Malin pebbles; some of them are of considerable value, and are set in seals, rings, necklaces, and other ornaments. Here is the lough or harbour of Strabregagh, which separates the parish from those of Donagh and Clonmany: west by Strabregagh bay, and comprises, according to the Ordnance survey, 19,643 statute it is unfit for vessels that draw much water, though small vessels can find shelter any where along the Runevad Point, and is often mistaken for Lough Swilly, which has caused many shipwrecks. The coast on each side of the entrance is very rocky, and the tides rapid. From Strabregagh to Coolort, and from Malin to Glengad, it presents a series of picturesque precipices, among which is Malin Head, the most northern point of the mainland of Ireland, being in N. Lat. 550 20′ 40″, and W. Lon. 70 24′. Eight miles east of the Head, and five from the shore, is the island of Ennistrahul, on which is a light-house, exhibiting a bright revolving light, visible only once in two minutes. To the east of the Head, and a mile and a half from the shore, are several small isles, called the Garve Islands. In the townland of Ballyhillian, at Malin Head, there is an admiralty signal tower; and at Malin Head and Glengad are coast-guard stations. Strabregagh abounds with salmon, and seals are sometimes found in it. At Portmore, near Slieve Ban, a pier and harbour are being constructed, at the expense of Capt. Hart, to whom the property of Malin Head belongs, The principal seats are Malin Hall, the residence of J. Harvey, jun., Esq., situated in a beautiful demesne embellished with flourishing plantations, which are highly ornamental in this bleak and exposed district; Rockville, of the Rev. J. Canning; and Goorey Lodge, of J. Harvey, sen., Esq.

The living is a rectory and vicarage, in the diocese of Derry, and in the patronage of the Marquess of Donegal: the tithes amount to £555; the glebe comprises 370 acres, of which 110 are barren. The church is at Malin, and was built in 1827, by aid of a loan of £200 from the late Board of First Fruits, and a gift of £100 each from Bishop Knox and Mr. Harvey, of Malin Hall: it is a neat plain building, with a handsome square tower. In the R. C. divisions part of this parish is united to part of Culdaff, forming the union or district of Cloncha; the remaining portions of the two parishes are also united and form the district of Culdaff. There are chapels at Lag and Aughacloy, in the former district, and at Bogan in the latter, all in this parish. At Goorey is a large Presbyterian meeting-house connected with the Synod of Ulster, of the third class. The parochial schools, which are in the town of Malin, are principally supported by the Harvey family. There is a female working school at Malin, also schools at Keenagh and Tully, both built on the estate of Mr. Harvey, of Malin Hall, who is the principal landed proprietor in the parish; and one near Malin Head. In these schools about 400 boys and 230 girls are educated; and there are also five private schools, in which are about 190 children, and three Sunday schools. At Larachrill are ten upright and two prostrate stones, about six feet high, so disposed as to form part of a druidical circle of 60 feet in diameter. At Umgal is shewn what is called Ossian's grave, and near it are places bearing the names of many of the events recorded in his poems. There are likewise traces of a monastery, and several churches or cells, whose names are unknown. Both history and tradition mention a conventual church at Malin, of which the only vestiges are a heap of stones, Pilgrimages are still performed to this place, which terminate by bathing in a small hollow in the rocks at Malin Head, which is filled at every tide and is reputed to possess the power of curing diseases. The old church of Cloncha, which has been disused since 1827 and is falling into ruin, appears to have been an abbey or priory. Near it is a stone pillar, 18 feet high, which was apparently the shaft of a cross, and is ornamented with scrolls and emblems; the upper part is broken off, and lies at some, distance. At Ballyahillon is a natural cave in the rocks, of considerable extent: it is here known as "Hell's hole," and is the subject of many extraordinary tales. – See MALIN.

CLONDEHORKY, a parish, in the barony of KILMACRENAN, county of DONEGAL, and province of ULSTER; containing, with the post-town of Dunfanaghy, 6477 inhabitants. This Parish is situated on the bay of Sheep Haven, on the north-western coast, and comprises, according to the Ordnance survey, 29,632$^3/_4$ statute acres, of which 26,859 are applotted under the tithe act, and 421$^1/_2$ are water. A small portion is woodland, a considerable portion arable and rough pasture, and there is a large tract of waste land and bog, of which much might be easily reclaimed. Near Rough Point is an extensive rabbit-warren. There are quarries producing slates of tolerable quality, and an inferior kind of marble is also found in the parish. Silicious sand of excellent quality is obtained from Muckish mountain, where iron ore is found: this mountain rises to an elevation of 2190 feet above the level of the sea. The gentlemen's seats are Horn Head, the residence of W. Stewart, Esq.; Marble Hill, of G. Barclay, Esq.; Ards, of A. Stewart, Esq., attached to which is a beautiful demesne; and Castle Doe, of Capt. Hart, formerly the residence of the Sandford family, and described as a very strong castle surrounded hy a bawn 40 feet square and 16 feet high. Fairs are held on the 10th of every month at Creaslough, and there are others at Dunfanaghy which see. A manor court is occasionally held, at which small debts are recoverable. At Sheep Haven is a coast-guard station, one of the seven constituting the district of Dunfanaghy. Within the limits of the parish is the point called Horn Head, in latitude 55° 12′ 50″ (N.), and longitude 7° 58′ 20″ (W.); and between it and the peninsula of Rossgull, or Rosguill is Sheep Haven, off the eastern side of which are several rocks above water, the outermost of which, nearly two miles west of Melmor Point, is called Carrickavrank rock.

The living is a rectory and vicarage, in the diocese of Raphoe, forming the corps of the prebend of Clondehorky, in the cathedral church of Raphoe, and in the patronage of the Provost and Fellows of Trinity College, Dublin, The tithes amount to £280. There is no glebe-house; the glebe comprises 400 acres, of which 200 are a barren sandy tract. The church is a neat plain structure, built hy aid of a gift of £300 from the late Board of First Fruits. The R. C. parish is co-extensive with that of the Established Church: the chapel, a spacious building, was erected in 1830, at an expense of £600, and there is a place of worship for Presbyterians in connection with the Synod of Ulster, of the third class. The parochial school is supported partly from Col. Robertson's fund and by annual donations, and a school at Cashelmore is supported hy Mr. Stewart, of Ards. In these schools about 120 boys and 70 girls are instructed; and there are three pay schools, in which are about 170 boys and 90 girls. At Ballymacswiney are some ruins of a monastery for Franciscans, founded by McSwine; and near the coast is "McSwine's Gun," a perforation in the rock, through which the sea is forced, during or immediately after a storm from the north-west, to a height of between 200 and 300 feet, with so great a noise as to be heard for 10 miles. – See DUNFANAGHY.

CLONDEVADOCK, or CLONDEVADOGUE, a parish, in the barony of KILMACRENAN, county of DONEGAL, and province of ULSTER, 15½ miles (N. by E.) from Letterkenny; containing 9595 inhabitants. This parish, which comprises, according to the Ordnance survey, 27,367¼ statute acres, of which 627¾ are water, is situated on the north-western coast; it comprehends the greater part of the peninsular district of Fannet, or Fanad, extending northward into the ocean, and terminating in the points called Maheranguna and Pollacheeny. The surface is for the most part occupied by mountains of considerable altitude, among which Knockalla is 1196 feet above the level of the sea: these are separated by deep and narrow vales, of which the soil is tolerably good, consisting of a brown gravelly mould, sometimes inclining to clay, on a basis of white gravel, brownish or reddish clay, slate of various colours, and sometimes soft freestone rock. The parish contains about 60 quarter lands of good arable and bad pasture, with much waste and barren land: many acres have been covered and destroyed by the shifting sands. The point of Fannet is in lat. 55° 15′ 50″ (N.) and lon. 7° 39′ (W.): it is on the western side of the entrance of Lough Swilly, and a lighthouse has been erected on it, of which the lantern has an elevation of 90 feet above the level of the sea at high water; it consists of nine lamps, displaying a deep red light towards the sea, and a bright fixed light towards the lough or harbour, and may be seen in clear weather from a distance of 14 nautical miles. The seats are Croohan House, the residence of R. H. Patton, Esq.; Greenfort, of H. Babington, Esq.; and Springfield, of M. Dill, Esq.

The living is a rectory and vicarage, in the diocese of Raphoe, and in the patronage of the Provost and Fellows of Trinity College, Dublin: the tithes amount to £463.5.4½. The glebe-house was built by aid of a loan of £100 from the late Board of First Fruits, in 1795; the glebe comprises 240 acres, of which 160 are uncultivated. The church is a plain structure, towards the repairs of which the Ecclesiastical Commissioners have recently granted £371.10.3. The R. C. parish is co-extensive with that of the Established Church, and contains two large chapels. There are five schools, one of which, the parochial school, is partly supported by annual donations from the rector and the late Col. Robertson's school fund. In these about 250 boys and 130 girls are instructed; and there are two pay schools, in which are about 70 boys and 11 girls, and five Sunday schools.

CLONMANY, or CLUINMANAGH, a parish, in the barony of ENNISHOWEN, county of DONEGAL, and province of ULSTER, 5 miles (W. by N.) from Carne; containing 6450 inhabitants. According to Archdall, a very rich monastery existed here, built by St. Columb in the 6th century, of which there is now no trace, but the festival of that saint is observed on the 9th of June. The parish, which is bounded on the north by the Atlantic ocean, comprises 23 divisions, called quarter lands, and, according to the Ordnance survey, 23,376 statute acres, two-thirds of which are irreclaimable mountain land, and 127¼ are water, The shore forms a semicircle of nearly nine miles, and abounds with sea-weed, which is used as manure. The mountains, of which the largest is Raghtin, rising to an elevation of 1656 feet above the level of the sea, are chiefly composed of whinstone and clay-slate, and near the pass to Desertegney a valuable deposit of limestone has been recently discovered. In the mountain of Ardagh are veins of lead ore, which have not yet been worked. The land is not generally favourable for cultivation. There are three corn-mills. Fairs are held on Jan. 1st, March 24th, June 29th, and Oct. 10th, for horses, cattle, sheep, flax, yarn, &c. Within its limits are the rivers Clonmany and Ballyhallon: the former has its rise in Meendoran lough, and the latter from a small spring in the western part of the parish; they contain trout and eels, and in autumn, salmon. Within the parish also is Dunaff Head, between which and Fanet Point, in the parish of Clondevadock, is the entrance to Lough Swilly. On Dunree Point an artillery station was erected in 1812, in which a small garrison is still maintained. At Rockstown is a coast-guard station, and at Strand, or Clonmany, one for the constabulary police. The principal seats are Dresden, the residence of T. L. Metcalfe, Esq.; Glen House, of M. Doherty, Esq.; and the glebe-house, of the Rev. Mr. Molloy.

The living is a rectory and vicarage, in the diocese of Derry, and in the patronage of the Marquess of Donegal: the tithes amount to £400. The glebe-house, which is on a glebe of five acres, was built in 1819, by aid of a gift of £100, and a loan of £675, from the late Board of First Fruits: the glebe at Cherbury comprises 365 acres, of which 300 are uncultivated, The church is a neat structure, with a low square tower: it is situated in the vale of Tallaght, and the Ecclesiastical Commissioners lately granted £368.4.3 for its repair. The R. C. parish is co-extensive with that of the Established Church, and has a large and well-built chapel. The parochial school is aided by an annual donation from the incumbent; and at Garryduff is a very large and handsome school-house, built in 1835. There is a school at Urras, aided by an annual donation from Mrs. Merrick, in which are educated 35 boys and 17 girls; and there are four pay schools, in which are 170 boys and 30 girls. On the north-east of the parish are the ruins of a castle, called Carrick-a-Brakey, consisting of a circular tower, 25 feet high and 8 feet in diameter, and a square building, 30 feet high and 10 feet in diameter. A mile south-east of this is another castle, called in Irish Caislean na Stucah; it stands on a pyramidal rock, insulated by spring tides, the top of which is 80 perches above the level of the sea, and is inaccessible except by long ladders. Tradition states that it was built by Phelemy Brasselah O'Doherty. At Magheramore is a very perfect cromlech, consisting of a table stone of above 20 tons, supported by three upright pillars: it is called Fion McCuil's finger stone. Among the natural curiosities is a chink in a rock at Tallaght, under which is a cavern: and at Leenan Head is a beautiful cave, 70 yards long and 5 or 6 broad, excavated by the sea, through which boats can pass; besides a waterfall dashing over a perpendicular rock 50 feet high, and several caves. Here are also some chalybeate springs; and on the lofty mountains eagles still build their nests, and are very destructive, particularly in the lambing season.

CONVOY, a parish and village, in the barony of RAPHOE, county of DONEGAL, and province of ULSTER. 3 miles (W. S. W.) from Raphoe; containing 5380 inhabitants, of which number, 356 are in the village. It is situated on the river Dale, and on the road from Stranorlar to Raphoe, from which latter parish it was separated in 1825, and formed into a distinct parish, comprising, according to the Ordnance survey, 20,082 statute acres. At its north-western extremity is the mountain of Cark, 1198 feet above the level of the sea. The village consists of one long street, compris ing 73 houses; and has fairs on May 17th, Oct. 26th, and Nov. 3rd. The village of Cornagillagh is also in this parish. Convoy House is the residence of R. Montgomery, Esq. The living is a perpetual curacy, in the diocese of Raphoe, and in the gift of the Dean of Raphoe: the curate's income consists of £75 paid by the dean, and £25 from Primate Boulter's augmentation fund. The church is a handsome structure, in the ancient English style of architecture, and was erected by aid of a gift of £420, and a loan of £300, from the late Board of First Fruits, in 1822. In the R. C. divisions the parish forms part of the union or district of Raphoc, and has a large plain chapel near the village. There is a meeting-house for Presbyterians, in connection with the Synod of Ulster, of the second class; also one for Covenanters. The parochial school is aided by a grant from Col. Robertson's fund; and there are seven other public schools in the parish, in all of which more than 500 children are taught; also four Sunday schools.

CONWALL, a parish, partly in the barony of RAPHOE, but chiefly in that of KILMACRENAN, county of DONEGAL, and province of ULSTER; containing, with the post-town of Letterkenny, 12,978 inhabitants. This parish is situated on the road from Lifford to Dunfanaghy, and contains, according to the Ordnance survey, 45,270 statute acres, of which 32,715 are in the barony of Kilmacrenan; there is much wasteland and bog. Among the seats are Ballymacool, the residence of J. Boyd, Esq.; and Gortlee, of J. Cochran, Esq. The living is a rectory and vicarage, in the diocese of Raphoc, and in the patronage of the Provost and Fellows of Trinity College, Dublin, The tithes amount to £800. The glebe-house was built in 1816, by aid of a gift of £100 and a loan of £1500 from the late Board of First Fruits: the glebe comprises 868 acres, of which 328 are arable. The church, to the repairs of which the Ecclesiastical Commissioners have recently granted £273.11.7, is a small plain structure with a spire, in the town of Letterkenny. In the R. C. divisions this parish forms part of the district of Aughnish, and has chapels at Letterkenny and Glen-Swilly. There are two Presbyterian meeting-houses in Letterkenny, one in connection with the Synod of Ulster, of the first class, the other is connected with the Seceding Synod, and is of the second class. There are also places of worship for Covenanters and Methodists, The parish school is aided by £12 per annum from the late Col. Robertson's school fund, and an annual donation from the rector; and there are a Presbyterian free school and eight other public schools in the parish, in all of which about 850 children are taught; also eight Sunday schools. An abbey existed here so early as the 6th century, and continued at least till the 13th. There are still some ruins of the old parish church. – See LETTERKENNY.

CULDAFF, or COOLDABH, a parish, in the barony of ENNISHOWEN, county of DONEGAL, and province of ULSTER, 6 miles (N. W.) from Moville; containing 5995 inhabitants. It is bounded on the north-east by the Atlantic ocean, and contains, according to the Ordnance survey, including detached portions, 20,089½ statute acres, about two-thirds of which are mountain and bog, and 55½ acres are water including the tideway of Culdaff river. The surface is generally mountainous, intersected with occasional districts of cultivated land. The mountains of

Crucknanionan, Clonkeen, Carthage, and Glengad, the highest summit of which is called Croagh, are covered with black heath, intermixed with coarse grass and bog; that called Squire Carn, on the southern boundary of the parish, is 1058 feet above the level of the sea. The land is generally cold, and cultivation is not in an advanced state, except in the neighbourhood of Culdaff House, where an improved practical system of agriculture has been advantageously introduced, as also near Carthage House, the residence of the Rev. James Knox. Limestone abounds, and is carried hence to a considerable distance. Prior to the year 1812, large quantities of cod were taken off this coast, but that species of fish has since almost wholly disappeared. Salmon of excellent flavour is, during the summer months, taken in the river and for several miles along the coast, but it also is now scarce; in a small lake at Moneydarragh the char, or Alpine trout, is found in considerable numbers. In the several detached bogs of this parish great quantities of timber, chiefly fir and oak, are imbedded; the oak is generally black and in a good state of preservation. These bogs occupy a low tract of country, extending westward to Malin, with small elevated knolls of firm cultivated land rising from amid the bog, and known here as the "Isles of Grelagh:" it is supposed that the sea once flowed either over or around the whole, as marine exuvivae are every where found beneath the bog. The village of Culdaff, generally called Milltown, is situated on the eastern bank of the river, and contains about 30 houses. Fairs are held on the 10th of Feb., May, Aug. and Nov., for general farming stock. It enjoys an advantageous position for carrying on a considerable coasting trade, but very little business is done. Several good roads intersect the parish; and there is a penny post to Moville. Culdaff House, the residence of George Young, Esq., with an extensive and highly improved demesne, well fenced, planted, and cultivated, nearly adjoins the village; and not far distant is Redford, the residence of the Rev. R. Hamilton, by whose exertions a barren rocky district has been converted into a comparatively fertile plain.

The living is a rectory, in the diocese of Derry, and in the patronage of the Marquess of Donegal: the tithes amount to £482. The glebe-house stands a mile east of the village, on a glebe comprising 105 acres, of which 40 are uncultivated land. The church is a small neat edifice, in the early English style, with a square tower of modern erection. In the R. C. divisions part of this parish is united to part of Cloncha, forming the union or district of Culdaff, and the remainder forms part of the district of Cloncha: there is a large chapel at Bogan, in the latter parish, which serves for both. The parochial school for boys is principally supported by the rector, aided by local contributions. A school in the village of Culdaff was built and is principally supported by George Young, Esq., and his lady; and at Ballyharry is a school in connection with the National Board, and another at Caramora: in these schools about 140 boys and 100 girls are educated; and there are five private schools, in which are about 400 children, and three Sunday schools. On the summit of a steep rock, on the coast near Carthage are the remains of a circular fort, called Doonowen: it is nearly surrounded by the sea, and is supposed to have been the residence of the ancient proprietor of the barony of Ennishowen. At Cashel is a curious elevation, which appears to have been the site of a religious house; close adjoining are two perfect stone crosses of great antiquity, and near them the plinth of a third cross; at Baskil are two upright stones, supporting a horizontal one; and in several other parts of the parish are considerable remains of antiquity. The parish is said to have been the birth-place of the celebrated comedian Macklin.

CURROHILL and MENTAUGHS, an extra-parochial district, in the barony of ENNISHOWEN, county of DONEGAL, and province of ULSTER; containing 311 inhabitants. This district was formerly part of the lands appertaining to the abbey of Derry, or Templemore, and is locally situated in the parish of Clonmany.

DESERTEGNEY, a parish, in the barony of ENNISHOWEN, county of, and province of ULSTER, 13 miles (N. N. W.) from Londonderry; containing 1890 inhabitants, This parish is situated on the northern coast, amid the barren mountains of Ennishowen, and is bounded on the north by the Atlantic ocean, and on the west by Lough Swilly; it comprises, according to the Ordnance survey, 7577 statute acres, of which 5834 are applotted under the tithe act; the arable land includes 1794 acres; the remainder is mountain pasture. Some of the lower lands produce good crops of oats, flax, and potatoes; and wherever the mountains afford vegetation, they are depastured by numerous herds of small cattle and sheep. There are indications of copper and lead ore within the parish; and iron ore is abundant. The gentlemen's seats are Lensfort, the elegant residence of the Rev. W. Henry Hervey; and the glebe-house, of the Very Rev. Dean Blakeley. The living is a rectory, in the diocese of Derry, and in the patronage of the Marquess of Donegal: the tithes amount to £135; the glebe-house stands on a glebe of 166 acres, of which 88 are uncultivated. The church is a small neat edifice, with a square tower, situated close to the shore of Lough Swilly. In the R. C. divisions the parish forms part of the union or district of Upper and Lower Fahan and Desertegney; there is a small chapel, occupying the site of the old parish church. The parochial school, near the church, in which are about 30 boys and 15 girls, is a very neat edifice, erected in 1829 by the Rev. W. H. Hervey, and supported by him and a small donation from the rector. There are also two private schools, at Leaugin and Gortlick, in which are about 50 children; and a Sunday school. The gap of Mamore is a remarkable natural curiosity on the confines of this parish, opening to the Atlantic ocean, and most extensive and magnificent views are obtained from the mountains near it. In the Erwys and other lofty mountains of this district, the eagles continue to build, and they prove very destructive to the young lambs on the mountains.

DONAGH, a parish, in the barony of ENNISHOWEN, county of DONEGAL, and province of ULSTER, containing, with the post-town of Carn, 5357 inhabitants. The ancient name given to Donagh by St. Patrick was Domnach-Glinne-Tochuir, "the Sabbath-House of the Glen with Fountains:" there is but a slight variation in the former, portion of this title, and the latter is still the name of the valley where the silver mines were formerly worked. From the book of Armagh and other authorities it appears that a religious establishment was founded here, in 412, by St. Patrick, of which he appointed McCarthen, brother of the saint of Clogher, bishop, or abbot: of the several crosses which marked the limits of its sanctuary one only remains; the saint's penitential bed, and other relics, having been preserved here, this place was much resorted to by pilgrims on St. Patrick's day. The parish is situated on the shore of the bay of Straghbregagh, or Strabreagy, and is intersected by the roads leading from Londonderry to Malin and Malin Head, from Moville to Buncrana. and from Londonderry to Clonmany. It comprises, according to the Ordnance survey, 25,259$^1/_4$ statute acres, the greater part of which are mountain and bog, incapable of being cultivated; small detached portions of land, under tillage, at the foot of the numerous mountains, extending from Glen Tocher to Strabreagy, yield oats, flax, potatoes, and some wheat and barley. Slieve Snaght, or the mountain of Snow, is the highest; according to the above survey, it rises 2019 feet above the level of the sea. From its northern side issues a small river, which runs through the town of Carn, and near the foot of this mountain is a pretty cascade, called Earmaceire. The mountains are mostly of schist, and slate and excellent flagstones are also found in them, besides extensive knolls and ranges of blue limestone. The limestone in Glen Tocher is remarkably good; the silver mines there were worked by an English company about 1790, but owing to the intimidation of the miners they were abandoned, and the attempt to work them has not been resumed. Two small tuck-mills employ about 12 people, but the greater part of the inhabitants are engaged in agricultural pursuits and in fishing. The parish contains numerous good houses, the principal of which are noticed under the head of Carn, which see.

The living is a rectory, in the diocese of Derry, and in the patronage of the Marquess of Donegal: the tithes amount to £365. The glebe-house is situated in the midst of a bog, one mile from the church, on the shore of the bay: sixty acres of good land were reserved, for the glebe of this parish, in the grant of the barony of Innishowen, by Jas. I., to Sir Arthur Chichester; the glebe now comprises 162 Cunningham acres, about 50 of which are under cultivation, and more are being reclaimed. The church is a small neat edifice, erected in 1769; the walls were newly raised, newly roofed, and otherwise improved in 1812. The R. C. parish is coextensive with that of the Established Church, and is called Carndonagh; there is a large and handsome chapel in the town of Carn, built in 1826, at a cost of £1200. At Carn is also a large meeting-house for Presbyterians in connection with the Synod of Ulster. Besides the school at Carn, there are others under the National Board at Glen Tocher, Glengennan, and Glasalts; also one private and two Sunday schools, one of which is in connection with the Presbyterian meeting-house. A stone cross, six feet high, hewn out of a solid block, and ornamented with numerous scrolls and sham-rocks, stands near the church; close adjoining which are the square shafts of two others, having on each side the figure of a human head. There are several forts in the parish.

DONAGHMORE, a parish, in the barony of RAPHOE, county of DONEGAL, and province of ULSTER; containing, with the post-town of Castlefin, 13,257 inhabitants. It is situated on the river Finn, and comprises, according to the Ordnance survey, 46,378 statute acres, of which 45,630 are applotted under the tithe act, and valued at £14,331 per annum, and 330 are water, More than one-third is mountainous and uninhabited; and, with the exception of a small portion of woodland, roads, and water, the remainder is good arable and pasture land. The living is a rectory and vicarage, in the diocese of Derry, and in the patronage of the Lighton family. The tithes amount to £1440. The glebe-house is a comfortable residence; the glebe comprises 750 acres. The church, situated near Castlefin, is a plain old edifice, towards the repairs of which the Ecclesiastical Commissioners have recently granted £273: there is also a chapel of ease opened for divine service in 1833. The R. C. parish is co-extensive with that of the Established Church; there are three chapels, situated respectively at Crossroads, Castlefin, and Sessaghoneel. The Presbyterians have three places of worship, two in connection with the Synod of Ulster, namely, one at Donaghmore of the first class, and the other at Raws; and one belonging to the Seceding Synod. There are eight schools, in which about 300 boys and 250 girls are instructed; and nine pay schools, in which are 620 boys and 220 girls, and 10 Sunday schools, with six classes of adults established by one of the curates, who instructs 180 males and 80 females. – See CASTLEFIN.

DONEGAL, a sea-port, market and post-town, and parish (formerly an incorporated parliamentary borough), in the barony of TYRHUGH, county of DONEGAL, and province of ULSTER, 24 miles (S. w.) from Lifford, and 113 (N. w.) from Dublin; containing 6260 inhabitants, of which number, 830 are in the town. In 1150 Murtogh O'Loghlen burnt this town and devastated the surrounding country. A castle was built here by the O'Donells about the 12th century; and a monastery for Franciscan friars of the Observantine order was founded in 1474, by Hugh Roe, son of O'Donell, Prince of Tyrconnell, and by his wife, Fiongala, daughter of O'Brien, Prince of Thomond. O'Donell, in 1587, bade defiance to the English government and refused to admit any sheriff into his district. The council at Dublin not having sufficient troops to compel his submission, Sir John Perrot, lord-deputy, proposed either to entrap him or his son. He accomplished his object by sending a ship freighted with Spanish wines to Donegal, the captain of which entertained all who would partake of his liberality. Young O'Donell and two of his companions accepted his invitation, and when intoxicated were made prisoners and conveyed to Dublin as hostages for the chief of Tyrconnell. After remaining a prisoner in the castle for a considerable time, he, in company with several other hostages, effected his escape and returned to Donegal, where he was invested with the chieftaincy of Tyrconnell, and married a daughter of O'Nial, chief of Tyrone. In 1592, an English force under Captains Willis and Convill took possession of the convent and the surrounding country, but were quickly expelled by the young Hugh Roe O'Donell, with the loss of their baggage. In 1600, O'Nial met O'Donell and the Spanish emissary, Oviedo, here, on the arrival of supplies from Spain at Killybegs, to concert the plan of a rebellion. Shortly after this, the English, taking advantage of O'Donell's absence in Connaught, marched a strong party to Donegal, and took possession of the monastery, which was unsuccessfully assaulted by O'Donell; and the debarkation of the Spaniards at Kinsale, about this time, occasioned him to go to their assistance, leaving the English in undisturbed possession. In 1631, the annals of Donegal, generally called the "Annals of the Four Masters," were compiled in the convent: the original of the first part of this work is in the Duke of Buckingham's library at Stowe, and of the second in the collection of the Royal Irish Academy; part of these interesting annals have been published by Dr. O'Conor, under the title of "Rerum Hibernicarum Scriptores." The castle was taken, in 1651, by the Marquess of Clanricarde, who was, however, soon obliged to surrender it to a superior

Donegal castle. Drawn by T. Creswick and engraved by C.Radclyffe. From S.C. Hall, Ireland: its scenery, character &c. *vol.iii (London, 1846).*

force. On the 15th of October, 1798, a French frigate of 30 guns anchored close to the town, and two more appeared in the bay; but the militia and inhabitants of the town and neighbourhood showing a determination to resist a landing, they left the harbour.

The town is pleasantly situated at the mouth of the river Esk, and consists of three streets, comprising 150 houses, and a large triangular market-place. The market is held on Saturday; and fairs on the 2nd Friday in each month. Here is a constabulary police station. The harbour is formed by a pool on the east side of the peninsula of Durin, where, at the distance of two miles below the town, small vessels may ride in two or three fathoms of water, about half a cable's length from the shore. There is a good herring fishery in the bay, in summer. The borough was incorporated by a charter of Jas. I., dated Feb. 27th, 1612, in pursuance of the plan of forming a new plantation in Ulster. The corporation consisted of a portreeve, twelve free burgesses, and an unlimited number of freemen; and the charter created a borough court, of which the portreeve was president, but it has long since been disused. From its incorporation till the Union the borough returned two members to the Irish Parliament, and on the abolition of its franchise, £15,000 was paid as compensation to the Earl of Arran and Viscount Dudley. Since that period the corporation has ceased to exist. By a grant to Henry Brook, in 1639, a manor was erected, comprehending the town of Donegal, with a court leet and a court baron, to be held before a seneschal appointed by the patentee, having a civil jurisdiction to the extent of 405. The manorial court is still held monthly, on Mondays, except during the summer: petty sessions are held every alternate week; and the general quarter sessions for the county are held here in March, June, October, and December, in a small sessions-house. There is a small bridewell.

The parish comprises, according to the Ordnance Survey, 23,260 statute acres, including 503¼ in Lough Esk and 214¾ in small lakes: 23,089 acres are applotted under the tithe act, besides which there are about 900 acres of bog and a large tract of mountain land, in which is the beautiful lake of Lough Esk, at the upper end of which is the romantic and picturesque place called Ardnamona, the property of G. C. Wray, Esq., and from which the river Esk descends southward to its estuary, in the inmost recess of the bay of Donegal. About a quarter of the cultivated land is arable, the remainder pasture. The living is a vicarage, in the diocese of Raphoe, and in the patronage of the Bishop; the rectory is impropriate in Col. Conolly. The tithes amount to £338.9.2½, of which £107.13.10¼ is payable to the impropriator, and the remainder to the vicar. The glebe-house was rebuilt by aid of a gift of £100, from the late Board of First Fruits in 1816; and there is a glebe of 38 acres. The church is a handsome structure, built in 1825, by aid of a donation of £100 from John Hamilton, Esq., and a loan of £1300 from the same Board. The R. C. parish is co-extensive with that of the Established Church, and has a chapel at Donegal and one at Townawilly. There is a meeting-house for Presbyterians in connection with the Synod of Ulster, of the third class, and one connected with the Seceding Synod, of the second class; also two places of worship for Independents and one for Wesleyan Methodists. The parochial school was built on land given by the Earl of Arran. There are also a school on Erasmus Smith's foundation, one supported by Mrs. Hamilton, and nine others aided by different Societies and subscriptions. In these are about 600 children, and there are three Sunday schools, About the close of the last century, Col. Robertson, son of a clergyman of this town, bequeathed a sum of money, out of the interest of which, £15 per annum was to be paid to each of the parishes in the diocese of Raphoe, for the support of a school-master to instruct children of all religious denominations. This fund has so much increased as to enable the trustees to grant £40 to each parish, for the erection of a school-house, provided an acre of land on a perpetually renewable lease be obtained for a site. There is a dispensary in the town, supported in the customary manner. Manganese is found in the demesne of Lough Esk, the residence of Thomas Brooke, Esq. Pearls, some of great beauty, have been found on the river Esk. The remains of the monastery are still visible at a short distance from the town: the cloister is composed of small arches supported by coupled pillars on a basement; in one part of it are two narrow passages, one over the other, about four feet wide, ten long, and seven high, which were probably intended as depositories for valuables in times of danger. A considerable part of the castle remains, and forms an interesting feature in the beautiful view of the bay; although it and the other property granted to the patentee, at a rent of 13s. 4d. per annum, have passed into other families, one of his descendants still pays a rent to the crown for it. Within three miles of the town is The Hall, the residence of the Conyngham family. Donegal gives the titles of Marquess and Earl to the Chichester family.

DOUGHBEG, a village, in the parish of CLONDEVADOCK, barony of KILMACRENAN, county of DONEGAL, and province of ULSTER; containing 5S houses and 284 inhabitants.

DRUMHOLM, DRIMHOLM, or DRUMHOME, a parish, in the barony of TYRHUGH, county of DONEGAL, and province of ULSTER, 4 miles (N.) from Ballyshannon; containing 8502 inhabitants. St. Ernan, who died about 640, was abbot of a monastery here, where Flahertach O'Maldory, King of Tyrconnell, was buried in 1197. The parish is situated on Donegal bay, and, according to the Ordnance survey, comprises 35,433 statute acres, of which 15,482 are applotted under the tithe act. It is a vicarage, in the diocese of Raphoe, forming the corps of the prebend of Drumholm in Raphoe cathedral, and is in the patronage of the Bishop; the rectory is impropriate in Col. Conolly. The tithes amount to £735.3.6¾, of which £245.1.2¾ is payable to the impropriator. and the remainder to the vicar. The glebehouse was erected in 1792, by aid of a gift of £100 from the late Board of First Fruits. The glebe comprises 531 plantation acres, of which 400 are cultivated, and the remainder is a rabbit burrow. A church was built at Ballintra, in 1795, at an expense of £1098, of which £500 was a gift from the same Board, and the Ecelesiastical Commissioners have recently granted £252.13.9. for its repair. Another church was built at Rossnowlough, in 1830, by aid of a grant of £600 from the late Board of First Fruits, which also granted £350 towards building a chapel at Golard. The R. C. parish is co-extensive with that of the Established Church, and has a large plain chapel near Ballintra. There are places of worship for Presbyterians in connection with the Synod of Ulster, and for Wesleyan Methodists. About 690 children are educated in the public schools, and 20 in a private school; there are also eight Sunday schools. – See BALLINTRA.

DUNFANAGHY, a sea-port and post-town, in the parish of CLONDEHORKY, barony of KILMACRENAN, county of DONEGAL, and province of ULSTER, 32 miles (N. W.) from Lifford, and 137$^{1}/_{4}$ (N. N. W.) from Dublin; containing 464 inhabitants. It is situated on the bay of Sheephaven, and consists of one street, containing 85 houses; the inlet from Sheephaven forms a commodious bay, which takes its name from this place, and affords good anchorage to vessels of the largest burden, which find better shelter here than in Sheephaven, from the latter being too much exposed to the north and north-east winds. This place is the head of a coast-guard district, comprising also the stations of Rutland, Guidore, Innisboffin, Sheephaven, Mulroy, Rathmullen, and Knockadoon; and including a force of 7 officers and 53 men, under a resident inspecting commander. Fairs are held on the Thursday after Whit-Sunday, Aug. 5th, Oct. 2nd, and Nov. 17th. A constabulary police force is stationed in the town, and petty sessions are held every Friday. Nearly adjoining it, on the west, is a very extensive rabbit warren; and the neighbourhood is rich in mineral productions. The surrounding district, called Cloghanealy, consists chiefly of mountainous elevations covered with very indifferent herbage; and among its geological features are hills of sand and rocks of granite and crystal, rising to a great height. A commodious school-house has been built in the town, and there is also a dispensary.

DUNGLOE, or CLOGHANLEA, a post-town, in the parish of TEMPLECROAN, barony of BOYLAGH, county of DONEGAL, and province of ULSTER, 19$^{1}/_{2}$ miles (N.) from Ardara, and 154 (N. W.) from Dublin, on the north-west coast: the population is returned with the parish. Here are a market-house, constabulary police station, and dispensary; also the parochial church, and R. C. chapel. The post-office is subject to that at Ardara. Petty sessions are held on the first Tuesday in each month.

DUNKANELY, a village, in the parish of KILLAGHTEE, barony of BANNAGH, county of DONEGAL, and province of ULSTER, 9 miles (W.) from Donegal, near Inver bay, and on the road from Killybegs to Donegal: the population is returned with the parish. In 1618 this place was a settlement of ten British families, having a territory of 1500 acres, a bawn of lime and stone, and a castle, and able to muster 50 men at arms. It consists of one street, has a penny post to Donegal, a dispensary, a place of worship for Methodists, and a public school. Twelve fairs are held in the course of the year for farming stock, and a manor court monthly for the recovery of debts under £3. In the village are the ruins of the old parish church, and in the immediate vicinity is the present church. Half a mile to the west are the ruins of Castle MacSwine, occupying a point of land little broader than its foundation, which projects some yards into the sea at the head of MacSwine's bay. – See KILLAGHTEE.

EFFISHBREDA, an extra parochial district, in the barony of ENNISHOWEN, county of DONEGAL, and province of ULSTER, 2 miles (N. W.) from Buncrana, on the road to Clonmany; containing 32 inhabitants. It comprises a wild mountain district lying between Desertegney and Lower Fahan, chiefly occupied by small farmers, and is nominally in the parish of Desertegney.

ENNISTRAHULL, an island, in the parish of CLONCHA, barony of ENNISHOWEN, county of DONEGAL, and province of ULSTER, 8 miles (E.) from Malin Head, on the northern coast; the population is returned with the parish. It is situated in lat. 55° 26′ 20″, and lon. 7° 14′ 10″. Here is a lighthouse, built by the corporation for improving the port of Dublin, exhibiting a bright revolving light, which attains its greatest brilliancy every two minutes; the lantern is elevated 167 feet above the level of the sea at high water, and may be seen from all points 18 nautical miles in clear weather. About a quarter of a mile to the north is a rocky shoal, and fur ther northward lie the Tarmore rocks, around which are always from 11 to 18 fathoms of water. In the channel between this island and the small isles called the Garvilans the stream of tide does not flow eastward until nearly five hours after high water, nor westward until five hours after low water, when its velocity is nearly four miles an hour.

FAHAN, or FOCHAN (UPPER), a parish, in the barony of ENNISHOWEN, county of DONEGAL, and province of ULSTER, 7 miles (N. W.) from Londonderry, on the road to Buncrana; containing 3309 inhabitants. St. Columb founded here the Abbey of Fathenmura, also called Fochan Mor, or Fothenmor, which subsequently became richly endowed and for many centuries was held in great veneration: it contained many relics of antiquity, among which was the Book of the Acts of St. Columb, written by the Abbot St. Murus, or Muran, (to whom the great church was dedicated,) in Irish verse, some fragments of which still remain; also a very large and ancient chronicle, held in high repute. The parish is bounded on the west by Lough Swilly, and comprises, according to the Ordnance survey, 10,040$^{1}/_{4}$ statute acres; some of the land is very rich and well cultivated. The mountains afford good pasturage; the Scalp rises, according to the above survey, 1589 feet above the level of the sea. Near Fahan Point are slate rocks, lying close upon the shores of the Lough, which have not yet been much worked: there is also an abundance of millstone grit, which is quarried for making and repairing the roads, and excellent freestone, The principal seats are Glengollan, the residence of Charles Norman, Esq., proprietor of the greater part of the parish; Birdstown, of the Rev. P. B. Maxwell; Roseville, of Miss Schoales; Fahan House, of T. Kough, Esq.; and the Glebe-house, of the Rev. W. Hawkshaw. The living is a rectory, in the diocese of Derry, and in the patronage of the Bishop: the tithes amount to £360. The glebe-house was erected by aid of a gift of £100, in 1822, from the late Board of First Fruits: the glebe comprises 52 acres. The church is a large handsome edifice, built by aid of a loan of £1000, in 1820, from the same Board; it has a square tower with pinnacles. In the R. C. divisions the parish is united to Desertegney and Lower Fahan, and has a large chapel, built in 1833. At Cashel is a meeting-house for Presbyterians in connection with the Seceding Synod. The parochial school, in which are about 50 children, is aided by subscriptions; the school-house, a large and handsome building, was erected in 1828, by the Kildare-place Society. There are also two other public schools, one of which is aided by the Rev. P. B. Maxwell; and a national school is held at the R. C. chapel. About 220 children are taught in five private schools, and there are four Sunday schools. There are no remains of the abbey, but several valuable relics have been found, some of which are in the possession of the rector: the east window of the old church is nearly entire, affording an elegant specimen of the architecture of the 15th century. St. Murus's bed, or grave, and a holy well, are much resorted to by the peasantry.

FAHAN (LOWER), a parish, in the barony of ENNISHOWEN, county of DONEGAL, and province of ULSTER; containing, with the post-town of Buncrana (which is described under its own head), 5614 inhabitants. This parish originally formed the Lower, or Northern portion of the extensive parish of Fahan, from which it was separated in 1795; it is bounded on the west by Lough Swilly, and comprises, according to the Ordnance survey, 24,782$^3/_4$ statute acres. A great portion is mountain, affording good pasturage, of which Slieve Snaght, on the north-eastern boundary, rises, according to the above survey, 2019 feet above the level of the sea. The valleys are well watered and productive, and agriculture is improving. Freestone is abundant, and limestone is found in almost every part: there are also indications of lead, copper, and iron ore. There is a coast-guard station at Ballinary; and at Neids' point is a battery, erected in 1812, now under the care of a master-gunner and five artillerymen. Lough Swilly is very spacious and deep, affording anchorage for large ships; vast numbers of oysters, cod, and haddock are taken in it. Here are many gentlemen's seats, the principal of which are Buncrana Castle, the residence of Mrs. Todd, which was once the seat of the powerful sept of The O'Doherty, who governed the entire country for several centuries; the Lodge, unoccupied; Rockfort, of the Rev. W. H. Stuart; Townsend Lodge, of Col. Downing; River-View, of W. Camac, Esq.; and the Cottage, belonging to Dr. Evans. The living is a perpetual curacy, in the diocese of Derry, and in the patronage of the Rector of Upper Fahan: the tithes amount to £420. The church, in the town of Buncrana, was built in 1804, by aid of a gift of £500, and considerably enlarged by a loan of £390 in 1816, from the late Board of First Fruits; the Ecclesiastical Commissioners have recently granted £370 for its further enlargement and repair. In the R. C. divisions the parish forms part of the union or district of Upper and Lower Fahan and Desertegney; there is a large chapel at Cock Hill. At Buncrana is a meeting-house for Presbyterians in connection with the Synod of Ulster; and the Primitive and Wesleyan Methodists have each a place of worship. The parochial school, at Buncrana, is aided by the trustees of Erasmus Smith's charity: there are also male and female schools at Luddon, and a national school at Cock Hill. In these schools about 280 children are instructed; and there are eight private schools, in which are about 320 children, and a Sunday school. Not far from Ballinary is a very curious fort, or cairn, called Dooninary, chiefly composed of loose stones, having smaller ones as outposts.

GARTAN, a parish, in the barony of KILMACRENAN, county of DONEGAL, and province of ULSTER, 6 miles (N. W.) from Letterkenny, on the road to Dunfanaghy; containing 2109 inhabitants. St.Columb founded a monastery here in 521, of which the ruins still remain. The parish comprises, according to the Ordnance survey, 44,124 statute acres, including 1590 under water; there is a considerable extent of heathy mountain and bog. A silver and lead mine was worked here in 1835, in the townland of Warrenstown, but has been discontinued. Gartan is the residence of Capt. Chambers. The living is a rectory and vicarage, in the diocese of Raphoe, and in the patronage of the Bishop: the tithes amount to £150. The glebe-house was erected in 1828 by a gift of £400 and a loan of £380 from the late Board of First Fruits: the glebe comprises 25 acres. The church, which is a small plain building, was erected in 1819. In the R. C. divisions the parish is the head of a union or district, comprising also part of Kilmacrenan, in each of which is a chapel. The parochial school, in which about 50 children are educated, is aided by an endowment from Col. Robertson's fund, and subscriptions from the rector; there is also a Sunday school.

GLENCOLLUMBKILLE, a parish, in the barony of BANNAGH, county of DONEGAL, and province of ULSTER, 11$^1/_2$ miles (N. W. by W.) from Killybegs; containing 3752 inhabitants. This parish, which is on the northwest coast, includes within its limits Tellen head and Malin bay, and, according to the Ordnance survey, comprises 32,243$^3/_4$ statute acres, of which 329 are water, and 61$^3/_4$ are in Rathlin

O'Birne islands, belonging to Kilbarron parish. Agriculture is backward; the wasteland consists of large tracts of sand, bog, and mountain, among the last of which are Malin Beg, rising 1415, Glenlough 1513, and Slieve league 1964, feet above the level of the sea. Four fairs are held at Carrick annually. The living is a consolidated rectory and vicarage, in the diocese of Raphoe, and in the patronage of the Bishop: the tithes amount to £115. The glebe-house was erected by a gift of £369.4, and a loan of the same amount from the late Board of First Fruits, in 1828. The glebe comprises 40 acres, of which 15 are cultivated land, and the remainder bog, rock, and pasture. The church is a plain building, erected by aid of a gift of £553.16 from the late Board, in 1828. The R. C. parish is co-extensive with that of the Established Church, and contains two chapels. About 220 children are educated in three public schools, of which the parochial school is aided by an endowment from Col. Robertson's fund. On the summit of Slieve league are the remains of a religious house: here are also some ruins of a castle. On the site of the present church formerly stood a monastery, of which scarcely a vestige is left, except a subterraneous passage, which was discovered a few years since on digging a grave. A ruin is pointed out as having been the residence of St. Columb, and a cavity in an adjoining rock is called his bed. There is a well, dedicated to St. Columb, at which a patron is held, with twelve ancient stone crosses, placed a quarter of a mile apart, as preparatory stations to visiting the well. There is a remarkable echo in the mountains.

INCH, an island, and an ecclesiastical district, in the barony of ENNISHOWEN, county of DONEGAL, and province of ULSTER, 9 miles (N. W.) from Londonderry; containing 1135 inhabitants. This island, which is situated in Lough Swilly, comprises, according to the Ordnance survey, 6357$^{3}/_{4}$ statute acres, of which 3258$^{3}/_{4}$ are in Mintiaghs, or the Bar of Inch, and 60 are under water. Sir Cahir O'Dogherty, in the 15th century, built a castle near the southern extremity of the island, in which he confined O'Donell, one of the rival chieftains of Tyrconnell, who had been treacherously made prisoner in his own house. But O'Donell having prevailed upon his keeper to release him from his irons, made himself master of the castle, in which he was besieged by his rival Rory, whom he killed on the spot, by throwing down upon him a large stone from the battlements. After the flight of the Earl of Tyrone, the castle and the island, being part of the barony of Ennishowen, were granted to Sir Arthur Chichester, whose descendant, Lord Templemore, is the present proprietor. In the war of 1641, the island was in the possession of the insurgents, from whom it was taken and garrisoned for the king; and in 1689, Gen. Kirk, with two ships from England laden with supplies for the Protestants besieged in Londonderry, unable to pass the enemy's lines at Culmore, sailed into Lough Swilly and encamped on the island, where he remained from the 13th till the 28th of July, when again entering Lough Foyle he relieved the distressed citizens. The island is about a mile distant from the main land of Burt, Fahan Point, and Rathmullen, from each of which are ferries. The surface is very uneven towards the north, where are some mountainous elevations called the Gullions, or Gollans; towards the south it is more level, and the land is in a moderately good state of cultivation. The mountainous portions afford good pasturage, and the inhabitants are employed in agricultural pursuits and in the fishery. Inch House, the residence of J. Kennedy, Esq., is the only seat on the island. Near the north point, opposite Rathmullen, is a battery, erected in 1813 on the threatened invasion; and on the Rathmullen shore is another, which completely commands the lough, under the management of a master-gunner and five artillerymen. There are also barracks for one officer and 27 non-commissioned officers and privates of the artillery. The living is a perpetual curacy, in the diocese of Derry, and in the patronage of the Dean; it was erected in 1809, when seven townlands were separated from the parish of Templemore. The stipend is £100, of which £74 is paid by the patron and £26 from Primate Boulter's fund. The church, for the repair of which the Ecclesiastical Commissioners have recently granted £279, is a small neat edifice on the eastern side of the island. In the R. C. divisions the parish forms part of the union of Iskahan, Burt, and Inch; the chapel is a small building in the centre of the island. About 40 children are taught in the parochial school; and there are three private schools, in which are about 120 children, and a Sunday school.

INNISBOFFIN, an island, in the parish of TULLOGHOBIGLEY, barony of KILMACRENAN, county of DONEGAL, and province of ULSTER: the population is returned with the parish. It lies off the north-western coast, about a mile and a half from the main land, arid contains about 150 acres of arable and pasture land and about 250 of mountain. On the north-eastern side of the island is a small bay, and to 'the north are the islets Ennisduich and Ennisbeg.

INNISKEEL, a parish, partly in the barony of BANNAGH, but chiefly in that of BOYLAGH, county of DONEGAL and province of ULSTER; containing, with the post-town of Narin or Nairn (which is separately described), 8266 inhabitants. This parish, also called Innis-Coel, derives its name from a monastery founded on an island within its limits, of which St. Conald Coel was abbot about the year 590, when he was killed by pirates. It is on the north-west coast, and is 24 miles in length and about 8 miles in breadth, comprising 102,081$^{1}/_{2}$ statute acres, of which 80,453$^{3}/_{4}$ (including a detached portion) are in the barony of Boylagh, and 21,627$^{3}/_{4}$ in that of Bannagh; 730$^{1}/_{4}$ acres are in the tideway of the river Guibarra, and 1871$^{1}/_{4}$ in lakes. The surface is mountainous and uneven, and the soil various; the higher grounds consist chiefly of rocky pasture; the Aghla mountain rises 1958 feet above the level of the sea, and the mountain of Portnockan contains a vein of lead ore.

The island of Innis Coel, or Inniskeel, which is about a mile off the shore, comprises about 65 statute acres. On its eastern side is a good and safe harbour, called Churchpool, affording sheltered anchorage for vessels of 350 tons' burden, except in strong gales from the south-west or north-west, when a heavy sea sets in round the eastern point, sometimes breaking into the bay; the best anchorage is in the middle of the bay. Fairs are held at Fintown on May 16th, and 3rd of July, Sept., and Nov.; and it is a station of the revenue police. The living is a rectory and vicarage, in the diocese of Raphoe, and in the patronage of the Bishop; the tithes amount to £500. The glebe-house is a good residence, and the glebe comprises 40 acres, of which 12 are good arable land and 28 rocky pasture. The church was built in 1825, at an expense of £900. By act of council, in 1829, 49 townlands were severed from this parish, and 38 from that of Killybegs, to form the district curacy of Ardara. The R. C. parish is co-extensive with that of the Established Church, and contains two chapels, situated respectively at Glentis and Fintown. There is also a place of worship for Wesleyan Methodists. About 100 children are taught in two public schools, of which the parochial school is partly supported from Col. Robertson's fund; and there are two private schools in which are about 60 children. There are some remains of the monastery on the island of Inniscoel, consisting chiefly of the ruins of the church, near which is a well, dedicated to St. Conald Coel, to which numbers resort annually.

INNISMACSAINT, or CHURCHHILL, a parish, partly in the barony of TYRHUGH, county of DONEGAL, but chiefly in that of MAGHERABOY, county of FERMANAGH, and province of ULSTER; containing, with the post-town of Churchhill, the market-town of Derrygonnelly, and part of the post-town of Ballyshannon, (each of which is separately described), 14,801 inhabitants. The name Innismacsaint is derived from an island in Lough Erne, about half a mile from the shore, where a celebrated abbey was founded by St. Nenn, or Nennid, early in the sixth century. This afterwards became the parish church until, in the reign of Queen Anne, one was built at Drumenagh; part of the ancient building still exists. According to the Ordnance survey the parish comprises 52,994$^1/_4$ statute acres, of which 9505 are water, including a considerable portion of Lough Erne and part of Lough Melvin: of these, 45,867$^1/_4$, including several small islands, are in the county of Fermanagh, and 7127 in Donegal. About two thirds of it are arable and pasture, and the remainder waste and bog: 23,616 acres are applotted under the tithe act. Agriculture is in a backward state, especially in the Fermanagh part of the parish. There is a great quantity of bog, particularly on the Wyault mountains, where there is a basaltic dyke. Coal appears in several places in thin layers, and there are quarries of good sandstone used for building. The mountain of Glennalong rises 793, and Shean North 1133, feet above the level of the sea. Lough Erne affords a navigable communication with Enniskillen, Belturbet, and Ballyshannon. The living is a rectory and vicarage, in the diocese of Clogher, and in the patronage of the Marquess of Ely: the tithes amount to £500. The glebe-house at Benmore, the residence of the Rev. H. Hamilton, was built by a loan of £1000 and a gift of £100 from the late Board of First Fruits, in 1829; it is situated on a glebe of 540 acres. The church is a handsome building with a tower, erected in 1831 by a loan of £1385 from the same Board, and the Ecclesiastical Commissioners have recently granted £101 for its repair. There are also chapels of ease or district churches at Slavin and Finner. In the R. C. divisions parts of this parish are united to Bohoe and Devenish, and the remainder forms the union or district of Bundoran. There are plain chapels at Roscor, Knockaraven, Bundoran, and Carrickbeg. At Churchhill is a meeting-house for Wesleyan Methodists, and at Cosbystown one for Primitive Methodists. The parochial school was built by a bequest of £200 from the late Rev. J. Nixon, and is aided by an annual subscription of £5 from the rector; there is a school at the rector's gate-house, where girls are taught needlework by his family; a girls' school is supported by the Marchioness of Ely; and a school has been recently erected at Fasso, by the Marquess of Ely, who is proprietor of the parish. In these and another public school about 330 children are educated, and about 900 are taught in 19 private schools; there are also four Sunday schools. In the vicinity of Carricklake are the ruins of a church; and near Churchhill are the remains of Castle Tully, the inhabitants of which were slaughtered in the war of 1641. Several Danish raths or forts exist here, some of which are very perfect. There is a sulphureous spring at Braad, and a chalybeate spring at Rosslemonough.

INVER, a parish, in the barony of BANNAGH, county of DONEGAL, and province of ULSTER, 6 miles (W.) from Donegal; containing, with the town of Mount Charles (which is described under its own head), 11,785 inhabitants. This parish, which is also called Invernayle, is situated on the river and bay of Inver, on the north-west coast; and comprises, according to the Ordnance survey, 36,810$^3/_4$ statute acres, of which 35,943 are applotted under the tithe act, and 2051/3 are water. St. Natalis, who died in 563, was abbot of a monastery here, on the site of which was founded, in the 15th century, a monastery for Franciscans of the third order, which after the dissolution was granted by Jas. I. to Viscount Clandeboy. The bay of Inver lies between Doom Point and St. John's Point, both of which are included in this parish; and within the bay is Port harbour, on the south of which, at Ballymacdonnell, vessels may anchor in from three to six fathoms of water during north-west or south-east winds. In a precipice on the coast of the bay are indications of iron-ore, but none has yet been worked. Fairs are held at Mount Charles, which has a penny post to Ardara, Donegal, and Killybegs. The principal seats are White Hill, the residence of the Rev. Montgomery; Bonny Glen, of Murray Babington, Esq.; and the Hall, of Col. Pratt. The living is a consolidated rectory and vicarage, in the diocese of Raphoe, constituting the corps of the prebend of layer in Raphoe cathedral, and in the patronage of the Bishop; the tithes amount to £346.3.1. The glebe-house is a neat residence, and the glebe comprises 210 acres, of which 97 are cultivated. The church, for the repair of which the Ecclesiastical Commissioners have recently granted £186, is a spacious edifice with a spire. The R. C. parish is co-extensive with that of the Established Church: the chapel is a spacious edifice. About 360 children are taught in five public schools, of which the parochial school is partly supported by grants from Col. Robertson's fund, a school at Mountcharles by the trustees of Erasmus Smith's charity, and a school by the Wesleyan Missionary Society. There are also 12 private schools, in which are about 350 children, and four Sunday schools. In the bog of Drumkellin, in this parish, was found, in 1833, at a depth of 16 feet beneath the surface, a wooden house 12 feet square and 9 feet high, with a roof perfectly flat, completely framed and compactly joined; the frame-work consisted of large trunks of trees, the sides of cleft planks of oak about three inches thick, and the joints were 'cemented with a composition resembling tar and grease. The house rested on thick layers of sand and gravel spread on the bog, which was 15 feet deep beneath its foundation; and traces of a paved road leading to it, and resting on sleepers of timber, with numerous vestiges of domestic utensils, were found in several places around the building.

JOHNSTOWN (ST.), a village (formerly a parliamentary borough), in the parish of TAUGHBOYNE, barony of RAPHOE, county of DONEGAL, and province of ULSTER, 8½ miles (N. by W.) from Lifford: the population is returned with the parish. This place is situated on the river Foyle, which is here of considerable breadth and forms a boundary between the counties of Donegal and Tyrone. It originated in the plantation of Ulster, when a grant of the lands of Dromtoolan and Gollanogh, together containing about 210 acres and 80 acres of other lands, was made by Jas. I. to Louis Stewart, Duke of Lennox, and Earl of Richmond, on condition of his settling here 13 families of English or Scottish artisans or mechanics. For the use of this settlement the Earl was to assign 60 acres for the site of a town, to be called St. Johnstown, and to consist of one street of 13 houses, to each of which was to be allotted 5 acres of land, to be held of him in fee-farm at a trifling rent. This settlement was incorporated by charter of Jas. I. in 1618, under the designation of the "Provost and Burgesses of the Borough and Town of St. Johnstown," but never attained the local importance contemplated by the founder; and the corporation seems to have exercised scarcely any of its municipal functions, except that of returning two members to the Irish parliament, which it continued to do till the Union, when the borough was disfranchised. The village is situated on the western bank of the river Foyle. which is navigable to its junction with the lough for vessels of 50 tons, and consists only of one street containing a few neat houses; it has a penny post to Londonderry. The market granted by the charter is discontinued, and of the four fairs, only one is held on the 25th of Nov. It contains a place of worship for Presbyterians, the parochial school-house, and a dispensary. In the vicinity are some small vestiges of the castle of Montgevelin in which Jas. II. held his court till the termination of the siege of Londonderry.

KILBARRON, a parish, in the barony of TYR HUGH, county of DONEGAL, and province of ULSTER, on the road from Donegal to Enniskillen; containing, with the greater part of the sea-port, and market and post-town of Ballyshannon, 10,521 inhabitants. St. Columb founded a church here, of which Barrind was bishop about 590. According to the Ordnance survey, the parish comprises 23,932¾ statute acres, of which 915¼ are water. About half is arable; the remainder is meadow, pasture, and mountain land, and there is a sufficient extent of bog. In addition to the usual crops, great quantities of carrots and onions are raised in the open fields. The Abbey river, which flows into Abbey bay, in Ballyshannon harbour, contains eel, trout, and salmon; and off the coast most kinds of sea fish are abundant, but are preyed upon by a kind of small shark, or dogfish. During spring and summer here are many seals, and the coast is frequently visited by large whales, and great numbers of skate and thornback are taken with the long line. Sandstone and whinstone are found at Kildoney, and a kind of stone coal appears in the cliff overhanging the sea; the seam is about 7 inches thick and dips towards the land. In boring for coal, emery has been discovered about 12 feet below the surface. The principal seats are Parkhill, belonging to the representatives of the late J. O'Neil, Esq.; Cavan Garden, the residence of T. J. Atkinson, Esq.; Cherrymount, of Dr. Crawford; Camlin Tredennick, of I. Tredennick, Esq.; Fort William, of W. Tredennick, Esq.; Danby, of J. Forbes, Esq.; Wardton, of J. Folliott, Esq.; Laputa, of J. F. Johnston, Esq.; and Cliff, of Col. Conolly, who has greatly benefited this part of the county, in which he is one of the largest proprietors, having for many years expended at least £1000 per annum in agricultural implements, flax seed, dispensaries, schools, and roads; in addition to which he has expended large sums on the improvement of Ballyshannon harbour. The living is a vicarage, in the diocese of Raphoe, and in the gift of Col. Conolly, in whom the rectory is impropriate. Of the 44 townlands comprised within the parish, only four pay full tithe, three are subject to a small modus, and the remainder are tithe-free: the tithes amount to £45, of which £26 is payable to the impropriator, and £19 to the vicar. The church was erected in 1745, on an eminence near the town, and is the principal landmark for vessels entering the harbour. Divine service is also performed in a school-house. There is a glebe-house, for the erection of which a gift of £100, and a loan of £675, were granted, in 1810, by the late Board of First Fruits:the glebe comprises 316 acres. The R. C. parish is co-extensive with that of the Established Church: the chapel, in Ballyshannon, is a large neat building, erected in 1795; another at Castleard was erected in 1832, and has a burial-ground. There are also places of worship for Presbyterians, in connection with the Synod of Ulster, of the third class, and for Wesleyan and Primitive Methodists. About 580 children are educated in seven public schools, to one of which Col. Conolly subscribes £8 annually; and about 310 are taught in ten private schools: there are also seven Sunday schools. Near the glebe-house, on a stupendous rock rising almost perpendicularly out of the sea, are the ruins of the castle of Kilbarron, which is supposed to have been inhabited by freebooters. Within the parish are fourteen Danish Raths; and in the harbour of Ballyshannon, at the mouth of the Erne, there was formerly an island, called Inis Samer, where, according to the Munster annals, was a religious house, in which Flaherty O'Maoldora, King of Conall, or Tyrconnell, having renounced the world, died in 1197. There is a chalybeate spring in the parish. – See BALLYSHANNON.

KILCAR, or KILKARAGH, a parish, in the barony of BANNAGH, county of DONEGAL, and province of ULSTER, 5 miles (W.) from Killybegs; containing 4319 inhabitants. St. Carthach, whose festival is kept on the 5th of March, is supposed to have presided over a monastery here so early as 540. According to the Ordnance survey, it comprises 18,883 statute acres, about one-sixth of which are arable, the remainder bog and mountain land. Agriculture is in a very backward state, and there is not a single tree in the parish. Fairs are held quarterly for cattle, yarn, and flannel. The living is a rectory and vicarage, in the diocese of Raphoe, and in the patronage of the Bishop: the tithes amount to £125. The church is a small handsome building, erected in 1828. There is a glebe-house, with a glebe of 840 acres. The R. C. parish is co-extensive with that of the Established Church, and has a large new chapel. The parochial school, in which are about 100 children, is endowed with a grant from Col. Robertson's fund; and there are three other schools and a dispensary.

KILLAGHTEE, a parish, in the barony of BANNAGH, county of DONEGAL, and province of ULSTER, 3 miles (E.) from Killybegs, on the north-west coast; containing, with the village of Dunkanely, 4760 inhabitants. According to the Ordnance survey, it comprises, with a detached portion, 13,368 statute acres, of which about half is mountain land; there is a great quantity of bog, also of coarse limestone and freestone, used for building. Within the parish is St. John's Point, on which is a lighthouse, in lat. 54 33′ 15″, and lon. 8 26′, with a bright fixed light, 104 feet above the level of the sea at high water, and visible fourteen nautical miles. Inver bay commences at this Point, and extends to Devrin Point, and to the westward of it is Mac Swine's bay. Many of the parishioners are employed in fishing, and on the 12th of Feb., 1814, twenty fishing-boats and forty-three men were lost in a squall. The principal seats are Brucklees, the residence of Capt. Nesbit; Upper Brucklees, of A. Cassidy, Esq.; and Spa Mount, of M. Stevens, Esq. The living is a rectory and vicarage, in the diocese of Raphoe, and in the patronage of the Bishop: the tithes amount to £260. The church is a neat building, erected in 1826, at a cost of £1000, granted by the late Board of First Fruits. There is a neat glebe-house, with a glebe of 635 acres, of which 335 are unprofitable land, and which contains a strong sulphureous spa. In the R. C. divisions the parish forms part of the union or district of Killybegs, for which a large chapel is in course of erection. There is a place of worship for Wesleyan Methodists at Dunkanely. About 360 children are educated in six public schools, one of which is aided by donations from Primate Robinson's fund; and about 30 children in a private school. – See DUNKANELY.

KILLEA, a parish, in the barony of RAPHOE, county of DONEGAL, and province of ULSTER, 4 miles (S. W.) from Londonderry, on the road from that place to Letterkenny; containing 930 inhabitants. According to the Ordnance survey, it comprises 1869 statute acres, of which 1792 are applotted under the tithe act and valued at £1285 per ann., and 80 acres are bog. At Carrigans are some large corn-mills: it is a constabulary police station, and has a penny post to Londonderry. Dunmore House is the seat of R. McClintock, Esq. The living is a rectory and vicarage, in the diocese of Raphoe, and in the patronage of the Bishop; the tithes amount to £170. The church is a small plain building, for the repairs of which the Ecclesiastical Commissioners have recently granted £273. There is a glebe-house, with a glebe of 40 acres In the R. C. divisions the parish forms part of the union or district of Lagan. About 120 children are educated in two public schools, of which the parochial school is supported from Col. Robertson's fund, and there is a Sunday school.

KILLYBEGS, a sea-port, market, and post-town, and a parish, (formerly a parliamentary borough), partly in the barony of BOYLAGH, but chiefly in that of BANNAGH, county of DONEGAL, and province of ULSTER, 38 miles (S. W.) from Lifford, and 127 miles (N. W.) from Dublin, on the road from Ballyshannon and Donegal to Rutland; containing 4287 inhabitants, of which number, 724 are in the town. This place, which is situated on the north-west coast, was at a very early period one of the principal sea-ports in this part of the country, and formed a portion of the territories of the chiefs of Tyrconnell. The emissary of Philip II., King of Spain, landed here in 1596, and in April of the following year, a vessel from that country, laden with supplies for O'Donnell, and having some confidential agents on board, arrived for the purpose of conferring with that chieftain. In 1600, another vessel from Spain, with supplies for O'Donnell and O'Nial, landed here, and brought also a large sum of money, in order to promote the object they had in contemplation. On the plantation of Ulster, 200 acres of land were granted by Jas. I. to Roger Jones, Esq., on condition of his laying out the site of a town, building 20 houses with lands for burgesses, and assigning convenient spots for market-places, a church and churchyard, a public school and playground, and 30 acres of common. The town is situated at the head of a beautiful and safe harbour, to which it gives name, and at the base of a vast mountainous tract extending northward; and consists of 126 houses. It is the head of a coast-guard district, comprising the stations of Dooran, Tribane, Tiellen-East, Tiellen-West, Mallinbeg, Daurus Port Noo, and Neptune Tower, with a force of four officers and 56 men, under the control of a resident inspecting commander. A constabulary police force is also stationed here. The market is on Tuesday, and fairs are held on Jan. 15th, Easter-Monday, May 6th, June 21st, Aug. 12th, Sept. 15th, and Nov. 12th, for general farming stock. The harbour is nearly circular in form, well sheltered, and accessible to ships of considerable burden; vessels not drawing more than ten feet of water may anchor near the town, but the best anchorage is in 8½ fathoms near the west side. At sea the harbour is known by the remarkably sharp pointed summit of Cruanard Hill, which is higher than any other in the neighbourhood, and to the south of which is the entrance. By charter of Jas. I., in the 13th year of his reign, the inhabitants were incorporated by the designation of the "Provost, Free Burgesses, and Commonalty of the Borough of Calebegg." The corporation consisted of a provost (elected annually) and twelve free burgesses appointed for life, who had the power of admitting freemen; and under their charter the portreeve and free burgesses continued to return two members to the Irish parliament till the Union, when the borough was disfranchised, and the £15,000 awarded as compensation was paid to Henry, Earl of Conyngham. A court of record, with jurisdiction extending to £2, was also held every third Thursday; but it has been discontinued for many years, and the corporation has become altogether extinct. Petty sessions are held irregularly.

The parish, from which a portion has been separated to form the district parish of Ardara, is for civil purposes distinguished into Upper and Lower Killybegs. It comprises, according to the Ordnance Survey, 30,962¼ statute acres, of which 4304¼ are in that part of Lower Killybegs, which is in the barony of Boylagh; 11,074¼, including a detached portion, and 51 covered with water, are in the other part, in the barony of Bannagh; and 15,583¾, including 41¾ covered with water, are in Upper Killybegs, in the barony of Bannagh: 30,160 statute acres are applotted under the tithe act, of which about two-thirds are mountain and uncultivated land: agriculture is in a very unimproved state. The principal seats are Wood Hill, the residence of Major Nesbitt; and Fintra, of J. Hamilton, Esq. The living is a consolidated rectory and vicarage, in the diocese of Raphoe, and in the patronage of the Bishop; the tithes amount to £300. The church, a neat small edifice, was built on rising ground to the east of the town in 1829, at an expense of £1000. The glebe-house is of recent erection, and the glebe comprehends six townlands, comprising together 2000 Irish acres. In the R. C. divisions the parish is the head of a union or district, comprising also the parish of Killaghtee; the chapel here is a spacious and neat building, and there is also a chapel in Killaghtee. About 250 children are taught in two public schools, of which the parochial school is supported by an annual donation from Col. Robertson's fund, and the other by - Murray, Esq., of Broughton; there are also three private schools, in which are about 140 children, and a Sunday school. A small Franciscan friary was founded here by Mac Swiny Bannig, but there are no remains. Some ruins of the ancient castle of St. Catherine yet exist.

KILLYGARVAN, a parish, in the barony of KILMACRENAN, county of DONEGAL, and province of ULSTER; 12 miles (N. E. by N.) from Letterkenny; containing, with the town of Rathmullen, 3643 inhabitants. According to the Ordnance survey it comprises 9132 statute acres. It is in the diocese of Raphoe, and was formerly part of the corps of the deanery, from which it was separated by act of council, in 1835, and is now a rectory and vicarage, in the gift of the Crown: the tithes amount to £154. The church is a plain building, for the erection of which the late Board of First Fruits gave £300, and lent £500, in 1813. The Board also gave £450, and lent £50 for the erection of a glebe-house, in 1818: the glebe comprises 5a. 1r. 17p. In the R. C. divisions it forms part of the union or district of Tullyaughnish, and has a chapel. There is a meeting-house for Presbyterians in connection with the Synod of Ulster, of the third class, and one for Wesleyan Methodists. About 110 children are educated in two public schools, one of which is supported by donations from Col. Robertson's fund, and about 70 in a private school; there is also a Sunday school.

KILLYMARD, a parish, in the barony of BANNAGH, county of DONEGAL, and province of ULSTER, on the western side of the town of Donegal, from which it is separated by the river Esk; containing 4798 inhabitants. It comprises, according to the Ordnance survey (including a detached portion), 28,230 statute acres, of which 472¼ are in Lough Esk and 202¼ in smaller loughs: about 18,000 are barren mountain and waste land. The principal seats are Lough Esk, the residence of T. Brooke, Esq., and Rosselongan, of R. Steele, Esq. The living is a rectory and vicarage, in the diocese of Raphoe, forming the corps of the prebend of Killymard in the cathedral of Raphoe, and in the patronage of the Bishop: the tithes amount to £276.18.5½ per ann. The late Board of First Fruits, in 1830, granted a loan of £800 for the erection of the church, and, in 1816, gave £200 and lent £600 for the erection of the glebe-house, which has a glebe of 643 statute acres, valued at £205 per annum. The R. C. parish is co-extensive with that of the Established Church, and has a small chapel. Here is also a place of worship for Presbyterians of the Seceding Synod, and one for Wesleyan Methodists. About 440 children are educated in six public schools, to one of which Mr. Murray, of Broughton, gives £5 annually; and 20 are educated in a private school. Here is a fine sulphureous spa of great efficacy in cutaneous diseases, over which Mr. Murray, its proprietor, has erected a pump-room, and hot, cold, and shower-baths.

KILMACRENAN, a post-town and parish, in the barony of KILMACRENAN, county of DONEGAL, and province of

ULSTER, 6 miles (N. N. W.) from Letterkenny, on the road to Dunfanaghy; containing 9251 inhabitants. St. Columb founded an abbey here, which was richly endowed; and one of the O'Donells, princes of Tyrconnell, also founded an abbey for conventual Franciscans, which at the dissolution was granted to Trinity College, Dublin: the present church is supposed to be part of it, and has a mitred head sculptured in relief over the door. Near the village is the rock of Doune, on which the O'Donells were always inaugurated by priests whom they regarded as descendants of St. Columb: the last inauguration was that of Sir Niall Garbh O'Donell, the successor of Hugh Roe O'Donell, but the ceremony being performed without the lord-lieutenant's consent, he was degraded from his chieftainship. The parish comprises, according to the Ordnance survey (including detached portions), 35,617 statute acres, of which 7821/4 are in small loughs, and 6 in the tideway of the river Lackagh. The system of agriculture is improving, and there is some mountain and bog; fine granite is obtained. The village has a sub-post-office to Letterkenny, and is a constabulary police station; fairs are held in it on the first day of every month, and there is a dispensary. The living is a rectory and vicarage, in the diocese of Raphoe, and in the patronage of the Provost and Fellows of Trinity College, Dublin: the tithes amount to £675. There is a glebe-house, for the erection of which the late Board of First Fruits gave £100, and lent £1125, in 1815. The glebe comprises 150 acres. The church is a very old structure, which the Ecclesiastical Commissioners intend to rebuild. In the R. C. divisions this parish is partly the head of a union or district, and partly united to Gartan, and has a chapel in each portion. There is a meeting-house for Presbyterians in connection with the Synod of Ulster, of the third class. There are two public schools, of which the parochial school is supported by donations from Col. Robertson's fund, and in which about 210 children are educated; also nine private schools, in which are about 480 children, and five Sunday schools. Lough Salt mountain 1541 feet high is in this parish, and commands a magnificent prospect. The lough, which is 815 feet above the level of the sea, and 204 feet deep, is on the side of the mountain, and from its vicinity fine views of Lough Swilly to the east, and Letterkenny and the surrounding country to the south and west, are obtained. In the neighbourhood of the lake is a rocking-stone; there is a cromlech at Lough Keil, and at Milford the Giant's grave.

KILTEEVOCK, or KILTEEVOGE, a parish, in the barony of RAPHOE, county of DONEGAL, and province of ULSTER, 5 miles (N. W.) from Stranorlar, on the river Finn; containing 4365 inhabitants. This parish, which was formed by separating some townlands from Stranorlar, comprises, according to the Ordnance survey, 41,131$^3/_4$ statute acres, of which 91 are water. The land is of middling quality and principally in pasture; there is a considerable quantity of reclaimable bog and some mountain land, which is used for grazing. A lead mine was opened here in 1775, but was soon relinquished as unprofitable. Fairs are held at Cloghanbeg on Feb. 1st, May 19th, Aug. 25th, and Nov. 19th, for cattle, yarn linen, and drugget. The principal seats are Cloghan Lodge, the residence of Sir T. C. Style, Bart., and Glenmore, of C. Style, Esq. A manorial court formerly held here was discontinued in 1831. The living is a perpetual curacy, in the diocese of Raphoe, and in the patronage of the Rector of Stranorlar, to whom the rectory is appropriate: the tithes amount to £126. The perpetual curate's income consists of £50 late currency from the rector of Stranorlar, £25 from Primate Boulter's fund, and the gLebe, valued at £16 per ann. The glebe-house was built in 1799 by a gift of £450 and a loan of £50 from the late Board of First Fruits; the glebe comprises 30 acres. The church is a plain building. The R. C. parish is co-extensive with that of the Established Church, and is called Glenfin, at which place is the chapel, a plain building, erected in 1825 by subscription. About 240 children are educated in three public schools, one of which is aided by donations from Col. Robertson's fund, and 30 in a private school; there are also a Sunday school and a dispensary.

LECK, a parish, in the barony of RAPHOE, county of DONEGAL, and province of ULSTER, 1 mile (E.) from Letterkenny, on the road to Strabane; containing 4046 inhabitants. According to the Ordnance survey it comprises, including a detached portion, 10,744$^3/_4$ statute acres, of which 10,393 are applotted under the tithe act and valued at £4047 per annum, and 264 are in the tideway of the river Swilly, which is navigable through the whole of the parish. A large cattle fair is held at Old Town on June 8th. Here is Rock Hill, the beautiful seat of J. Vandeleur Stewart, Esq. The parish formed part of the corps of the deanery of Raphoe, but was separated from it by act of council in 1835, and is now a rectory and vicarage, in the diocese of Raphoe, and in the patronage of the Crown: the tithes amount to £324. The glebe-house was erected by aid of a gift of £450 and a loan of £50 from the late Board of First Fruits, in 1820; the glebe comprises 32 statute acres, valued at £25 per annum. The church is an ancient structure, and is about to be rebuilt. In the R. C. divisions it forms part of the union or district of Conwall. The parochial school is aided by an annual donation from Col. Robertson's fund; and there are two other public schools, one of which is supported by Sir E. Hayes, Bart,; about 160 children are educated in these schools, and there are two Sunday schools.

LETTERKENNY, a market and post-town, in the parish of CONWALL, barony of KILMACRENAN, county of DONEGAL, and province of ULSTER, 13 miles (W.) from Lifford, and 118 (N. W.) from Dublin, on the road from Lifford to Ramelton and Dunfanaghy; containing 2160 inhabitants. It is situated on the river Swilly, over which is a bridge of one arch, and consists of one street with a spacious market-square, containing 416 houses. The market is on Friday, and is well supplied with provisions; the fairs are on the first Friday in January, May 12th, July 10th, the third

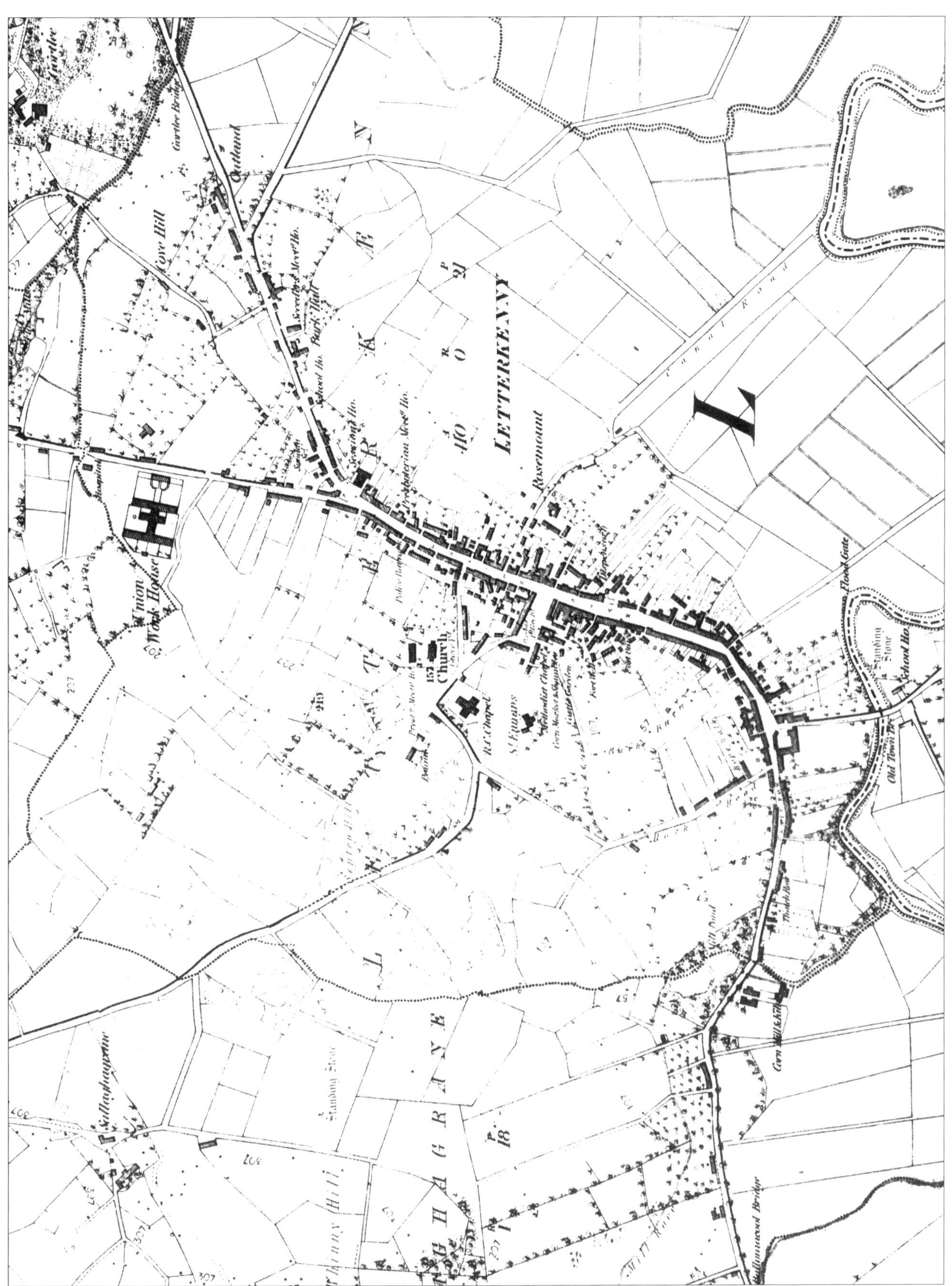

Letterkenny. Part of the O.S. map of Co.Donegal, sheet 53, published 1836 (reproduced at 140%).

Friday in August, and Nov. 8th. A constabulary police force is stationed here; petty sessions are held every Wednesday, and the quarter sessions for the county are held here in April and October; the court-house is a neat building, and there is a bridewell, containing six cells and two day-rooms, with two airing-yards. In the mountains in the vicinity are great quantities of stone of good quality, and marl; about half a mile from, the town, and about the same distance from Lough Swilly, is a good quarry of slate; and on the shores of the lough are great quantities of potters' clay and clay for bricks. The river is navigable from Lough Swilly to this place for vessels of 150 tons burden. The parish church, and the R. C. chapel of the district of Aughnish, a plain small building, are situated in the town; and there are three places of worship for Presbyterians respectively of the Ulster and Seceding Synods and for Covenanters. There are also a national school, a dispensary, and a small fever hospital. Near this place were the ancient English settlements of Drummore and Lurgagh, comprising about 2000 acres, with a bawn of brick and a castle of stone in a strong position, also a village at some distance, in which were 29 British families able to muster 64 men-at-arms; and Dunboy, a territory comprising 1000 acres, where, at the time of Pynnar's survey, in 1619, Mr. John Cunningham had a strong bawn, 70 feet square and 14 feet high, defended with two lofty towers, with a castle and 26 houses and a mill within the enclosure, the houses tenanted by British families, able to muster 50 armed men.

LETTERMACWARD, a parish, in the barony of BOYLAGH, county of DONEGAL, and province of ULSTER, 21 miles (W. S. W.) from Letterkenny, on the road from Killybegs to Rutland Island; containing 2039 inhabitants. This parish, which is situated on the river Guibarra, comprises, according to the Ordnance survey, 20,800$^1/_2$ statute acres, of which 512 are in the tideway of the river, and 503 in lakes; of the remainder, a very large portion is mountain waste and bog. The system of agriculture is in an unimproved state, a very small portion of the land being under tillage; there are strong indications of rich lead ore, in which silver ore has been found. Fairs are held on Feb. 20th, May 20th, Aug. 20th, and Oct. 1st, for cattle and sheep; and manorial courts are held occasionally. Prior to the 25th of March 1835, this parish formed part of the corps of the deanery of Raphoe, from which it was then separated. The living is a rectory and vicarage, in the diocese of Raphoe, and in the patronage of the Crown: the tithes amount to £89.8.7. The glebe-house was built by a gift of £415 and a loan of £46.3 from the late Board of First Fruits, in 1828; the glebe comprises 4 acres. The church is a plain edifice, erected about 60 years since. In the R. C. divisions, the parish is the head of a union or district, comprising also a portion of the parish of Templecroan; the chapel is a small building, and there is also a chapel at Templecroan. About 13 children are taught in the parochial school, which is partly supported from Col. Robertson's fund; and there is a private school, in which are about 18 children. A school-house was also built with the surplus funds granted by the late Board of First Fruits for erecting the glebe-house, but has not been opened. Very large seals are taken in the river Guibarra. Near the glebe house is a large moat.

LIFFORD, an assize town (formerly a parliamentary borough) and parish, in the barony of RAPHOE, county of DONEGAL, and province of ULSTER, 1 mile (W.) from Strabane, and 102 (N. by W.) from Dublin, on the road from Strabane to Letterkenny; containing 5941 inhabitants, of which number, 1096 are in the town. This place, formerly called Ballyduff and Liffer, and of which the parish still retains its ancient name of Clonleigh, was first distinguished as the residence of the chiefs of the sept of the O'Donells, who had a strong castle here, in which Manus O'Donell, Prince of Tyrconnell, after being detained prisoner for the last eight years of his life by his own son Calvagh, died in 1563. Hugh O'Donell, called Red Hugh, in 1596, entertained in this castle Don Alonzo Copis, emissary of Philip III. of Spain, who had been sent to ascertain the state of Ireland previously to the embarkation of a Spanish force for its assistance against the English. In 1600, Nial Garbh O'Donell, who had abandoned the cause of Hugh, led 1000 men of the English garrison of Derry to this place, which, from the previous destruction of its castle, was defended only by ramparts of earth and a shallow ditch. On the approach of the English, the garrison of Hugh O'Donell abandoned the place and encamped within two miles of it, and the English took possession of the post, which they fortified with walls of stone. Nial O'Donell, after some weeks had elapsed without any action taking place, observing some disorder in the camp of Hugh, advised the English to attack it; but after an obstinate battle, in which many were killed on both sides, the English retreated to their fortifications, and O'Donell soon after led his forces into Connaught to oppose the young Earl of Clanrickarde. Under the protection of this English fortress the present town first arose, and in 1603 had attained such importance that a market was granted by Jas. I. to Sir Henry Docwra, Knt., governor of Lough Foyle. In 1611, the village of Liffer, with the fortress and about 500 acres of land adjoining, were, on the settlement of Ulster, granted by Jas. I. to Sir Richard Hansard, with right to hold two fairs in the town, on condition that he should within five years assign convenient portions of land to 60 inhabitants for the erection of houses with gardens, and 200 acres for a common, and that he should also set apart 100 acres for the keep of 50 horses, should His Majesty think proper to place a garrison of horse in the town. The same monarch, in the 10th of his reign, granted to the inhabitants a charter of incorporation, under the designation of the "Warden, Free Burgesses, and Commonalty of the Borough of Liffer," from which time its progress was gradual.

The town is situated in a beautiful valley at the base of an extensive range of mountains, and on the western bank of the river Foyle, over which is a stone bridge of twelve arches leading into the county of Tyrone. It consists of two streets, and contains 161 houses, of which several are neat and well built: the market and fairs have been discontinued. There are infantry barracks for 3 officers and 54 non-commissioned officers and privates. A penny post to Strabane has been established, and there is a constabulary police station in the town. The corporation by the charter consisted of a warden, 12 free burgesses, and an indefinite number of freemen, assisted by two serjeants-at-mace and other officers. The warden, who was also clerk of the market, was annually elected from the free burgesses, who were chosen for life from the commonalty or freemen by a majority of their own body, by whom also the freemen were admitted and the serjeants-at-mace and other officers appointed. The borough returned two members to the Irish parliament till the Union, when it was disfranchised. A court of record for the recovery of debts to the amount of £3.6.8 was granted by the charter to be held weekly before the warden; but no proceedings appear to have issued from it for a long period; the corporation seems to have ceased to exercise any other municipal function except that of returning members to the Irish parliament, and since the Union it has become quite extinct. The assizes and December quarter sessions are held in the town. The court-house and county gaol is a very spacious and handsome building in the castellated style; the former is well adapted for holding the various courts; and the latter, which is divided into six wards, is well arranged for classification, and capable of receiving 124 prisoners; the men are employed in breaking stones and in pounding bones for manure, for which there is a large demand, and the women in needlework, spinning, and washing; there is a good school, and the discipline and interior economy have been recommended to the imitation of the managers of other prisons.

The parish, which is also called Clonleigh, comprises, according to the Ordnance survey, 12,517½ statute acres, of which 153 are in the tideway of the river Foyle, and 12,227 are applotted under the tithe act and valued at £8520 per annum. The principal seats are Clonleigh, the residence of the Rev. W. Knox; and Cavanacor, of B. Geale Humfrey, Esq. The river Foyle is navigable for vessels of 20 tons from Derry to this place. The living is a rectory, in the diocese of Derry, and in the patronage of the Bishop: the tithes amount to £840, and the glebe comprises 427 acres, of which 177 are uncultivated land. The church is a neat edifice of stone with a square tower, and contains a monument to Sir Richard Hansard and Dame Anne, his wife, enumerating his various benefactions to the town. In the R. C. divisions the parish forms the head of a union or district, comprising also the parish of Camus-juxta-Morne: the chapel, within a mile of the town, is a neat edifice. There is a place of worship for Presbyterians in connection with the Synod of Ulster, of the second class. About 450 children are taught in seven public schools, of which one is endowed by Sir Richard Hansard with £30 per ann. for a master and £20 for an usher, to be appointed by the Bishop of Derry, who is visiter; the parochial schools are partly supported by a bequest of the late Lord Erne and by the Rector, and another is supported by the Creighton family. There are also four private schools, in which are about 80 children, and a Sunday school. Mr. Blackburn, in 1806, bequeathed £200, the interest of which he appropriated to be annually distributed among poor householders, but the legacy has not yet been made available to the purpose. There are remains of three religious houses, at Ballibogan, Churchminster, and Clonleigh; the monastery of Cluanleodh, according to Archdall, was founded at a very early period by St. Columb, and St. Carnech was bishop and abbot of this establishment in 530. Lifford gives the titles of Baron and Viscount to the family of Hewitt.

MALIN, a village, in the parish of CLONCHA, barony of ENNISHOWEN, county of DONEGAL, and province of ULSTER, 3 miles (N.) from Carn, to which it has a penny post: the population is returned with the parish. It is situated at the extremity of a creek of Strabreagy bay, on the road from Londonderry to Malin Head, and comprises 28 well-built modern houses, in the form of a square: at the east end is a large bridge leading towards Carn and Culdaff. Malin Hall, the residence of J. Harvey. Jun., Esq., is situated a little above the village in a well-planted demesne, which forms a great ornament in this bleak neighbourhood. Malin has a patent for a market on Tuesday, not now held, but there are fairs, principally for the sale of cattle and sheep, on Easter-Tuesday, June 24th, Aug. 1st, and Oct. 31st, which are well attended. It is a constabulary police station; and petty sessions are held on alternate Wednesdays. The parish church of Cloncha was erected here in 1827; it is a neat edifice, in the early English style, with a square tower surmounted with pinnacles. The male and female parochial schools were built by J. Harvey, Esq., and there is a female work school. Here was formerly a conventual church, the only remains of which are a heap of stones; and there are numerous vestiges of antiquity and natural curiosities in the neighbourhood, which are described under Cloncha.

MANOR-CONYNGHAM, a village, in the parish of RAYMOCHY, barony of RAPHOE, county of DONEGAL, and province of ULSTER, 4 miles (E. N. E.) from Letterkenny, on the road to Londonderry: tho population is returned with the parish. This place, which consists of one street, is situated on the banks of Lough Swilly, and contains the parochial church, a neat structure; and meeting-houses for Presbyterians and Seceders, both of the second class. It has a penny post to Letterkenny and Strabane. Fairs on the 6th of Jan. and the 6th of every alternate month have been lately established, for the encouragement of which the landed proprietors give small premiums to the owners and buyers of the best farming stock, yarn, flax, &c., exhibited for sale.

MEVAGH, or MOYVAGH, a parish, in the barony of KILMACRENAN, county of DONEGAL, and province of ULSTER, 14 miles (N. by W.) from Letterkenny; containing 4794 inhabitants, This parish comprises, according to the Ordnance Survey, 21,026$^1/_2$ statute acres, of which 382$^1/_2$ are water, and 18,393 are applotted under the tithe act; the greater part of the land is poor, a small portion only being considered very good. There is a great quantity of bog and wasteland; the latter consists of large tracts of sand thrown up by the sea. Lead has been discovered but is not at present worked. It is situated on Mulroy bay, and within its limits is the peninsula of Rossgul, bounded on the west by Sheephaven, on the north by the ocean, and on the east by the arm of the sea called Mulroy: in the centre this peninsula rises into great elevations, and near the shore presents a stunted verdure. The harbour of Mulroy, by the line of coast, is 5 miles to the west of Lough Swilly; it has water sufficient for the largest ships, and is well sheltered, but part of the channel is narrow and difficult. On the 14th of every month a fair is held in Glen; and petty sessions are held on alternate Saturdays. The living is a rectory and vicarage, in the diocese of Raphoe, and in the patronage of the Bishop: the tithes amount to £375; the glebe, about two miles from the church, comprises 184$^1/_4$ statute acres, valued at £30 per ann., of which 25$^1/_4$ acres are arable, and the remainder rocky pasture and mountain, with the exception of 2$^1/_4$ consisting of streets and commons. The church is in good repair; it was built about 160 years since. The R. C. parish is co-extensive with that of the Established Church: the chapel is a good slated building. About 230 children are educated in four public schools, of which the parochial school is aided by an annual donation from Col. Robertson's fund; and in three private schools are about 130 children: there are also three Sunday schools. At the time of Pynnar's survey, a strong bawn of lime and stone, sixty feet square, with flankers, stood here; and there were 23 British families, capable of mustering forty-two fighting men.

MOUNT-CHARLES, a town, in the parish of INVER, barony of BANNAGH, county of DONEGAL, and province of ULSTER, 3 miles (W.) from Donegal, on the road from Donegal to Killybegs; containing 508 inhabitants. It consists of only one street, in which are 83 houses, a small market-house (in which divine service is performed every Sunday), a school-house under the trustees of Erasmus Smith's charity, and a dispensary; it is a constabulary police station, and has a penny-post to Ardara, Donegal, and Killybegs. Fairs are held on Jan. 18th, March 28th, May 10th, June 9th, Aug. 20th, Sept. 22nd, Oct. 22nd, and Nov. 18th. Near the town is the Hall, the property of the Marquess of Conyngham, but at present occupied by Col. Pratt. Mount-Charles gives the inferior titles of Earl and Viscount to the Marquess of Conyngham.

MOVILLE, a market and post-town, in the parish of LOWER MOVILLE, barony of ENNISHOWEN, county of DONEGAL, and province of ULSTER, 16 miles (N.) from Londonderry; the population is returned with the parish. This town, which was formerly called Bonafobble, is neat and flourishing, having of late rapidly grown into importance from its being resorted to as a fashionable bathing-place. It is pleasantly situated on the western shore of Lough Foyle, and consists of a square and three principal streets, with numerous elegant detached villas and bathing lodges in the immediate vicinity, chiefly near the shore. During the summer season, steam-boats arrive daily from Derry, Portrush, and other places, and for their accommodation two wooden piers projecting into deep water have been constructed, which they can approach at all times of the tide. A market on Thursday has been recently established, and is well supplied with general provisions, fish, and fowl; and fairs are held on the 28th of Jan., April, July, and Oct., for cattle, sheep and pigs. Petty sessions for the Moville district are held every fourth Tuesday, and a constabulary and a revenue police force, and a coast-guard are stationed here. Here is a national school; also a school for females, chiefly supported by subscription. The town is favourably situated, being sheltered from the north and westerly winds by the lofty mountains of Ennishowen, and commanding on the south a fine view of the fertile tracts of Myroe and the Faughan vale, backed by the noble mountains of Benbradagh and Benyevenagh, in the county of Londonderry. To the east is the splendid palace of the late Earl of Bristol, Bishop of Derry, with its temples and mausoleum; and beyond are numerous headlands, extending to the cape of Bengore. Among the principal residences in the vicinity are Moville Lodge, that of H. Lyle, Esq.; Gortgowan, of the Rev. Chas. Galway; Ballybrack House, of G. H. Boggs, Esq.; and Drumawier House, of John Grierson, Esq.: the others are noticed in the account of Upper Moville.

MOVILLE (LOWER), a parish, in the barony of ENNISHOWEN, county of DONEGAL, and province of ULSTER, 17 miles (N. N. E.) from Londonderry; containing 5785 inhabitants, This parish is situated on the western shore of Lough Foyle, and bounded on the north by the Atlantic ocean; it comprises, according to the Ordnance survey, including a detached portion, 15,950$^1/_2$ statute acres. Prior to 1788 it formed part of the parish of Moville (anciently called Mobhuile), when it was separated from the southern or upper division of the old parish. The land is in general of inferior quality, and a large portion of the parish consists of rocky barren mountain, from which circumstance, and that of the population being partly employed in fishing, agriculture is in a backward state; but in the neighbourhood of Moville the land has been brought into a good state of cultivation and well planted, and is embellished with several handsome residences, which, together with the principal features of the scenery, are noticed in the article on that town; and to the west of Greencastle a slope of cultivated land ascends towards the neighbouring mountains. The coast of this parish extends from the town of Moville to Glenagivney, including the headlands of Shrove and Ennishowen; nearly the whole line consists of rocky cliffs of a bold and romantic character, and between Shrove Point and the point of Magilligan, on the opposite coast of Londonderry, is the entrance to Lough Foyle, a capacious harbour, where the largest ships may ride in safety in all kinds of weather. Two light-houses are now in course of erection at Shrove Head by the Ballast Board, in consequence of the numerous shipwrecks that have taken place on the sand banks called "the Tons," near the entrance of the lough. Close on the shore of Lough Foyle, and nearly adjoining the church, are the magnificent ruins of Greencastle, built by Sir Caher O'Dogherty in the 15th century: it stands on a boldly prominent rock near the entrance of the lough, and, from the great strength and extent of the building, which covers the whole surface of the rock (100 yards long and 56 broad), flanked by octagonal and square towers, inaccessible from the sea, and strongly fortified towards the land, was rendered almost impregnable; it was, notwithstanding, said to have been the first castle abandoned by O'Dogherty, and seized upon by the English, and was afterwards granted to Sir Arthur Chichester. The walls are in some places twelve feet thick, and several of them are still in a good state of preservation; the eastern portion of one of the towers has fallen and lies in an unbroken mass on the ground. The eligibility of this situation in commanding the entrance to Lough Foyle induced the Government, on the apprehension of an invasion, to erect a fortress, nearly adjoining the castle, consisting of a tower, battery and magazine, with accommodation for 4 officers and 42 men, and, together with another battery on the opposite side of the harbour, mounting 26 guns: the establishment now consists only of a master gunner and five artillerymen. A court for the manor of Greencastle is held monthly, for the recovery of debts under 40s. late currency. Here are stations of the constabulary and revenue police, and of the tide-waiters and pilots of the port of Londonderry; and at Greencastle and Portkennigo are stations of the coast-guard, included in the district of Carn. The living is a rectory, in the diocese of Derry, and in the patronage of the Bishop: the tithes amount to £553.17 per annum. The church is a small but neat edifice, built in 1782, in the early English style, with a tower at the east front; it stands on a rocky eminence near the shore of Lough Foyle. In the R. C. divisions the parish is united with Upper Moville; there are chapels at Ballybrack and Ballynacree. Near the church is the parochial school, chiefly supported by the rector; at Moville is a female school; and at Glenagivney, Moville, and Gallaghdaff are national schools; in these collectively about 260 children are instructed: there are also two private schools, in which are about 80 children; and three Sunday schools. Near Greencastle are some extensive ruins, called Capel Moule, having the appearance of a military edifice, and supposed to have formerly belonged to the Knights Templars; and on a detached rock, about a mile distant, are the ruins of Kilblaney church: previously to 1620 Kilblaney formed a separate parish. Near Ennishowen Head is an extensive natural cave, often visited in the summer season.

MOVILLE (UPPER), a parish, in the barony of ENNISHOWEN, county of DONEGAL, and province of ULSTER, 15 miles (N. N. E.) from Londonderry, on the road to Greencastle; containing 4902 inhabitants. St. Patrick founded a monastery here, called Maghbhile and Domnachbhile, over which he placed Aengusius, the son of Olild; it soon became celebrated for its wealth, and notices of its abbots occur from the year 590 to 953, among whom was the celebrated St. Finian. The remains are called Cooley, meaning "the City," probably from a large number of persons having settled around this famous pile, which appears, from what is left of the western and southern walls, to have been a very extensive edifice. For some time before the reformation it was used as the parish church, and so continued until destroyed during the civil war of 1688. In the adjoining cemetery is a very ancient tomb, said to be that of St. Finian; and outside the walls stands a very lofty and handsome stone cross, hewn out of one block, and in good preservation. These ruins occupy a gentle eminence, near the shores of Lough Foyle, commanding a full view of the Atlantic. The parish, which is situated on the western shore of Lough Foyle, comprises, according to the Ordnance survey, $19,081\frac{3}{4}$ statute acres: one-half is mountainous, and the remainder consists of good and middling arable land with detached pieces of bog scattered all over the parish. The land is generally light, and everywhere encumbered by rocks, heath, and whins; the greater portion of the rocks are clay-slate. Near Whitecastle is excellent sandstone, and there are strong indications of coal, near which is a curious and extraordinary whin dyke. Here the system of rundale is still kept up, and the land, being divided into very small holdings, is much neglected, nearly all the population being employed in the weaving of linen cloth and fishing, combined with agricultural pursuits: the produce of the land is chiefly corn and flax, wheat having only been grown since 1830, but it is found to answer very well. The parish is within the jurisdiction of the manor court held at Greencastle, The principal seats are Red Castle, the residence of Atkinson Wray, Esq.; White Castle, of L. Carey, Esq.; Foyle View, of R. Lepper, Esq.; Greenbank, of J. Robinson, Esq.; Ballylawn, of S. Carmichael, Esq.; Beech Cottage, of the Rev. A. Clements; and the Glebe-house, of the Rev. J. Molesworth Staples. The living is a rectory, in the diocese of Derry, forming the corps of the prebend thereof, in the patronage of the Bishop; the tithes amount to £555. The glebe-house was built in 1775, at a cost of £590, by the then incumbent; the glebe comprises 74 Cunningham acres, valued at £66.12.0 per annum. The church is an ancient, small, and inconvenient edifice, on the shore of the lough; it was built by the Carey family, in 1741, as a private chapel, and afterwards became a chapel of ease, and eventually the parish church; but, being much too small, a larger is about to be erected, In the R. C. divisions this parish and Lower Moville form the union or district; there is a chapel at Drung. Near Castle Carey is a very neat meeting-house for Presbyterians in connection with the Synod of Ulster. About 400 children are educated in seven public schools, of which the parochial school at Ballylawn is being rebuilt; it is partly supported by the rector, and with five other schools, is in connection with the National Board; the school-house of one of the latter, at Terryroan, was erected by the Earl of Caledon, and the rector contributes £5 per ann. for its support. There are also four Sunday schools. Not far from Drung are eight upright stones, near which are several lying down, the remains of an ancient cromlech. Part of a fosse and some terraces and remains of former mansions are to be traced near Red and White castles, and at Castle Carey.

MUFF, an ecclesiastical district, in the barony of ENNISHOWEN, county of DONEGAL, and province of ULSTER, 5 miles (N. N. W.) from Londonderry, on the road to Moville; containing 5915 inhabitants. Aileach castle, now only a noble ruin, stands on the summit of a lofty hill, and appears to have been the residence of the princes of the country for many centuries; in the reign of Elizabeth it was occupied by the O'Dohertys, who, in 1601, were conquered by Sir H. Docwra, who afterwards held their lands from the queen. Sir Cahir O'Doherty, the chieftain of Ennishowen, on May 1st, 1608, invited Capt. Hart, the English Governor of Culmore fort, and his lady, to the castle, under the guise of friendship; when he seized and made them prisoners, exacting such orders from the governor as secured the chieftain's own admittance into Culmore fort; having succeeded in obtaining which he massacred the garrison, took possession of the fort, and, on the same night, captured Derry, putting Sir G. Paulett, the governor, to death. Aileach castle was, shortly afterwards, retaken by the English, under Lord-Deputy Wingfield, by whose orders it was dismantled, and it has ever since remained in ruins. This district is bounded on the east by Lough Foyle, and comprises, according to the Ordnance survey, 15,030 statute acres, of which 14,988 are applotted under the tithe act, and valued at £8658 per ann.; about four-fifths are good arable land under an excellent system of cultivation; the remainder is mountainous and unproductive. The village has a neat appearance, the houses being clean and well built. Fairs are held on May 4th, Aug. 5th, Oct. 25th, and Dec. 11th. It has a penny post to Londonderry and Moville, a dispensary, and a constabulary police station; petty sessions are held once every fortnight; and a court for the manor of Muff is held on the second Tuesday in every month, for the recovery of debts under 40s. Ballynagarde is the residence of Capt. Hart, and Birdstown, of the Rev. P. B. Maxwell. The living is a perpetual cure, in the diocese of Derry, and in the patronage of the Dean; it was erected in 1809, when thirteen townlands were separated from the parish of Templemore, The tithes belong to the Dean: the income of the curate is £100, late currency, arising from £26 paid out of the Augmentation funds of the Ecclesiastical Commissioners, and a stipend from the Dean. The church is a small neat edifice, in the Gothic style of architecture, built about a century since by the ancestor of the late Gen. Hart, of Kilderry; and the Ecclesiastical Commissioners have lately granted £379 for its repair. In the R. C. divisions Muff forms part of the union or district of Templemore. About 100 children are educated in a school principally supported by the dean, and a school at Culmore is supported by the Hart family; there are also two private schools, in which are about 90 children; and two Sunday schools. The fort of Culmore is nominally within this district, though usually considered to be extraparochial.

NARIN, or NAIRN, a post-town, in the parish of INNISKEEL, barony of LOWER BOYLAGH, county of DONEGAL, and province of ULSTER, 5½ miles (N. N. W.) from Ardara, and 140 (N. W.) from Dublin: the population is returned with the parish. It consists of a few scattered houses on the north-western coast, and has a sub-post-office to Ardara. A pier has been built for the accommodation of the fishermen.

NEWTOWN-CONYNGHAM, a village, in the parish of ALL SAINTS, barony of RAPHOE, county of DONEGAL, and province of ULSTER 6½ miles (W.) from Londonderry, on the road to Letterkenny: the population is returned with the parish. It consists of a few scattered houses, situated near Lough Swilley, and has a penny post to Londonderry, a station of the constabulary police, a fair on the 29th of October, and a chapel belonging to the R. C. district of Lagan. According to Ware, a friary once existed at Bellaghan, of which there are no vestiges.

OWEY, or WYE, an island, in the parish of TEMPLECROAN, barony of BOYLAGH, county of DONEGAL, and province of ULSTER, 5 miles (N.) from Rutland; containing 76 inhabitants. It forms one of the group of islands called the Rosses, situated off the north-western coast.

PETTIGOE, a town, partly in the parish of DRUMKEERAN, barony of LURG, county of FERMANAGH, but chiefly in the parish of TEMPLECARNE, barony of TYRHUGH, county of DONEGAL, and province of ULSTER, 4 miles (W. by N.) from Kesh, on the road to Ballyshannon and Donegal; the population is returned with the respective parishes. It is situated on the united rivers of Pettigoe and Omna, which are here crossed by two bridges in their course to Lough Erne. It is a station of the constabulary police, and has a penny post to Kesh. Fairs are held on the 25th of each month, besides which there are three large markets (here called "Marga More") on the Wednesdays respectively preceding All Saints'-day, Christmas-day, and Lent. The parochial church of Templecarne, the R. C. chapel, and a meeting-house for Presbyterians of the Seceding Synod, are in the town.

RAIGH, or ROY, an island, in the parish of MEVAGH, barony of KILMACRENAN, county of DONEGAL, and province of ULSTER, 5 miles (N. E.) from Glen: the population is returned with the parish. It is situated in

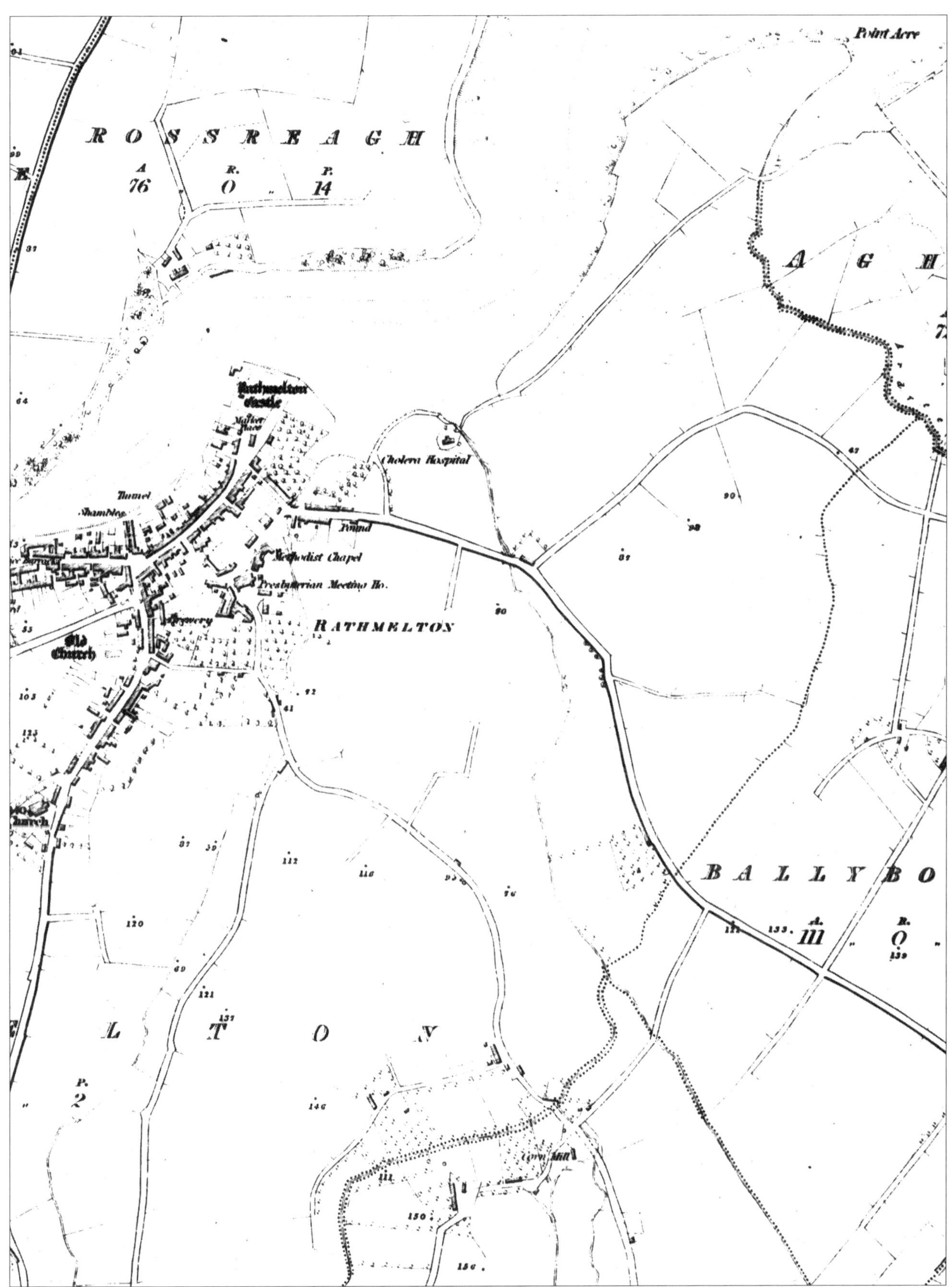

Rathmelton. Part of the O.S. map of Co.Donegal, sheet 45/46, published 1836 (reproduced at 140%).

Mulroy bay, and contains about 86 statute acres of pasture land. At low water the strand between it and the mainland is dry.

RAMELTON, a market and post-town, in the parish of AUGUNISH, barony of KILMACRENAN, county of DONEGAL, and province of ULSTER, 19 miles (N. N. W.) from Lifford, and 123$^1/_2$ (N. W. by N.) from Dublin; containing 1783 inhabitants. Sir Wm. Stewart, Knt., who was much in favour with Jas. I., became an undertaker for the plantation of escheated lands, of which he obtained a grant or patent of 1000 acres in this vicinity, and was created a baronet of Ireland in 1623. At the time of Pynnar's Survey he had built a strong bawn here, 80 feet square and 16 feet high, with four flankers and a strong and handsome castle; and contiguous to these he had built the town, then containing 45 houses, inhabited by 57 British families; he had also nearly completed the erection of a church: the place was then considered well situated for military defence. The town stands on the river Lenon, which here empties itself into Lough Swilly, and is navigable for small vessels: it consists of three streets, containing 341 houses, and is admirably adapted for manufactures of every description. Here are extensive corn-mills, a brewery, bleach-green, and linen manufactory, and a considerable quantity of linen is made by hand in the vicinity. A market for provisions is held on Tuesday, and on Thursday and Saturday for corn; and fairs are held on the Tuesday next after May 20th, Nov. 15th, and on the Tuesday after Dec. 11th. A chief constabulary police force is stationed in the town, and petty sessions are held on alternate Thursdays. There is a small salmon fishery, producing about £500 annually; the fish are considered to be in season throughout the year, and are mostly exported to England. In the town are the parochial church, meeting-houses for Presbyterians in connection with the Synod of Ulster (of the first class) and for Methodists, a small fever hospital, and a dispensary. A loan fund has been established; also a ladies' society and a shop for the sale of clothes at reduced prices to the poor. The parochial and Presbyterian schools, noticed in the article on Aughnish, are also in the town. On the shore of Lough Swilly is Fort Stewart, the residence of Sir Jas. Stewart, Bart., surrounded by an extensive and well planted demesne; and at a short distance to the north-east is Fort Stewart Castle, erected by Sir Wm. Stewart, the original patentee of the surrounding lands. Pearls of considerable value are occasionally found in the river Lenon.

RAPHOE, a market and post-town, a parish, and the seat of a diocese, in the barony of RAPHOE, county of DONEGAL, and province of ULSTER, 5 miles (N. W.) from Lifford, and 113$^3/_4$ (N. by W.) from Dublin, on the road from Strabane to Stranorlar; containing 6227 inhabitants, of which number, 1408 are in the town. This place, anciently called Rathboth, appears to have derived both its early and present importance from the foundation of an extensive monastery here by St. Columb, which, after its restoration by St. Adamnanus, who died in 703, continued to flourish and was soon after made the seat of a bishoprick. The town consists chiefly of three small streets branching off from a market-place of triangular form, and contains 288 houses, which are neatly built. An agricultural society has been established, which holds its meetings here. The whole of the surrounding scenery is agreeably diversified, and in the neighbourhood are some interesting views. The market is on Saturday, chiefly for meal and potatoes, and occasionally for linen yarn; besides which large markets are held on the first Saturday in Jan., Feb., March, April, and December; and fairs are held on May 1st, June 22nd, Aug. 27th, and Nov. 4th. The market-house is a neat building and well-arranged. The town is the head-quarters of the constabulary police for the county, and the residence of the sub-inspector; and petty sessions are held on alternate Saturdays. The parish, which is situated in the centre of the champaign district of the county, comprises, according to the Ordnance survey, 13,224$^1/_2$ statute acres, as applotted under the tithe act; the land is generally of good quality and in a state of profitable cultivation. The only seat, exclusively of the Episcopal palace and Deanery, is Green Hills, the residence of W. Fenwick, Esq.

The SEE appears to have originated during the Abbacy of St. Eunan, who converted the church of the monastery into a cathedral, and became the first bishop, but at what date cannot be precisely ascertained; nor is any thing more recorded of his successors prior to the English invasion than the mere names of one or two prelates, of whom the last, Aengus, died in 957. Gilbert O'Laran, who was consecrated in 1160, was a subscribing witness to a charter of confirmation granted by Maurice McLoughlin, King of Ireland, to the abbey of Newry, and is in that deed described as Bishop of Tirconnel, from the name of the territory in which the church of Raphoe is situated. During the prelacy of Carbrac O'Scoba, who succeeded in 1266, part of the diocese was forcibly taken away by German O'Cherballen, Bishop of Derry, and added to that see; and in 1360, Patrick Magonail erected episcopal palaces in three manors belonging to the see. The last R. C. bishop, previously to the Reformation, was Donat Magonail, who assisted at the Council of Trent in 1563; and the first Protestant bishop was George Montgomery, a native of Scotland, who was Dean of Norwich and Chaplain of Jas. I., and was consecrated to this see in 1605. Robert Huntington, celebrated for his extensive attainments in oriental literature and his assiduity in collecting, during 12 years residence at Aleppo, a valuable series of oriental manuscripts, of which many are in the Bodleian library at Oxford, and who had, while provost of Dublin University, been instrumental in printing the Old Testament in the Irish language, was appointed Bishop of Raphoe in 1701, but lived only 12 days after his consecration. John Pooley, who succeeded in 1702, repaired the palace and enlarged the cathedral by the addition of a north and south transept, rendering it perfectly cruciform.

Since 1605 the see had been held as a separate diocese till the passing of the Church Temporalities act of the 3rd of Wm. IV., by which it was enacted that, on the next avoidance, it should be united to the see of Derry, which union, on the decease of the late W. Bisset, D. D., in 1835, was carried into effect and the temporalities became vested in the Ecclesiastical Commissioners. It is one of the ten suffragan bishopricks that constitute the ecelesiastical province of Armagh; and comprehends the greater part of the county of Donegal, extending for 55 miles in length and 40 miles in breadth, and comprising an estimated superficics of 515,250 statute acres. The lands belonging to the see comprise 1392 acres of profitable land, consisting of the town parks; and the gross annual revenue, on an average of three years ending on Jan. 1st, 1832, amounted to £5787.8.2. The chapter consists of a dean, archdeacon, and the four prebendaries of Drumholm, Killymard, Inver, and Clondehorky. The consistorial court is held at Raphoe, and consists of a vicar-general, two surrogates, a registrar, deputy-registrar, and two proctors. The registrar is keeper of the records, which are of modern date; all prior to 1691 are supposed to have been destroyed when the castle was taken by Cromwell, or when it was afterwards plundered and burned by the soldiers of Jas. II. The total number of parishes is 34, of which 5 are district parishes, comprehended in 34 single benefices, of which 5 are perpetual curacies; of these, 5 are in the patronage of the Crown, 15 in that of the Bishop, 2 in the patronage of incumbents, and the remainder in lay and corporation patronage: there are 34 churches and 28 glebe-houses. The cathedral, which is also the parochial church, and to the repair of which the Ecclesiastical Commissioners have recently granted £1005, is a plain, ancient, cruciform structure with a square tower, which was added to it by Bishop Forster in 1737, as appears by that date on a stone over the door: there is no economy fund. The Episcopal palace, formerly a strong castle, is about a quarter of a mile from the town: it is a handsome and spacious castellated building, pleasantly situated in tastefully disposed grounds. The deanery-house, which is also the glebe-house of the parish, was built in 1739, at an expense of £1680, and has been subsequently enlarged and improved from their own funds by various successive incumbents; it is pleasantly situated about a mile from the town. In the R. C. divisions the diocese is co-extensive with that of the Protestant see; it comprehends 24 benefices, containing 36 chapels, which

Bishop of Raphoe's Castle. Drawn by R. O'C. Newenham and engraved by J.D. Harding. From R.O'C. Newenham, Picturesque views of the antiquities of Ireland, *vol.1, (London, 1830).*

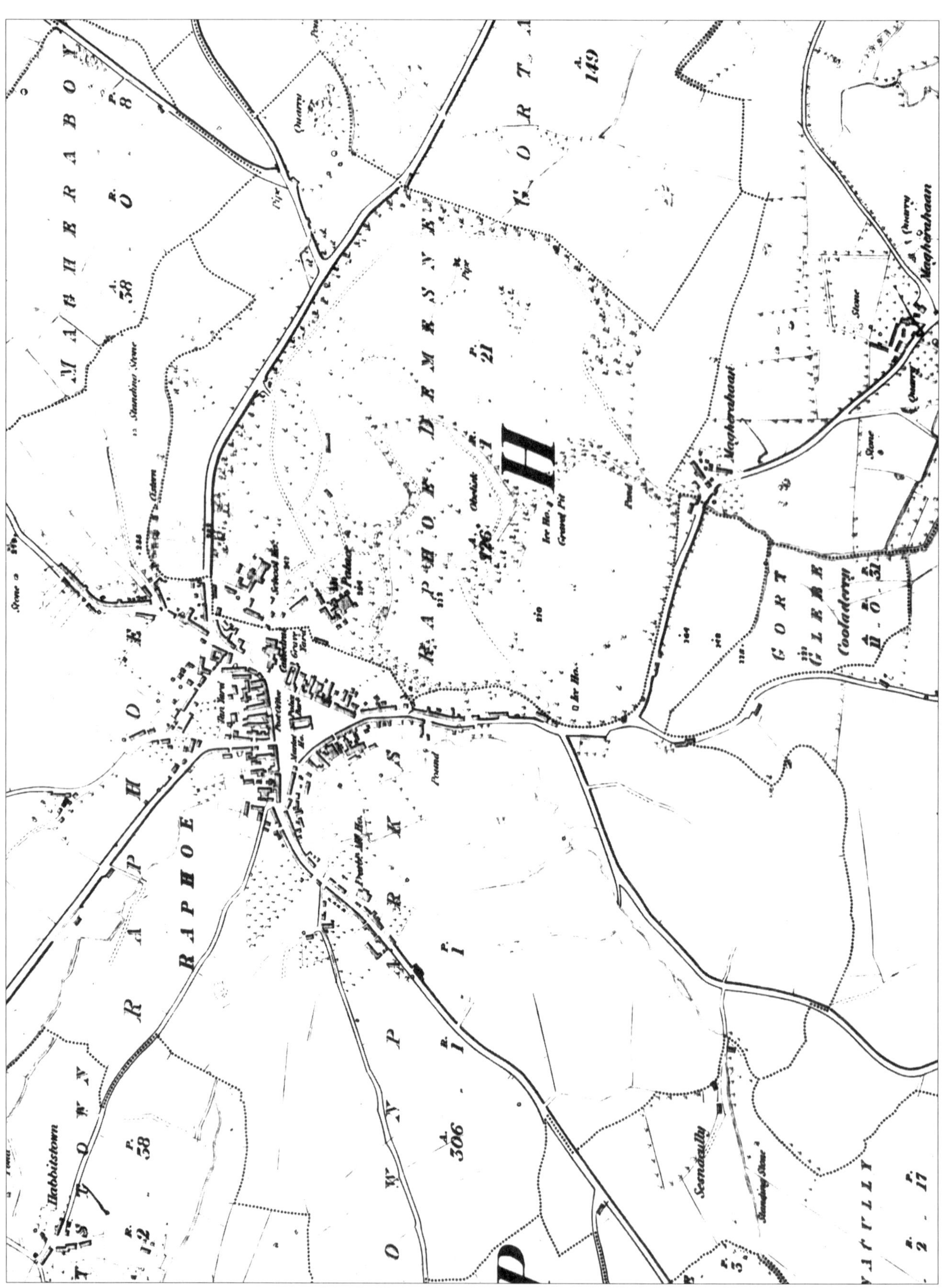

Raphoe. Part of the O.S. map of Co. Donegal, sheet 70, published 1836 (reproduced at 140%).

are served by 50 clergymen, of whom 24 are parish priests, and 26 are coadjutors or curates; the bishop's parishes are Conwal and Aughnish; the cathedral is at Letterkenny where is also the bishop's residence.

The living is a rectory and vicarage, in the diocese of Raphoe, formerly united to the rectories of Stranorlar, Leck, and Killygarvan, and the chapelry of Lettermacaward, from which, by act of council in 1835, it was separated, and now solely constitutes the corps of the deanery, The tithes amount to £900; and the glebe comprises 150 acres, valued at £150 per ann,; the other lands belonging to the deanery comprise 2701$^1/_2$ statute acres, extending over several parishes, which, with the rents and renewal fines, produce £426.5.10 per ann., making the gross annual revenue of the deanery £1476.5.10. In the R. C. divisions the parish is the head of a union or district, including also the parish of Conwal, in which is a chapel. There is a place of worship for Presbyterians in connection with the Synod of Ulster, of the second class. The Royal free grammar school was founded by Chas. I., who endowed it with lands in the western part of the county, comprising from 5000 to 6000 acres, of which 1400 are profitable, and the remainder bog and mountain, producing together an annual income of £550: the school-house was rebuilt in 1737, and enlarged in 1830, and is a spacious and handsome building; attached to it is a valuable library, containing more than 3000 volumes, founded by Bishop Forster and Dr. Hall for the use of the clergy of the diocese, In this and in three other public schools, of which the parochial school is partly supported by annual donations from Col. Robertson's fund, about 280 children are taught; an infants' school and a female working school are also supported by the Dean, and there are six private schools, in which are about 200 children, and four Sunday schools. An asylum for four poor clergymen's widows was founded by Bishop Forster, who endowed it with lands now producing to each £50 per ann.; the house, which is spacious and well adapted for the purpose, was purchased by the founder during his lifetime, and is situated in the town: there is also a dispensary.

RATHMULLEN, a small sea-port, in the parish of KILLYGARVAN, barony of KILMACRENAN, county of DONEGAL, and province of ULSTER, 5 miles (N.) from Ramelton: the population is returned with the parish. It is situated on the western shore of Lough Swilly, and consists of one main street: it has a penny post to Ramelton, and is both a constabulary police and coast-guard station, the latter being included in the district of Dunfanaghy: petty sessions are held here. There are some remains of a religious house built by Mac Swine Fanagh, for Carmelites or White friars, and dedicated to the Blessed Virgin; also of a castle, said to have been built by him, which was destroyed at the time of' the Reformation, but afterwards rebuilt by Bishop Knox. Part of this castle was for some time used as the parish church, previous to the erection of the present edifice.

RAYMOCHY, or RAY, a parish, in the barony of RAPHOE, county of DONEGAL, and province of ULSTER, 4 miles (E. by N.) from Letterkenny; containing 5756 inhabitants. This parish, also called Raghniohie, is situated on Lough Swilly, and comprises, according to the Ordnance survey, 14,820 statute acres. The land is chiefly arable, and there is some bog and mountain: agriculture is much improving. Fairs are held at Manor-Cunningham, on the 6th of every second month, commencing in January, principally for cattle. Lough Swilly is navigable to the sea for vessels of 200 tons burden. Leslie Hill is the seat of J. Beers, Esq. The living is a rectory and vicarage, in the diocese of Raphoe, and in the patronage of the Provost and Fellows of Trinity College, Dublin: the tithes amount to £650, and the glebe comprises 505 Cunningham acres, valued at £254.13.10 per ann. The glebe-house was built in 1775 by the then incumbent. The church is a plain building, erected in 1792 at a cost of £646, of which £554 was contributed by the landed proprietors, and £92 by parochial assessment; the Ecclesiastical Commissioners have recently granted £167.6.4 for repairs. In the R. C. divisions the parish forms part of the union or district of Lagan, or All Saints; there is a chapel at Drimairghill. There are two Presbyterian meeting-houses in connection with the Synod of Ulster, and one for Seceders, all of the second class. About 240 children are educated in three public schools, of which the parochial school receives an annual donation from Col. Robertson's fund; and another is endowed with a house and 20 acres of land by one of the family of Beers. There are also nine private schools, in which are about 270 children, and five Sunday schools.

RAYMUNTERDONY, or RAYMUNTERDOYNE, a parish, in the barony of KILMACRENAN, county of DONEGAL, and province of ULSTER, 4 miles (S. W.) from Dunfanaghy, on the road to Dungloe; containing 2193 inhabitants, This parish is situated on the north-western coast, and, according to the Ordnance survey, comprises 12,017 statute acres; more than two-thirds is mountainous, the remainder being tolerably good land; agriculture is in an improving state: here is a fine slate quarry. Fairs are held on the last Thursday in every month at Falcarogh, on the Crossroads. Ballyconnell is the residence of the Rev. J. Olphert; and Carrow-Cannon, of T. Olphert, Esq. The living is a rectory and vicarage, in the diocese of Raphoe, and in the patronage of the Bishop: the tithes amount to £102.12, and the glebe comprises 1804 Cunningham acres, valued at £227 per annum. The glebe-house was erected in 1815, at a cost of £1025, of which £250 was a gift and £500 a loan from the late Board of First Fruits. The church is a plain neat building, erected by aid of a gift of £500 from the same Board, in 1803. In the R. C. divisions the parish is called Tullaghobigley-East, being united to part of the parish of Tullaghobigley-East, in which place is the chapel. A school is aided by an annual donation from Col. Robertson's fund, and another is partly supported by Mr. Olphert and the Rector. At Crossroads there is a dispensary, maintained in the usual manner. In the old church-yard is a remarkable cross, measuring 21 feet in length, which lies on the ground.

RONANISH, an island, in the parish of INNISKEEL, barony of BOYLAGH, county of DONEGAL, and province of ULSTER, 3 miles (N. W.) from Narin, on the north-west coast.

ROSSNOWLOUGH, an ecclesiastical district, in the barony of TYRHUGH, county of DONEGAL, and province of ULSTER, 3 miles (N. W.) from Ballyshannon, on the west of the road to Donegal and on the sea coast; containing 1006 inhabitants. In the year 1830, nine townlands, comprising 2403$^1/_2$ statute acres, were separated from the parish of Drumholm and constituted the ecclesiastical district parish of Rossnowlough. It is a perpetual curacy, in the diocese of Raphoe, and in the patronage of the Vicar of Drumholm: the gross value of the benefice is £108.8.9, of which £75 is paid by the vicar, and £25 from Primate Boulter's fund; the remainder is the annual value of the glebe. The church was erected in 1831, by aid of a gift of £800 from the late Board of First Fruits. In the R. C. divisions it is in the district of Drumholm. About 360 children are educated in six public schools, of which one is supported by the trustees of Erasmus Smith's charity, one from Col. Robertson's endowment, and the remainder chiefly by subscription. There are also two private schools, in which are about 130 children; and two Sunday schools.

RUTLAND, an island, in the parish of TEMPLECROAN, barony of BOYLAGH, county of DONEGAL, and province of ULSTER, 18 miles (N.) from Narin: the population is returned with the parish. This island, anciently called Innismacdurn, received its present name from its proprietor, an ancestor of the Marquess of Conyngham, in compliment to Charles, Duke of Rutland, who was at that time Lord-Lieutenant of Ireland. At the time of Pynnar's survey there was a small old castle with a bawn, where a few English families had settled. It is situated off the north-western coast, forming one of the group of islands called the Rosses, and contains about 180 acres, chiefly rocky and coarse mountain land, with a considerable quantity of bog. The harbour is narrow and fit only for small vessels. The inhabitants, in each of the years 1784 and 1785, realised £40,000 from the herring fishery off the coast; and the great abundance of herrings found here at that time induced Col. Conyngham to expend £50,000 in building houses and stores and forming a town here, and in constructing roads through the mountains on the coast to the champaign country in the interior. From that period the fishery began to decline, and in 1793 it entirely failed; and though it afterwards began to revive, it never regained its former prosperity. The females are employed in knitting coarse yarn stockings. On the 16th of September, 1798, James Napper Tandy landed here from the French brig Anacreon from Brest, with three boats full of officers and men, accompanied by Gen. Rey and Col. Blackwell; but after remaining for a day and a night, hearing that the French, who had landed at Kilcummin, had surrendered and been made prisoners, they re-embarked. On the island is a coast guard station, forming one of the seven that constitute the district of Dunfanaghy; a dispensary is maintained in the usual way.

STRANORLAR, a market and post-town, and a parish, in the barony of RAPHOE, county of DONEGAL, and province of ULSTER; 10$^1/_4$ miles (W. by S.) from Lifford, and 118 (N. W. by N.) from Dublin, on the road from Strabane to Ballyshannon, and on the river Fin; containing 6114 inhabitants, of which number, 641 are in the town. The parish, according to the Ordnance survey, comprises 15,509 statute acres, of which 159 are under water. That part which forms the estate of Sir Edmund Hayes is under an improved system of agriculture, but the other part appears to be neglected. Here appear two veins containing spar, ochre, and apparently lead ore; they are in a limestone rock, and in the vicinity are great bodies of decomposed limestone, forming excellent manure, and some is quarried for building. The stupendous mountains of Barnesmore, alike remarkable for their perpendicular ascent and for their beautifully varied rocks and herbage, form the Gap of the same name, situated at the south-western extremity of the parish; through this gap a fine stream flows into Lough Esk, and it is also the pass between the north and west of Ireland, coastwise, and on the leading road to Donegal. The town comprises 116 houses, of which 20 are well built, the remainder being occupied by labourers and artisans. Here is a good hotel; also a market and court-house. The market, at which fine brown linen is sold, is held every Saturday; and there are fairs on March 29th, June 11th, July 6th, Aug. 12th, Oct. 10th, and Dec. 9th and 10th. Manor courts are held in the court-house before the seneschal on the first Saturday in every month; and petty sessions are held on alternate Wednesdays. The linen manufacture is partially carried on; there are two extensive bleach-greens near the town, one belonging to J. Johnston, Esq.; the other, adjoining Summer Hill, to J. and C. Johnston, Esqrs. In the neighbourhood are numerous gentlemen's seats, among which are Drumboe Castle, the residence of Sir E. Hayes, Bart,, M.P., situated on a pretty lawn in the centre of an improved demesne; Tyrcallen, of H. Steevens, Esq., in a beautiful and extensively planted demesne, on the principal elevation in which the proprietor has erected an observatory; Edenmore, of J. Cochran, Esq., J.P., a neat mansion, in a small but handsome demesne, on the south bank of the Fin; Woodlands, a handsome modern residence, of J. Johnston, Esq., J.P.; Summer Hill, of C. Johnston, Esq.; Glenmore, of C. Style, Esq., a handsome mansion in improved grounds; the Glebe-house, of the Rev. T. Fullerton; and Cloghan Lodge, the occasional residence of Sir T. C. Style, Bart,, near the romantic waterfall and salmon leap of this name on the Fin.

The living is a rectory and vicarage, in the, diocese of Raphoe, and in the patronage of the Crown; the tithes amount to £485. The glebe-house was built in 1812, at a cost of £692, British currency, of which £46 was a loan, and the remainder a gift from the late Board of First Fruits. The church is an old building, to which the same Board, in 1825, granted a loan of £300 for the erection of a gallery. Prior to the 24th of March, 1835, this parish, forming part of the deanery of Raphoe, consisted of the two perpetual cures of Stranorlar and Kilteevock, but by an order in council of the above date it was disappropriated from the deanery, and erected into a separate and distinct parish, or benefice. It was provided, however, that the incumbent should pay to the perpetual curate of Kilteevock the same salary as had been paid by the dean. The R. C. parish is co-extensive with that of the Established Church; there are two chapels, one in the town, and one about five miles westward. There are places of worship for Presbyterians, in connection with the Synod of Ulster (of the third class), for Seceders (of the second class), and for Wesleyan Methodists; also a dispensary. The parochial school has an endowment from Col. Robertson's charity; there is another under the trustees of Erasmus Smith's charity; and four more are aided by subscriptions; in these schools are about 350 children, There are also two private schools, in which are about 130 children; and two Sunday schools.

TAUGHBOYNE, a parish, in the barony of RAPHOE, county of DONEGAL, and province of ULSTER, 5 miles (W. S. W.) from Londonderry, on the road to Haphoe; containing, with the village and ancient disfranchised borough of St. Johnstown, 6335 inhabitants. St. Baithen, son of Brendan, a disciple and kinsman of St. Columb, and his successor in the abbey of Hy, founded Tegbaothin in Tyrconnell: he flourished towards the close of the sixth century. The parish, according to the Ordnance survey, comprises an area of 15,773$^3/_4$ statute acres, including a large portion of bog: the land is chiefly arable, and of good quality. There are some extensive slate quarries, but the slates are small and of a coarse quality. The river Foyle, which bounds the parish on the east, is navigable for small boats to St. Johnstown, where a fair is held on Nov. 25th. The living is a rectory and vicarage, in the diocese of Raphoe, and in the patronage of the Marquess of Abercorn: the tithes amount to £1569.4.7$^1/_2$; and the glebe, comprising 317 acres, is valued at £260.6.5$^1/_2$ per annum. The glebe-house was originally built in 1785, at a cost of £1313 British, and subsequently improved at an expense of £1399 by the then incumbent. The church was erected in 1626; the Ecclesiastical Commissioners have lately granted £268 for its repair. In the R. C. divisions the parish forms part of the union or district of Lagan, or Raymochy; the chapel was built about 50 years since. In the parochial school partly supported by an endowment of Col. Robertson, a school under the London Hibernian Society, and two schools supported by subscription, about 200 children are educated; there are also nine private schools, in which are about the same number of children, and five Sunday schools: two school-houses have been lately erected by the Marquess of Abercorn. There is a dispensary for the poor.

TEMPLECARNE, or TEMPLECOIN, a parish, partly in the barony of LURG, county of FERMANAGH, but chiefly in the barony of TYRHUGH, county of DONEGAL, and province of ULSTER, 4 miles (W.) from Kesh; containing 5461 inhabitants. The parish, which is also called Termoncerin-Magrath, from its having been the residence of Magrath, the first Protestant bishop of Clogher, is bounded on the south by Lough Erne, and comprises, according to the Ordnance survey, 45,868 statute acres, of which 7719 are in the county of Fermanagh. Of these, 2140$^1/_2$ are in Lough Derg, which is wholly within the parish; 4400 are in Lower Lough Erne, and 1085$^1/_2$ are in small loughs. About three-fourths of the land consist of heathy mountain, affording during the summer only a scanty pasturage to a few black cattle; the remainder, with the exception of a moderate portion of meadow, is principally under tillage. The soil is but indifferent, and the system of agriculture backward; though some improvement has taken place in the low lands, its general progress has been greatly retarded by the want of convenient roads through the mountainous district. Limestone abounds, and is quarried for agricultural uses; there are also large quarries of excellent freestone, of millstones of peculiar hardness, and of a coarse kind of dark marble; iron ore is found here, and mines were formerly worked to advantage. The rivers Pettigoe, Omna, Letter, and Rossharbor, all of which abound with trout, pike, and eels, intersect the parish in various directions and fall into Lough Erne. The principal mountains, among which are some small lakes well stored with fish, are Crocknacunny, Minchifin, Rushen, and Rossharbor. Lough Derg, a noble expanse of water, bordering on the eastern confines of the county of Donegal, is thickly studded with picturesque islands, of which the chief are Saints' Island, called also St. Dabeoc's, or St. Fintan's island, from the supposed founder of a monastery upon it, of which there are some remains; Turres or Station island, so called from its being the resort of pilgrims on penance; Innishtoesk, and Goat, Eagle, Ash, Kelly's, Grouse, Lodge, and the Prior's islands. The shores of the lake are precipitously steep, except in that part where the ferryboat plies to convey visiters to the several islands; and the scenery of the parish is strikingly diversified. Waterfoot, the residence of Lieut.-Col. Barton, is pleasantly situated. Fairs are held on the 25th of every month except December, in which month the fair is held on the Wednesday next before Christmas-day, for cattle, sheep, pigs, and linen yarn. A manorial court and petty sessions are held every other week.

The living is a rectory and vicarage, in the diocese of Clogher, and in the patronage of the Bishop: the tithes amount to £300. The glebe-house was built in 1813, at an expense of £978.9.2$^3/_4$, of which £623.1.6$^1/_2$ was a loan from the late Board of First Fruits, and the remainder was defrayed by the then incumbent: the glebe comprises 141 acres of good land, valued at £176.16.8 per annum. The church, situated at Pettigoe, is a small, old, and dilapidated structure, towards the rebuilding of which Mrs. Leslie (the proprietor of the estate), the rector, and the Protestant parishioners have contributed a large sum; and a subscription has been raised to build a chapel of ease about four miles from the town, In the R. C. divisions the parish, called also Pettigoe, is the head of a union or district, comprising also the parish of Belleek. There are two chapels in this parish; one at Pettigoe, a large and well-built edifice; and one about four miles from the town, on the Strabane road: there is also a chapel in the parish of Belleek, In the town there is a place of worship for Presbyterians of the Seceding Synod; and near it, though within the verge of the adjoining parish, are two for Wesleyan Methodists. About 460 children are taught in four public schools, of which the parochial school is supported by the rector, and others by Mrs. Leslie; and there are four private schools, in which are about 250 children, and five Sunday schools. Near the glebe-house are the ruins of an ancient castle, said to have been the residence of the first Protestant Bishop of Clogher; it was battered by Ireton in the parliamentary war, from the neighbouring hill, on which are still traces of the works thrown up by that officer. There are also several Danish raths and mineral springs in the parish. On Saints' Island, in Lough Derg, are the remains of an Augustinian priory, dedicated to St. Peter and St. Paul, the foundation of which is ascribed to St. Dabeoc, brother of St. Canoe, who flourished towards the close of the fifth century; notwithstanding its celebrity, it was plundered and reduced to ashes by Bratachus O'Boyle and Mc Mahon, in 1207. It was subject to the great abbey of Armagh, and for several ages was celebrated for its miraculous cell, called St. Patrick's purgatory, an invention attributed to a saint of that name who was prior here in the ninth century: this cell was much resorted to by pilgrims from all parts of Europe, who were supposed to suffer in imagination, while lying within its narrow precincts, all the pains endured by the wicked in the purgatory of the Romish church. Its proximity to the shore, with which it was connected by a neck of land, affording too great facility of access, the cave was stopped up, and another opened in a smaller island, now called the Station Island, about half a mile from the shore, to which access is obtained by a ferry boat constantly plying for that purpose. Such was the reputation this place maintained, that safeguards were frequently granted by the Kings of England to foreigners of distinction who came to visit it; among others to Raymond, Viscount de Perilleux, and Knight of Rhodes, with a train of 20 men and 30 horses, in 1397. This purgatory was repeatedly suppressed by the Popes, and also by the Lords-Justices of Ireland, who banished the friars and broke up the cell; but it was as frequently revived, and is still visited by multitudes of pilgrims, who assemble here during what is called "the station," which commences on the first of June and continues to the 15th of August, during which time the friars are constantly engaged in hearing confessions, enjoining penance, and performing other devotional rites. The number annually resorting hither during that period exceeds 10,000; each pays the ferryman 6½d. for taking him to the island and bringing him back; and the proprietor of the lake receives £165 per annum for allowing the ferryman to ply. The term of continuance on the island is three, six, or nine days, and each pilgrim spends the last twenty-four hours of his term in the chapel of the purgatory, which receives light only from a small window in one of the angles. About ten years since a boat having eighty pilgrims on board swamped and went to the bottom, and only three of the number were saved; the bodies of the rest were afterwards found and interred on Saints' Island.

TEMPLECROAN, a parish, in the barony of BOYLAGH, county of DONEGAL, and province of ULSTER; containing, with the post-town of Dungloe and the islands of Arranmore and Rutland (which are separately described), 8198 inhabitants. The parish is situated on the north-western coast, and is bounded on the north by the Gwidore river; it comprises, according to the Ordnance survey, 52,921 statute acres, of which 989½ are in the tideway of the Gwidore, and 2896 in lakes. Within its limits is the greater part of the district called "the Rosses," consisting of a dreary wilderness of rugged mountain wastes and heath is broken on the west into abrupt rocky heights, and including many islands separated by inlets of the sea. Some of these islands are thinly covered on the summits with moss and heath, and a few present specimens of verdure produced by cultivation; Arranmore, the largest, forms a shelter for the rest and a barrier against the western ocean. On the shores of Cruit grows a kind of long and broad-leaved grass having a saline taste, which the cattle readily feed on at ebb tide. The district is unfavourable either for grazing or tillage; the produce raised is inconsiderable and there is often a scarcity of food. Throughout the parish agriculture is in a very backward condition, the greater portion of the land consisting of sands, mountain rocks, and bog: the mountain of Crovehy rises 1033 feet above the level of the sea. Indications of iron ore may be observed in the precipitous face of the mountains. Petty sessions are held at Dungloe, at which place there is a constabulary police station. The living is a rectory and vicarage, in the diocese of Raphoe, and in the patronage of the Marquess of Conyngham; the tithes amount to £235. The glebe-house was erected by aid of a gift of £100, in 1763, from the late Board of First Fruits; the glebe comprises 815 acres, valued at £152.16.3 per ann. The church is a small plain building, erected in 1760 by aid of a gift of £400 from the same Board. In the R. C. divisions this parish forms part of the union or district of Lettermacward, and is partly a district in itself: it contains three good, plain, slated chapels, one at Dungloe belonging to Lettermacward; the others in Arranmore and Kincaslagh, belonging to Templecroan. There are two parochial schools, situated at Dungloe and Carrenbuoy, aided by annual donations from Col. Robertson's fund and from the rector, who also contributes to the support of two schools at Maghera and Dungloe: in these schools are about 160 children. There are also six private schools, in which are about 120 children. A dispensary is supported at Dungloe. Here are the ruins of the ancient castle of Dungloe, near which have been brought up out of the sea several brass cannon, bearing the Spanish arms, said to have belonged to the Armada.

TERRYRONE, a village, in the parish of UPPER MOVILLE, barony of ENNISHOWEN, county of DONEGAL, and province of ULSTER, 8 miles (N.) from Londonderry, on the road to Moville; the population is returned with the parish. This village was formerly of some importance, having been then inhabited by the farmers of the adjoining lands on the system of "Rundale," but that system having been broken up by the proprietor, the Earl of Caledon, the farmers now reside on their respective lands, and the village has in consequence been almost deserted. Though the land in the vicinity is in general poor, the state of agriculture has been lately much improved under the patronage of its noble proprietor. Here is a school established by Lord Caledon, and now in connection with the National Board; the school-house was built at his lordship's expense.

TORY, or TORRE, an island, in the parish of TULLAGHOBIGLY, barony of KILMACRENAN, county of DONEGAL, and province of ULSTER, on the north-west coast, three leagues (N. W.) from Horn Head, two leagues (N. E.) from Bloody Forland Point, and 12 miles (S. W.) from Dunfanaghy; containing, in 1835,70 families. It is about three miles in length and one in breadth, comprising about 1200 acres, of which 205 are arable or pasture, the remainder being mountain or barren sands. Here is a lake called Lough Altin, of considerable extent. Clay is found of different kinds and colours, some of which is made by the inhabitants into earthen vessels capable of resisting a strong heat. The spinning of flax and wool is carried on to some extent, the females commencing as soon as they are able to sit at the wheel; the men are employed in agriculture and fishing. On the north point of the island is a lighthouse, in lat. 55 16′ 10″ and lon. 8 15′ erected by the corporation for improving the port of Dublin in 1832: it is a bright fixed light, the lantern elevated 122 feet above the sea at high water, and may be seen for 17 nautical miles when the atmosphere is clear. With southerly winds a vessel may stop on the east side of the island in fair weather. The clay found in one of the churches is held in veneration as a preservative from injuries of any kind, particularly from fire. Ruins of several ecclesiastical buildings exist here, including those of an abbey of which St. Ernan, the son of St. Colman, was abbot about 650; another yet presents a steeple 64 feet high and 54 feet in circumference. Here are also two stone crosses, one 7 feet, the other 3 feet, in length. About a mile further off are the ruins of an old building, called by the inhabitants Ballaas Castle.

TULLAGHOBIGLEY, a parish, in the barony of KILMACRENAN, county of DONEGAL, and province of ULSTER, 7 miles (S. W.) from Dunfanaghy, on the north-west coast, and on the rivers Gwidore and Clady; containing 8464 inhabitants. For civil purposes it is divided into east and west; the former contains 5202, and the latter 3262, inhabitants. It is said to derive its name from Tully O'Bighey, who founded a monastery here, of which the remains exist. According to the Ordnance survey it comprises 68,608 statute acres, of which 785 are in Tory Island, $92\frac{1}{2}$ in the tideway of the Gwidore, and 1720 in small loughs; 19,811 are applotted under the tithe act. About one-fourth of the entire superficies is arable, and the remainder mountain and bog; agriculture is but little improved. Within the limits of the parish are the district of Cloghanheely and part of that of the Rosses; and the islands of Tory, (about two leagues to the north-east), Innisboffin, Island Dowey, or Innisduck, (comprising about 20 acres of arable and pasture and a quantity of mountain land), Innisbeg, Inisinney, and Innismanan, of which the two first are inhabited, and the rest only during the summer; also Bloody-Foreland-Point, in lat. 55° 8′, and lon. 8° 17′; and the mountains of Errigal, 2462 feet, Carntreena 1396 feet, and Bloody-Foreland 1035 feet, above the level of the sea. In the Rosses, at a place called Rosapenna, so lately as 1784, the district was well cultivated, planted and improved, particularly around the mansion of Lord Boyne, whose demesne excited general admiration; but now the house, park, garden and even the tallest trees are covered with sand blown in from the Atlantic; even the chimneys are only visible at times, and, added to this, 1400 acres of land lie buried beneath the sand, which is every year increasing. On the townland of Tullaghobigley iron ore has been found in large lumps; and in the Errigal mountain, extensive lead mines, belonging to the Earl of Leitrim, have been successfully worked, but are at present abandoned. Fairs are held at Gortahock on the first Tuesday, at the Cross Roads the last Thursday, and at Derrybeg on the last Monday in every month, but they are only indifferently attended. The gentlemen's seats are Cashel, the residence of R. Johnston, Esq.; and Dunloey, of Capt. Dambrene, where is a fine marble quarry. The living is a rectory and vicarage, in the diocese of Raphoe, and in the patronage of the Bishop: the tithes amount to £220, and the glebe comprises 40 acres, valued at £30 per annum. The roof of the church fell in in 1834, which having left it a ruin, divine service is now performed in the rector's house. In the R. C. arrangements the parish is divided into East and West Tullaghobigley, the former being united to the parish of Raymunterdoney: the chapel at Gortahork, in the eastern division, is a large slated building, erected about 50 years since; and at Cottern, in the western division, is a chapel, which has been built 87 years. The parochial school, in which are about 50 children, is aided by an annual donation from Col. Robertson's fund: there are also five private schools, in which are about 80 children. At Maghragallan are the ruins of an old church and a burial-ground.

TULLY, or TULLAFERNE, a parish, in the barony of KILMACRENAN, county of DONEGAL, and province of ULSTER; containing, with part of the post-town of Ramelton, 6096 inhabitants. It is situated on a branch of Lough Swilly, and comprises, according to the Ordnance survey, 16,612 statute acres, of which 383 are water, and

14,908 are applotted under the tithe act and valued at £4585 per annum. There is a considerable portion of bog, also part of a lake, upwards of a mile in length, called Lough Ferne: about 100 acres of land have been lately reclaimed from the sea at Mulroy bay; this bay admits the approach of vessels to within half a mile of the village of Milford. Several of the inhabitants are employed in linen-weaving at their own houses. The gentlemen's seats are Glenalla, the residence of the Rev. G. V. Hart; Clara, of Jas. Watt, Esq.; and Ballyare, of John Cochrane, Esq. The parish is in the diocese of Raphoe, and is a rectory, forming part of the union of Aughnish, or Tullyaughnish: the tithes amount to £590.12.8; and there is a glebe, comprising 512 Cunningham acres, valued at £256 per annum. In the R. C. divisions it is the head of a union or district, comprising also the parish of Killygarvan, by which name the district is also called: each parish contains a chapel. There are two meeting-houses for Covenanters and one for Presbyterians. At Milford is a school on the foundation of Erasmus Smith, in which, and in two other public schools, about 260 children are educated; and about 290 children are taught in six private schools; there are also five Sunday schools.

Acknowledgements

Grateful acknowledgement is due to the following for the use of illustrations in their possession: the Linen Hall Library for the cover picture and the two Lewis maps; the map library of the school of geography at QUB for the O.S. maps: the Southern Education Library Board, local studies section, Armagh for the Moneymore and Draperstown views. Thanks must be expressed to Mr John Killen, Mrs Norah Essie, Mr Roger Dixon, Mr Colm Croker, Mrs Margaret McNulty, Ms Maura Pringle, Mrs Angelique Bell, Mr Patrick McWilliams and Ms Mary McVeigh.

Bunbeg harbour and store. Drawn by H. Clive and engraved by T. Picken. Printed by 'Day & Haghe, lithographers to the Queen'. This view of the mid 1840s shows a scene very different from that described by Samuel Lewis a few years earlier, in his account of the parish of Templecroan. It depicts the buildings constructed in the late 1830s and early 1840s by the landlord, Lord George Hill. The building on the right is a mill, while beyond it can be seen a warehouse and a residence (later used by the local doctor). On the hill is a signalling apparatus to link Bunbeg to Carrickfin Island.